MATH ADVENTURES

A Key to Academic Math Advancement

GRADE 8

Author: Ace Academic Publishing

Ace Academic Publishing is a leading supplemental educational workbook publisher for grades K-12. At Ace Academic Publishing, we realize the importance of imparting analytical and critical thinking skills during the early ages of childhood and hence our books include materials that require multiple levels of analysis and encourage the students to think outside the box.

The materials for our books are written by award winning teachers with several years of teaching experience. All our books are aligned with the state standards and are widely used by many schools throughout the country.

Prepaze is a sister company of Ace Academic Publishing. Intrigued by the unending possibilities of the internet and its role in education, Prepaze was created to spread the knowledge and learning across all corners of the world through an online platform. We equip ourselves with state-of-the-art technologies so that knowledge reaches the students through the quickest and the most effective channels.

For inquiries and bulk orders, contact Ace Academic Publishing at the following address:
Ace Academic Publishing
3031 Village Market Place,
Morrisville, NC 27560, USA
www.aceacademicpublishing.com

ISBN: 978-1-962517-15-7

Introduction

About the Book

Welcome to "**Math Adventures - A Key to Academic Math Advancement**"! This workbook is specifically designed to align with the school curriculum and help students improve their analytical and logical thinking skills. With over **750 questions and several word problems**, this book aims to cover all the required syllabus for students in Grade 8.

Our workbook is an excellent resource for end-of-the-year state tests given by schools, as well as a great review book during the summer. Whether you are looking to improve your math skills or simply keep them sharp, "**Math Adventures**" provides a comprehensive and challenging set of problems to help you achieve your goals.

Our authors have extensive experience in teaching and developing math curricula for students at all levels. **They have carefully crafted each problem to challenge students and help them develop key problem-solving and critical thinking skills.** The book covers a wide range of topics, including arithmetic, algebra, geometry, and data analysis, providing students with a well-rounded education in math.

We believe that with practice, anyone can master math. "**Math Adventures**" is designed to help students build confidence in their abilities and develop a love for the subject. With clear explanations, helpful hints, and detailed solutions, this book is an excellent tool for anyone looking to improve their math skills.

Thank you for choosing "**Math Adventures - A Key to Academic Math Advancement**". We hope that you find it useful and enjoyable!

Common Core Math Workbooks

Common Core English Workbooks

The One Big Book Workbooks

Math Adventures Workbooks

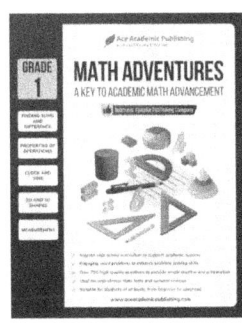 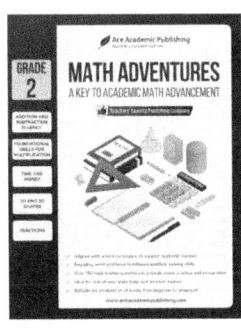  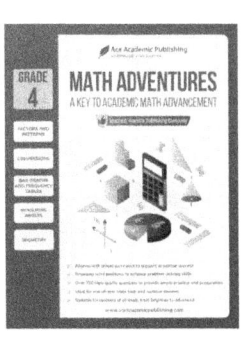

 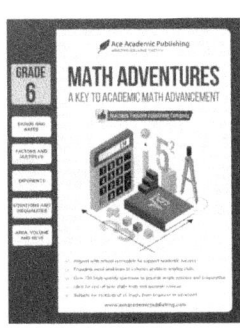  

Early Learning Workbooks

TABLE OF CONTENTS

TABLE OF CONTENTS

CHAPTER 1

EXPONENTS AND ROOTS

8		6			3		9	
	4			1			6	8
2			8	7				5
1		8			5		2	
	3		1				5	
7		5		3		9		
	2	1			7		4	
6				2		8		
	8	7	6		4			3

RATIONAL AND IRRATIONAL NUMBERS

Rational numbers:

Rational numbers are numbers that can be written in the form $\frac{p}{q}$, where p and q are both integers, and $q \neq 0$. For example, 4 and −1

- $\frac{4}{-1}$ is a rational number.
- $-\frac{4}{1}$ is also a rational number

For instances using 0, the placement of 0 determines whether the number is rational or not. For example, 0 and 6.

- $\frac{0}{6}$ is a rational number.
- $\frac{6}{0}$ is NOT a rational number because the denominator is zero.

It is important that the denominator of a rational number written as a fraction is not equal to zero or else it will be considered undefined.

Irrational numbers:

Irrational numbers are numbers that CANNOT be written in the form $\frac{p}{q}$, where p and q are both integers, and $q \neq 0$. Examples of irrational numbers are $\sqrt{2}$ and π.

Rational and irrational numbers can be written as decimals. Rational numbers include numbers with finite decimal expansion and repeating decimals.

Examples:

$\frac{1}{4} = 0.25$

$\frac{1}{3} = 0.333 = 0.\overline{3}$

Irrational numbers include numbers whose decimal expansion is neither finite nor infinite.

$$\sqrt{2} = 1.41421356237309504880168872420 97\ldots$$
$$\pi = 3.14159265358979323846264338 32795$$

EXPONENTS AND ROOTS

1.1 Rational and Irrational Numbers

1 Determine which of the following numbers is a rational number.

$$\frac{4}{5}, \sqrt{5}$$

(A) $\frac{4}{5}$　　(B) $\sqrt{5}$

2 Determine which of the following numbers is an irrational number.

$$\frac{\pi}{0}, \sqrt{3}$$

(A) $\frac{\pi}{0}$　　(B) $\sqrt{3}$

3 What type of number is $\frac{3\sqrt{6}}{3}$?

(A) Whole number　　(B) Integer

(C) Rational Number　　(D) Irrational Number

4 Which decimal is the equivalent of $\frac{17}{20}$?

(A) 0.75　　(B) 0.85　　(C) $0.\overline{75}$　　(D) $0.\overline{85}$

5 Which decimal is the equivalent of $\frac{44}{94}$?

(A) 0.4680851063829787　　(B) 0.467

(C) $0.\overline{444444444444444}$　　(D) $0.\overline{46464646}$

Rational and Irrational Numbers 1.1

6 Determine whether the expression below is rational or irrational.

$$7 + \sqrt{7}$$

(A) Rational (B) Irrational

7 The area of a rectangle is 100 square units, and its width is $2\sqrt{2}$ units. Is the height of a rectangle a rational or an irrational number?

(A) Rational (B) Irrational

8 Which fraction is equivalent to 0.321321?

(A) $\frac{321}{100}$ (B) $\frac{321}{99}$

(C) $\frac{107}{333}$ (D) The number cannot be written as a fraction.

9 Which fraction is equivalent to 0.757575?

(A) $\frac{75}{100}$ (B) $\frac{25}{33}$

(C) $\frac{25}{10}$ (D) The number cannot be written as a fraction.

10 Write $0.\overline{03}$ as a fraction.

(A) $\frac{1}{33}$ (B) $\frac{1}{3}$

(C) $\frac{1}{99}$ (D) The number cannot be written as a fraction.

1.1 Rational and Irrational Numbers

11 What type of number is π?

(A) Whole number (B) Integer

(C) Rational Number (D) Irrational Number

12 Which decimal is equivalent to $\frac{21}{33}$?

(A) $0.\overline{63}$ (B) 0.6464 (C) 0.11111 (D) $0.6\overline{2}$

13 Which decimal is equivalent to $\frac{62}{33}$?

(A) 1.878787 (B) $\overline{1.87}$ (C) 1.83 (D) 1.33432

14 The area of a circle is 3π. Is the radius of a circle a rational or an irrational number?

(A) Rational (B) Irrational

15 The perimeter of a mirror is $\frac{7\pi}{3}$ meters, and its width is $\frac{\pi}{2}$ meters. Is the height of a mirror a rational or an irrational number?

(A) Rational (B) Irrational

Rational and Irrational Numbers 1.1

16 The difference of m and n is a rational number. Is m a rational or an irrational number?

(A) Rational (B) Irrational

17 The quotient of m and n is an irrational number, and n is a rational number. Is m a rational or an irrational number?

(A) Rational (B) Irrational

18 The product of m and n is a rational number, and n is a rational number. Is m a rational or irrational number?

(A) Rational (B) Irrational

19 The sum of m and n is a rational number. Is m a rational or an irrational number?

(A) Rational (B) Irrational

20 Write $0.\overline{24}$ as a fraction.

(A) $\frac{6}{33}$ (B) $\frac{24}{10}$ (C) $\frac{8}{33}$ (D) $\frac{24}{33}$

Next Section: Expressions Using Properties of Exponents

EXPRESSIONS USING PROPERTIES OF EXPONENTS

Expressions using properties of exponents are expressions that involve numbers or variables raised to a power, and which can be simplified or manipulated using the laws of exponents. The properties of exponents are rules that allow us to perform operations on exponential expressions, such as multiplying, dividing, adding, and subtracting.

Product of a Power

$a^x a^y = a^{x+y}$

Example: $5^2 5^4 = 5^{2+4} = 5^6$

Zero Exponent

$a^0 = 1$

Example: $4^0 = 1$

Power of a Power

$(a^x)^y = a^{xy}$

Example: $(5^2)^4 = 5^{2\times 4}$

Quotient of Powers

$\dfrac{a^x}{a^y} = a^{x-y}$

Example: $\dfrac{4^5}{4^3} = 4^{5-3}$

Power of a Product

$(ab)^x = a^x b^x$

Example: $(5\times 6)^3 = 5^3 6^3$

Power of a Quotient

$\left(\dfrac{a}{b}\right)^x = \dfrac{a^x}{b^x}$

Example: $\left(\dfrac{4}{5}\right)^3 = \dfrac{4^3}{5^3}$

Negative Exponent

$a^{-x} = \dfrac{1}{a^x}$

Example: $2^{-3} = \dfrac{1}{2^3}$

Expressions Using Properties of Exponents

1.2

1 Simplify using the properties of exponents.

$$b^3 \times b^2$$

(A) b^6 (B) b^5 (C) b^1 (D) $\frac{1}{b^5}$

2 Simplify using the properties of exponents.

$$(4^3)^2$$

(A) 4^6 (B) 4 (C) -4 (D) 4^5

3 Simplify using the properties of exponents.

$$m^2 \times n^2$$

(A) $(mn)^4$ (B) 1 (C) 0 (D) $(mn)^2$

4 Simplify using the properties of exponents.

$$10^{-4}$$

(A) 10^4 (B) $\frac{1}{10}$ (C) $\frac{1}{10^4}$ (D) 10^3

5 Simplify using the properties of exponents.

$$(m^{-2})^4$$

(A) $\frac{1}{m^8}$ (B) m^8 (C) m^6 (D) m^2

EXPONENTS AND ROOTS

1.2 **Expressions Using Properties of Exponents**

6 Simplify using the properties of exponents.

$$m^0 \times n^0$$

(A) 0 (B) 1 (C) mn (D) $\dfrac{m}{n}$

7 The length of a rectangle is a^5 mm, and its width is a^3 mm. What is the area of a rectangle?

(A) a^8 mm² (B) a^{15} mm² (C) a^2 mm² (D) $a^{\frac{5}{3}}$ mm²

8 The side length of a square is 4^5 mm. What is the area of a square?

(A) 4^{25} mm² (B) 4^{10} mm² (C) 4^{15} mm² (D) 4^5 mm²

9 The radius of a circle is a^4 mm. What is the area of a circle?

(A) $a^{16}\pi$ mm² (B) $a^4\pi$ mm² (C) $a\pi$ mm² (D) $a^8\pi$ mm²

10 The side length of a cube is 7^4 mm. What is the volume of a cube?

(A) 7^7 mm³ (B) 7^8 mm³ (C) 7^{12} mm³ (D) 7^2 mm³

11 The length of a playground is a^6 m, and its width is a^2 m. What is the area of a playground?

A $a^8 m^2$ B $a^{12} m^2$ C $a^2 m^2$ D $a^3 m^2$

12 A man has b sons, and each of his sons have 3 sons. Write an expression that represents the total number of men.

_____

13 The radius of a coin is a^8 mm. What is the area of a coin?

_____

14 The area of the floor is a^7 m², and its length is a^3 m. What is the width of the floor?

_____

EXPONENTS AND ROOTS

1.2 **Expressions Using Properties of Exponents**

15 The side length of a square window is 6^3 cm.
What is the area of a window?

_____

16 The seats in the hall are arranged in such a way that the number of rows is equal to the number of seats in each row. There are a^7 rows. How many seats are there?

(A) a^{14} seats (B) a^9 seats (C) a^{49} seats (D) a^{21} seats

17 In the theater, there are a total of 8^4 seats and 8 seats in each row. How many rows are there?

(A) 8 rows (B) 8^2 rows (C) 8^3 rows (D) 8^4 rows

18 The edge length of a cube box is 4^3 cm. What is the volume of a box?

(A) 4^0 cm³ (B) 4^4 cm³ (C) 4^6 cm³ (D) 4^9 cm³

Expressions Using Properties of Exponents 1.2

19 The height of a cube aquarium is 6^5. What is the volume of the aquarium?

_____

20 Simplify: $\dfrac{a^4(a^2)^{-3}}{(a^4)+4^2}$

_____

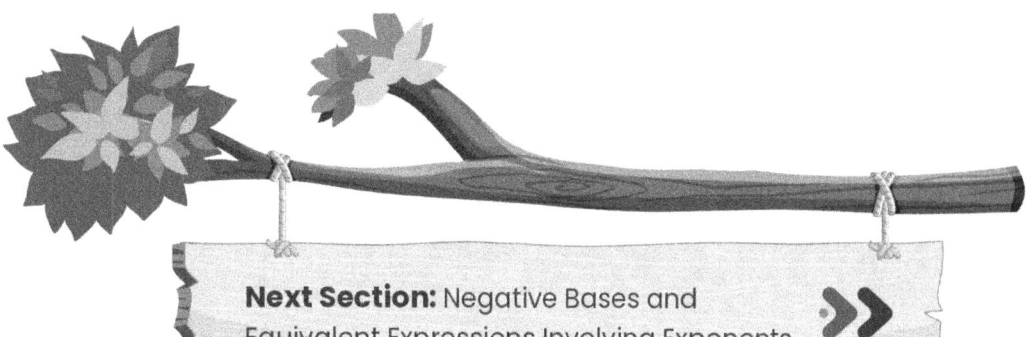

Next Section: Negative Bases and Equivalent Expressions Involving Exponents >>

NEGATIVE BASES AND EQUIVALENT EXPRESSIONS INVOLVING EXPONENTS

Negative bases:

A negative base refers to a situation where a number is raised to a negative power.

$$(-a)^x = a^x \text{ if } x \text{ is even}$$
$$(-a)^x = -a^x \text{ if } x \text{ is odd}$$

Example: $(-3)^4 = 3^4$, $(-3)^7 = -3^7$

Negative Exponent:

A negative exponent refers to a situation where a number or variable is raised to a negative power.

$$a^{-x} = \frac{1}{a^x}$$

Example: $6^{-3} = \frac{1}{6^3}$

1 Simplify using the properties of exponents.

$$(-a)^3 \times (-a)^7$$

(A) a^{-10} (B) a^{10} (C) a^4 (D) a^{-4}

2 Which of the following x values make the equation true?

$$5^2 \times x = 5^9$$

(A) 5^7 (B) 5^6 (C) 5^{12} (D) 5^3

3 The dimensions of a rectangular field are 4^5 yards by 4^6 yards. What is the area of the field?

(A) 4^{30} square yards   (B) 4^{10} square yards

(C) 16^{11} square yards   (D) 4^{11} square yards

4 If x can be any integer, what must be true about the value of 3^x?

(A) It can be a positive or negative value

(B) It can be any positive value, including zero

(C) It can be any positive value

(D) It must be a whole number

EXPONENTS AND ROOTS

1.3 Negative Bases and Equivalent Expressions Involving Exponents

5 The expression $3^2 \times 4^2$ is equivalent to which of the following?

(A) 24 (B) 144 (C) 124 (D) 98

6 What is the value of the expression x^4 when $x = -2$?

(A) 16 (B) −16 (C) 32 (D) −32

7 Are $(-3)^5$ and 3^{-5} equal? (A) Yes (B) No

8 Convert $|-b^{-4}|$ m to cm.

_____

9 The area of a rhombus is $|-b^{-2}|$, and the area of a rectangle is b^{-2}. Is the area of the rhombus equal to the area of the rectangle?

(A) Yes (B) No

10 The number of bacteria in Experiment #1 is 5^5. The number of bacteria in Experiment #2 is 4^5. Are there an equal number of bacteria in both experiments?

(A) Yes   (B) No

11 The edge length of a cube box is $|-a^4|$ cm. What is the volume of a box?

(A) a^2 cm^3 (B) a^7 cm^3 (C) a^{12} cm^3 (D) a^8 cm^3

12 Find x to make the equation true.

$$\frac{2^2}{2^3((-4)^{-2})^3} = 2^x$$

(A) 10   (B) 11   (C) 12   (D) 16

13 The width of a notebook is $(-4)^{-2}$ m. What is the width of a notebook in cm?

EXPONENTS AND ROOTS

1.3

**Negative Bases and Equivalent
Expressions Involving Exponents**

14

Determine if the expressions below are equal.
Fill in the blank with = or ≠.

$$(2^3)^2 \underline{\hspace{1cm}} 2^3 \times 2^2$$

(A) Equal   (B) Not equal

15

The area of the door is $|(-a)^{11}|$ cm², and its width is $(-a^2)$ cm .
What is the height of the door?

_____

16

Determine if the expressions below are equal.
Fill in the blank with = or ≠.

$$\left(\frac{5}{3}\right)^6 \underline{\hspace{1cm}} 5^6 \, 3^{-6}$$

(A) Equal   (B) Not equal

17

The length of a rectangle is 6^{-4} and its width is 4^{-6}. Is the length of the rectangle equal to its width?

(A) Yes   (B) No

Negative Bases and Equivalent Expressions Involving Exponents | **1.3**

18 The length of a matchbox is $(-2)^{-6}$ m. What is the length of a matchbox in cm?

_____

19 The length of Particle A is 4^{-20} and the length of Particle B is 2^{-40}. Is the length of both particles equal?

(A) Yes   (B) No

20 The area of a parallelogram is $|(-2)^{-6}|$, and the area of a rectangle is 2^{-6}. Is the area of the parallelogram equal to the area of the rectangle?

_____

Next Section:
Square Roots and Cube Roots

SQUARE ROOTS AND CUBE ROOTS

A **square root** of a number is a value that can be multiplied by itself to produce the original number. A **perfect square** is a square of an integer

The symbol for the square root is $\sqrt{}$.

$$8 \times 8 = 64$$
$$\sqrt{64} = 8$$

A **cube root** of a number is a value that can be cubed to produce the original number. The symbol for the cube root is $\sqrt[3]{}$.

A **perfect cube** is a cube of an integer.

Example:

$$4 \times 4 \times 4 = 64$$
$$\sqrt[3]{64} = 4$$

Integer	Perfect Cube
0	$0^3 = 0$
1	$1^3 = 1$
2	$2^3 = 8$
3	$3^3 = 27$
4	$4^3 = 64$
5	$5^3 = 125$
6	$6^3 = 216$
7	$7^3 = 343$
8	$8^3 = 512$
9	$9^3 = 729$
10	$10^3 = 1000$

The cube root of a perfect cube is an integer.

SQUARE ROOTS AND CUBE ROOTS

The cube root of an integer is not always an integer. In some cases, it can be simplified.

Example:

$$\sqrt[3]{16} = \sqrt[3]{8 \times 3}$$

A cube root that cannot be simplified further is called a surd. In the example above, $2\sqrt[3]{2}$ is a surd.

You can also find the cube root of a negative integer. A cube root of a negative integer will always be negative because multiplying an odd number of negative numbers gives a negative number.

Example:

$\sqrt[3]{} - 27 = -3$

EXPONENTS AND ROOTS

1.4   **Square Roots and Cube Roots**

1   Which of the following is an irrational number?

(A) $\sqrt{25}$ (B) $\sqrt{4}$ (C) $\sqrt{42}$ (D) $\sqrt{23}$

2   Which of the following has the largest value?

(A) 8.8   (B) $\sqrt{64}$ (C) $\sqrt{36}$ (D) $-\sqrt{36}$

3   Which of the following is a rational number?

(A) $\sqrt{81}$ (B) $\sqrt{21}$ (C) $\sqrt{32}$ (D) $\sqrt{6}$

4   Solve the equation: $x^2 = 49$

(A) ± 49 (B) 7   (C) -7 (D) ± 7

5   The area of a square is found using the equation $A = s^2$, where s is the length of one side. Mercy knows the area of a square to be 25 square feet. What is the length of one side of the square?

(A) 5   (B) 10   (C) 15   (D) 20

Square Roots and Cube Roots   1.4

6 The volume of a cube box is 0.320 m³. What is the height of the box?

_____

7 Find the square root.

$\sqrt{0.64}$ = _____.

8 Find the cube root of a perfect cube.

$\sqrt[3]{-1}$ = _____.

9 Find the square root.

$\sqrt{\frac{16}{144}}$ = _____.

10 Find the cube root of a perfect cube.

$\sqrt[3]{6561}$ = _____.

11 The volume of a cube room is 64 m³. What is the height of the room?

Ⓐ 8 m   Ⓑ 4 m   Ⓒ $2\sqrt[3]{2}$ m   Ⓓ $\sqrt[3]{3}$ m

1.4   Square Roots and Cube Roots

12 The area of a square-shaped mobile phone is 196 cm². What is the width of the mobile phone?

(A) 14 cm   (B) 13 cm   (C) 16 cm   (D) 24 cm

13 The volume of an ice cube is 0.049 cm³. What is the height of the ice cube?

(A) $\frac{\sqrt[3]{7}}{10}$ m   (B) $\frac{7}{10}$ m   (C) $\frac{\sqrt[3]{49}}{10}$ m   (D) $\frac{49}{10}$ m

14 The area of a square-shaped paper is 3600 cm². What is the side length of the paper?

(A) $6\sqrt{2}$ cm   (B) 6 cm   (C) $2\sqrt{6}$ cm   (D) 60 cm

15 The volume of a cube radio is 8000 cm³. What is the height of the radio?

Square Roots and Cube Roots · 1.4

16 The area of a square-shaped desk is 5.29 cm². What is the width of the desk?

_____

17 The volume of a cube sculpture is 384 m³. What is the height of the sculpture?

_____

18 Simplify. $(\sqrt{250} + \sqrt{810})^2$

_____

19 The area of a square-shaped painting is 0.36 m². What is the width of the painting?

(A) 0.6 m   (B) 0.06 m   (C) 6 m   (D) ± 0.06 m

1.4 Square Roots and Cube Roots

20 The volume of a cube TV is 0.512 m³. What is the height of the TV?

_____

Next Section:
Scientific Notation

SCIENTIFIC NOTATION

Scientific notation is a way to express numbers that are too big or too small. There are rules that allow you to add, subtract, multiply, and divide numbers written in scientific notation:

If we add numbers written in scientific notation with the same power of 10, we just add its coefficients and multiply by the power of 10.

Example: $3.2 \times 10^4 + 2.1 \times 10^4 = (3.2 + 2.1) \times 10^4 = 5.3 \times 10^4$

If we subtract numbers written in scientific notation with the same power of 10, we just subtract its coefficients and multiply by the power of 10.

Example: $3.2 \times 10^4 - 2.1 \times 10^4 = (3.2 - 2.1) \times 10^4 = 1.1 \times 10^4$

If we multiply numbers written in scientific notation, we multiply their coefficients and powers of 10.

Example: $3.2 \times 10^4 \times 2.1 \times 10^2 = (3.2 \times 2.1) \times (10^4 \times 10^2) = 6.72 \times 10^6$

If we divide numbers written in scientific notation, we divide its coefficients and powers of 10.

Example:
$$\frac{3.2 \times 10^4}{1.6 \times 10^2} = \frac{3.2}{1.6} \times 10^{4-2} = 2.0 \times 10^2$$

1.5   Scientific Notation

1   How should 423,000,000 be expressed in scientific notation?

- (A) 4.23×10^8
- (B) 42.3×10^8
- (C) 4.23×10^{-8}
- (D) 0.423×10^{-8}

2   How should 0.000000765 be expressed in scientific notation?

- (A) 76.5×10^7
- (B) 7.65×10^{-7}
- (C) 7.65×10^8
- (D) 76.5×10^8

3   Elisha rewrote the 53,090,000,000 in scientific notation as 5.39×10^{10}. What mistake did she make?

- (A) There are only 8 zeroes in the original number.
- (B) The first factor, 5.39, is too small to represent the original number.
- (C) She did not include the zero in the hundred million places in the first factor.
- (D) The second factor should not be expressed as 101^0.

4   Which number is 5 times larger than 90,000?

- (A) 9×10^7
- (B) 9×10^9
- (C) 9×10^8
- (D) 4.5×10^8

5 Eric wrote 0.000000000000978 as 9.78×10^{13}. What mistake did he make?

(A) The exponent should be negative.

(B) The exponent should be larger.

(C) The first-factor should be negative.

(D) The first-factor is incorrect.

6 The table below shows the weight of insects.

Name	Weight (kg)
Ant	2.0×10^{-6}
Grasshopper	4.4×10^{-4}
Spider	5.0×10^{-5}
Fly	1.5×10^{-5}
Mosquito	3.0×10^{-6}

How much more does a spider weigh than a fly?

_____

1.5   Scientific Notation

---

7   Compare. Fill in the blank using the following symbols: >, <, or =.

$$0.000054 \underline{\hspace{2cm}} 5.4 \times 10^{-5}$$

(A) >   (B) <   (C) =

8   Compare. Fill in the blank using the following symbols: >, <, =.

$$3.2 \times 10^{-6} \underline{\hspace{2cm}} 0.000032$$

(A) >   (B) <   (C) =

9   What is 0.0000025 expressed in scientific notation?

(A) 2.5×10^{-5} (B) 2.05×10^{-6} (C) 2.5×10^{-6} (D) 0.25×10^{-6}

10   Which expression is equivalent to $5.3 \times 0.1 \times 0.1 \times 0.1$?

(A) 5.3×10^{3} (B) 0.53×10^{3} (C) 0.53×10^{-3} (D) 5.3×10^{-3}

11 Which expression is equivalent to $6.9 \times 10 \times 10 \times 10 \times 10$?

(A) 6.9×10^3 (B) 6.9×10^2 (C) 6.9×10^{-3} (D) 6.9×10^4

12 The net of a rectangular prism is shown, where $a=9.0\times10^{-4}$, $b=4.0 \times 10^{-4}$ and $c=8.0 \times 10^{-4}$.

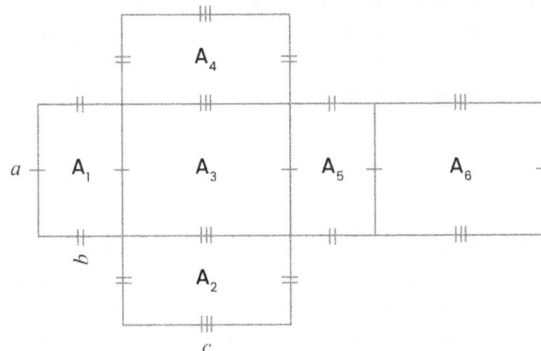

How many times is c greater than b

_____.

13 Write the number in standard notation.
The atomic radius of chlorine is 7.9×10^{-11} m.

(A) 0.000000000000079 (B) 0.00000000000079

(C) 0.0000000000079 (D) 0.000000000079

EXPONENTS AND ROOTS

1.5   Scientific Notation

14   Fill in the blank. $6.6 \times 10^{-3} \div$ _____ $= 3.0 \times 10^2$

15   Write the number in scientific notation.
The density of helium is 0.1785 g/L .

(A) 1.785×10^{-1} (B) 1.785×10^{-2} (C) 1.785×10^{-3} (D) 1.785×10^{-4}

16   Evaluate. $(6.4 \times 10^{-4}) \times (2.3 \times 10^{-3})$

(A) 1.472×10^{-5} (B) 1.472×10^{-6} (C) 1.472×10^{-7} (D) 14.72×10^{-8}

17   Select the number in standard notation equal to the number in scientific notation.

$$5.8 \times 10^3$$

(A) 580   (B) 5,800   (C) 58,000   (D) 580,000

18   Evaluate.

$7.5 \times 10^{-1} - 2.8 \times 10^{-1} =$ _____

Scientific Notation 1.5

19 Write the number in scientific notation.
The mass of a dust particle is 0.000000000753 kg.

(A) 7.53×10^{-8} (B) 7.53×10^{-9} (C) 7.53×10^{-10} (D) 7.53×10^{-11}

20 Evaluate. $(4.0 \times 10^9) \div (5.0 \times 10^8) =$ _____.

Next Section: Chapter Review ≫

EXPONENTS AND ROOTS

1.6 Chapter Review

1 Find the value of $3\sqrt{216}$.

Ⓐ 4　　　Ⓑ 6　　　Ⓒ 16　　　Ⓓ 32

2 Which of the following is an irrational number?

Ⓐ $3\sqrt{8}$　　　Ⓑ $3\sqrt{125}$　　　Ⓒ $3\sqrt{49}$　　　Ⓓ $3\sqrt{27}$

3 The volume of a cube can be found using the formula $V = s^3$, where s is the length of a side of the cube. If the volume of a cube is 729 cubic inches, what is the length of one of the sides of the cube?

Ⓐ 729　　　Ⓑ 18　　　Ⓒ 13　　　Ⓓ 9

4 Which strategy represents a possible first step for converting this number to scientific notation?

6,185,000

Ⓐ Divide the number by 10^3

Ⓑ Divide the number by 10^5

Ⓒ Divide the number by 10^6

Ⓓ Divide the number by 10^7

5 New York is granted 10 seats in the House of Representatives and the estimated population per seat is 6.22×10^5. What is the total estimated population of New York?

_____

6 When multiplying 3^3 and 3^8, what happens to the exponents in the product?

(A) They are added.   (B) They are multiplied.

(C) They are subtracted.   (D) They are divided.

7 When dividing 6^{14} by 6^9, what happens to the exponents in the quotient?

(A) They are added.   (B) They are multiplied.

(C) They are subtracted.   (D) They are divided.

8 Which symbol can be used to compare these two numbers?

$$2\frac{6}{4} \rule{2cm}{0.4pt} \sqrt{16}$$

(A) =   (B) <   (C) >   (D) ≈

1.6   **Chapter Review**

9   Which symbol can be used to compare these two numbers?

$$5.366 \text{_____} \sqrt{38}$$

(A) =   (B) <   (C) >   (D) ≈

10   Which symbol can be used to compare these numbers?

$$\sqrt{24} \text{_____} \sqrt{38}$$

(A) =   (B) <   (C) >   (D) ≈

11   Emily claims the $\sqrt{68}$ is greater than 8.12. Which statement explains why she is correct?

(A) The square root 68 is approximately 8.25.

(B) The square root 68 is approximately 8.34.

(C) The square root 68 is approximately 8.66.

(D) The square root 68 is approximately 8.46.

12   Which of these numbers is the greatest?

(A) $\sqrt{32}$ (B) 5.33   (C) $\sqrt{30}$ (D) 5.89

13 Which of these numbers is the least?

(A) 7.99   (B) $\sqrt{59}$ (C) 7.62   (D) $\sqrt{60}$

14 Which fraction is equivalent to $0.\overline{246}$?

(A) $\dfrac{82}{333}$ (B) $\dfrac{246}{1000}$ (C) $\dfrac{123}{500}$ (D) $\dfrac{123}{900}$

15 Which fraction is equivalent to $0.\overline{27}$?

(A) $\dfrac{27}{10}$ (B) $\dfrac{3}{11}$ (C) $\dfrac{27}{100}$ (D) $\dfrac{3}{99}$

16 Which rational expression is equivalent to $\sqrt{3}$?

(A) $\dfrac{3}{10}$ (B) $\dfrac{21}{8}$ (C) $\dfrac{18}{9}$

(D) The number cannot be written as a fraction.

17 Which number is equal to $2\sqrt{7} + 7$?

(A) $\dfrac{23}{99}$ (B) $\dfrac{564}{199}$ (C) $\dfrac{234}{999}$

(D) The number cannot be written as a fraction.

1.6 Chapter Review

18 The area of a rectangular tile is 75 square centimeters, and its width is $\sqrt{25}$ centimeters. Is the length of a tile a rational or an irrational number?

(A) Rational   (B) Irrational

19 The table below shows the masses of Earth and Pluto.

Planet	Mass (kg)
Earth	5.9736×10^{24}
Pluto	1.25×10^{22}

How much does Earth weigh more than Pluto?

_____

20 Is the result of the expression below a prime number?

$\sqrt[3]{512} - \sqrt[3]{-343}$ (A) Yes   (B) No

Next Chapter: Functions ›

CHAPTER 2

FUNCTIONS

5	3			7				
6			1	9	5			
	9	8					6	
8				6				3
4			8		3			1
7				2				6
	6					2	8	
			4	1	9			5
				8			7	9

EVALUATE FUNCTION AND LINEAR FUNCTION

Evaluating a function means finding the output value of the function for a given input value.

A linear function is represented by the equation $y = mx + b$, where the input values are the values of x, the output values are the values of y, and m and b are the coefficients.

A linear function can be represented by the table.

Example:

$$y = 2x + 1$$

x	1	2	3	4
y	3	5	7	9

The difference between any two successive values of x must be the same:

2-1=1

3-2=1

4-3=1

The difference between any two successive values of y must be the same:

5-3=2

7-5=2

9-7=2

A linear function can be represented by a graph. The graph of a linear function is a straight line.

2.1 Evaluate Function and Linear Function

1 Does the data in this table represent a function? Why or why not?

Time (seconds)	Height (meter)
0	6
2	9
4	4
6	0
7	0
8	5

(A) Yes, each input has exactly one output.

(B) Yes, there is an input and output value of 0.

(C) No, there is more than one input for each output.

(D) No, there is more than one output for each input.

2 Does the data in this table represent a function? Why or why not?

Age (years)	Income (Thousands)
18	22
19	33
19	24
20	37
22	40

(A) Yes, the input values are less than the output values.

(B) Yes, each input has exactly one output.

(C) No, there is more than one input for each output.

(D) No, there is more than one output for a given input.

3   Do the values on this graph represent a function?

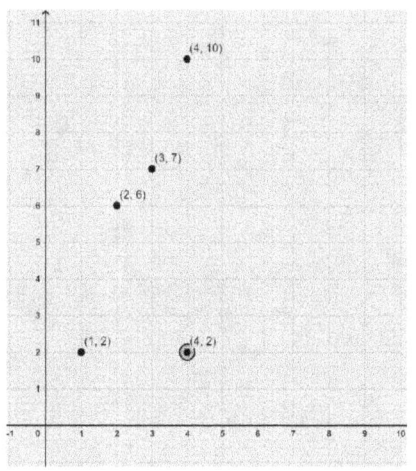

A   Yes, there is exactly one input for each output.

B   Yes, there is exactly one output for each input.

C   No, there is more than one input for each output.

D   No, there is more than one output for each input.

4   Do the values on this graph represent a function?

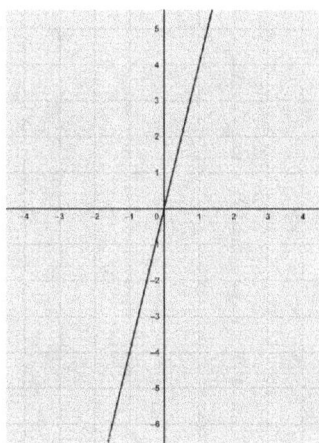

A   Yes, there is exactly one input for each output.

B   Yes, there is exactly one output for each input.

C   No, there is more than one input for each output.

D   No, there is more than one output for each input.

2.1   **Evaluate Function and Linear Function**

5   What is the domain of the function $y = 2x + 3$?

(A)   All real values of x

(B)   All real values of x such that $x \neq \dfrac{2}{3}$

(C)   All real values of x such that $x = \dfrac{2}{3}$

(D)   All real values of x such that $x > 0$

6   What is the domain of the function? $f(x) = \sqrt{4x-5}$?

(A)   All real values of x

(B)   All real values of x such that $x \geq \dfrac{5}{4}$

(C)   All real values of x such that $x \leq \dfrac{5}{4}$

(D)   All real values of x such that $x \geq 0$

7   What is the domain of the function? $f(x) = \dfrac{x+2}{1-x}$?

(A)   All real values of x

(B)   All real values of x such that $x \neq \dfrac{1}{2}$

(C)   All real values of x such that $x \neq 1$

(D)   All real values of x such that $x = 1$

Evaluate Function and Linear Function   2.1

8 What is the domain of the function $y = \frac{x+4}{3x-2}$?

(A) All real values of x

(B) All real values of x such that $x \neq \frac{2}{3}$

(C) All real values of x such that $x \neq \frac{3}{2}$

(D) All real values of x such that $x \leq 2$

---

9 Determine the domain of the function in the graph.

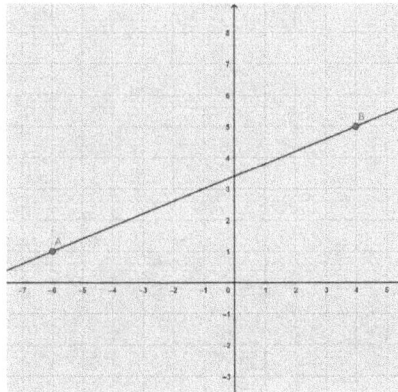

(A) $5 \leq x < 4$

(B) $-6 \leq x \leq 4$

(C) $-3 \leq x < 4$

(D) $6 \leq x \leq 8$

---

10 Select a number to fill in the table so that a table DOES NOT represent a function.

x	−6	−2		0	1
y	2	4	6	8	5

(A) −2   (B) −1

(C) 2   (D) 4

FUNCTIONS

11   Complete a table so that it represents a linear function.

x	1	3	5	7
y	2		6	8

(A) 1   (B) 2   (C) 3   (D) 4

12   Determine whether the graph represents a function.

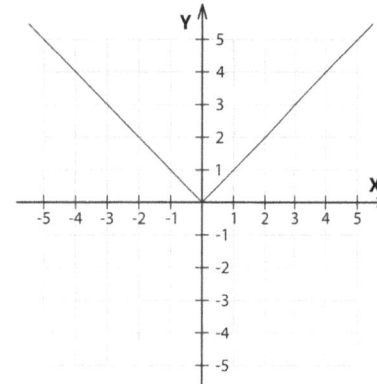

(A) Yes   (B) No

13   Determine whether the graph represents a function.

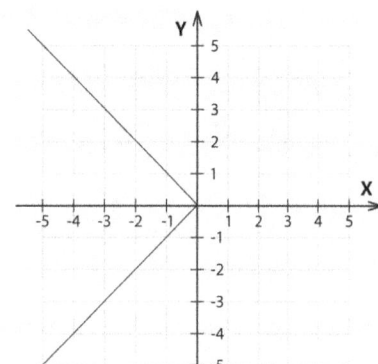

(A) Yes   (B) No

Evaluate Function and Linear Function | **2.1**

14 Parker earns $15 per hour, and charges a flat fee of $6. The total earnings, y, depend on the number of working hours, x. Fill in the table to represent this linear relationship.

x	0	2	4	6
y				

15 The perimeter of a square, y, depends on the length of a side of a square, x. Fill in the table to represent this linear relationship.

x	5	10	15	20
y				

16 Emma saved money in the bank for 5 years. The table below shows the amount of money in the bank account, y, in dollars, after x years.

x	0	1	2	3	4	5
y	300	1800	3300	4800	6300	7800

What are the domain and range of the function?

_____

2.1 **Evaluate Function and Linear Function**

17 James hiked for 4 hours. The table below shows the distance, y, in miles, that he passed after x hours. What are the domain and range of the function?

x	0	1	2	3	4
y	0	1.25	2.5	3.75	5

18 The equation $y = 5x + 2$ represents the level of water in the tank, y, in feet, after x hours. The tank is 32 feet high. What are the domain and range of the function?

19 A babysitter earns $30 per hour, and charges a flat fee of $10. The total earnings, y, depend on the number of working hours, x. Fill in the table to represent this linear relationship.

x	1	2	3	4
y				

20 Neha has a box of marbles. She gives an equal number of marbles to each child in the class. The equation $y = 60 - 3x$ represents the number of marbles left in the box, y, after Neha gave marbles to x children. What are the domain and range of the function?

_____

Next Section:
Compare the Linear Function

COMPARE THE LINEAR FUNCTION

A linear function is a function that can be written in form $f(x) = mx + b$, where m and b are constants. The variable x represents the input value, and the output value is obtained by multiplying the input value by the slope m and adding the y-intercept b.

A linear function can be represented by a table.

x	2	4	6	8
y	1	4	7	10

The rate of change can be found in the following way.

$$m = \frac{y_2 - y_1}{x_2 - x_1} = \frac{4-1}{4-2} = \frac{3}{2}$$

A linear function can be represented by a graph.

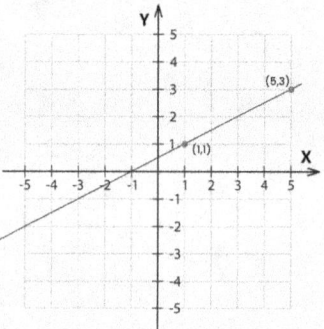

The rate of change can be found in the following way.

$$m = \frac{y_2 - y_1}{x_2 - x_1} = \frac{3-1}{5-1} = \frac{2}{4} = \frac{1}{2}$$

A linear function can be represented by an equation.

$$2x + 3y = 4$$

The rate of change m can be found in the following way.

$$2x + 3y = 4$$

$$y = -\frac{2}{3}x + \frac{4}{3}$$

$$m = -\frac{2}{3}$$

Compare the Linear Function   2.2

1   Find the rate of change for a linear function given by the table.

x	-4	-2	2	4
y	-2	-1	1	2

(A) $\dfrac{1}{4}$ (B) $\dfrac{1}{2}$ (C) 4   (D) 2

2   Find the rate of change for a linear function given by the table.

x	1	2	3	4
y	2	4	6	8

(A) -2   (B) $-\dfrac{1}{2}$ (C) $\dfrac{1}{2}$ (D) 2

3   Find the rate of change for a linear function given by the graph.

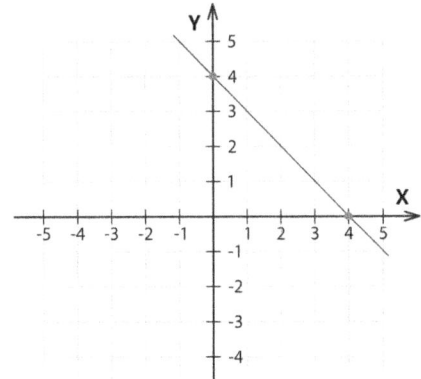

(A) -1   (B) 1

(C) 0   (D) $\dfrac{1}{4}$

2.2 Compare the Linear Function

4 Find the rate of change for a linear function given by the graph.

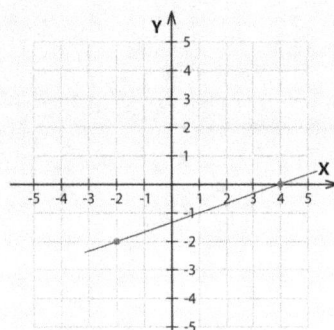

(A) 3

(B) −3

(C) $\dfrac{1}{3}$

(D) $-\dfrac{1}{3}$

5 The equation below shows the height of the bird, y in feet, after x minutes. How many feet does the height of the birds increase each minute?

$$y = 10 + 30x$$

(A) 10   (B) 20   (C) 30   (D) 40

6 The number of staff in the hotel is constant and the number of guests changes depending on the number of rooms rented. The graph below shows the total number of staff and guests at the hotel. How many guests are in each room?

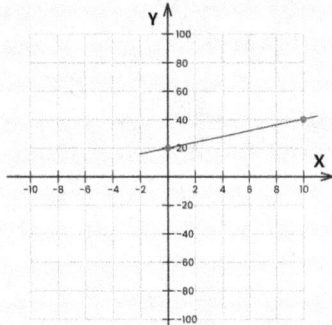

(A) 1

(B) 2

(C) 3

(D) 4

Compare the Linear Function **2.2**

7 Find the rate of change for a linear function given by the equation.

$$y = -4 - 10x$$

(A) −4   (B) $\dfrac{2}{5}$ (C) −10   (D) $-\dfrac{5}{2}$

8 Complete the table so that the rate of change is 3.

x	−2	2
y		24

9 Some students are waiting for a bus and the remaining students are transported by x vans. The equation below shows the total number of students, y. How many students are in each van?

$$y = 25x + 50$$

(A) 25   (B) 2   (C) −2   (D) 50

10 Noah and Peter are trying to make some money as dog walkers on their street. Noah charges $5 per walk for his services. Peter charges $10 per day and guarantees three dog walks each day. If a person wants to hire a dog walker for three dog walks per day for three days, who offers the better deal?

(A) Noah

(B) Peter

(C) They are the same cost.

(D) There is not enough information to determine which is a better deal.

2.2 Compare the Linear Function

11 John and James are trying to make some money as dog walkers on their street. John charges $5 per walk for his services. James charges $15 per day and guarantees three dog walks a day. If a person wants to hire a dog walker for two walks, who offers the better deal?

(A) John

(B) James

(C) They are the same cost.

(D) There is not enough information to determine which is a better deal.

12 The table below represents Function A.

x	y
2	10
4	20
6	40

What is the rate of change of Function A?

(A) $\frac{1}{5}$ (B) $-\frac{1}{5}$ (C) -5 (D) 5

13 The table below represents Function A.

x	y
3	6
6	7
9	8

Function B can be represented by the equation, $y = 5x + 10$. Compare the rate of change for each function.

(A) Function A has a smaller rate of change.

(B) Function B has a smaller rate of change.

(C) Both functions have an equal rate of change.

(D) It is impossible to tell the rate of change of each function based on the information given.

14 Ryan's mom is considering joining a movie club. The club requires members to pay a $40 yearly membership fee and charges 10 per movie purchased. When she buys movies at the store, and each movie costs $14. If she is considering purchasing 20 movies per year, which scenario is a better deal?

A) The movie club is a better deal.

B) Buying movies at the store is a better deal.

C) There is no difference between either option.

D) There is not enough information to determine which is a better deal.

15 Which representation of linear function has a greater rate of change? The equation or the table?

Equation: $2x + 5y - 3 = 0$

Table:

x	-5	-8	-11
y	-1	0	1

A) Equation   B) Table

2.2   Compare the Linear Function

16 Which representation of linear function has a greater rate of change? The graph or the equation?

Graph:

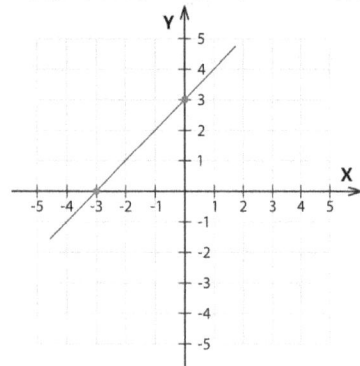

Equation: $2x + 4y = 8$

(A) Graph   (B) Equation

17 The initial number of bacteria in an experiment increases at a constant rate every minute. The equation below shows the total number of bacteria in an experiment, y, after x minutes. How many more bacteria are there in each minute?

$$y = 100 + 90x$$

18 The equation below shows the height of the bird y in feet, after x minutes. How many feet do the height of the birds increase in each minute?

$$y = 25 + 60x$$

(A) 25   (B) $\frac{60}{25}$ (C) $\frac{25}{60}$ (D) 60

19 Select a representation of a linear function that has the rate of change is greater.

Equation: $\frac{x}{2} + \frac{y}{3} = 1$

Table:

x	3	8	13
y	-8	-5	-2

(A) Equation   (B) Table

20 Function A is represented by the graph below.

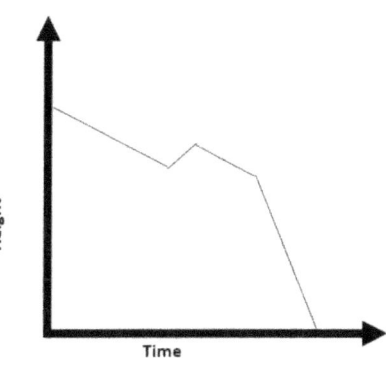

(A) Rain falls and fills a river with more water.

(B) A cold snap, snow falls and accumulates on the ground, then rapidly melts.

(C) A water faucet is opened, and a barrel of water is gradually emptied.

(D) A climber starts at the top of a mountain and descends in altitude.

Next Section: Identify and Rewrite Equations in Slope-Intercept Form

IDENTIFY AND REWRITE EQUATIONS IN SLOPE-INTERCEPT FORM

A slope–intercept form of a linear function is $y = mx + b$, where m is the slope and b is the y–intercept.

We can write an equation of a linear function in slope–intercept form if the coordinates of the two points are given.

Example:

Write an equation in slope–intercept form of a linear function that contains points A$(2,-3)$ and B$(1,-6)$.

$$A(2,-3) \rightarrow x_1 = 2, y_1 = -3$$
$$B(1,-6) \rightarrow x_2 = 1, y_2 = -6$$

Find slope.

$$m = \frac{y_2 - y_1}{x_2 - x_1} = \frac{(-6)-(-3)}{1-2} = \frac{-3}{-1} = 3$$

Find y–intercept.

$$b = -9$$

(You can also write an equation of a linear function in slope–intercept form with the graph of the linear function.)

1 Rewrite the equation in slope-intercept form.

$$4x - 5y = 3$$

(A) $y = \frac{4}{5}x + \frac{3}{5}$

(B) $y = -\frac{4}{5}x - \frac{3}{5}$

(C) $y = \frac{4}{5}x - \frac{3}{5}$

(D) $y = -\frac{4}{5}x + \frac{3}{5}$

2 Rewrite the equation in slope-intercept form.

$$-x - 2y + 3 = 0$$

(A) $y = -3x + \frac{3}{2}$

(B) $y = 3x + \frac{3}{2}$

(C) $y = -3x - \frac{3}{2}$

(D) $y = 3x - \frac{3}{2}$

3 Rewrite the equation in slope-intercept form.

$$5y - 11x - 22 = 0$$

(A) $y = -\frac{11}{5}x + \frac{22}{5}$

(B) $y = -\frac{11}{5}x - \frac{22}{5}$

(C) $y = -\frac{11}{5}x - \frac{22}{5}$

(D) $y = \frac{11}{5}x + \frac{22}{5}$

4 Write an equation in slope-intercept form given two points.

$$A(4,7), B(2,5)$$

(A) $y = 2x + 3$

(B) $y = x + 3$

(C) $y = x + 1$

(D) $y = 3x + 1$

FUNCTIONS

Identify and Rewrite Equations in Slope-Intercept Form

5 Write an equation in slope–intercept form given two points.

$$A(3,6), B(-1,2)$$

- (A) $y = 2x + 4$
- (B) $y = x + 4$
- (C) $y = 2x + 3$
- (D) $y = x + 3$

6 Write the equation in slope–intercept form given two points.

$$A(2,3), B(4,6)$$

- (A) $y = \frac{3}{2}x + \frac{4}{3}$
- (B) $y = \frac{3}{2}x + 3$
- (C) $y = \frac{3}{2}x + \frac{2}{3}$
- (D) $y = \frac{3}{2}x$

7 Write the equation in slope–intercept form given the graph.

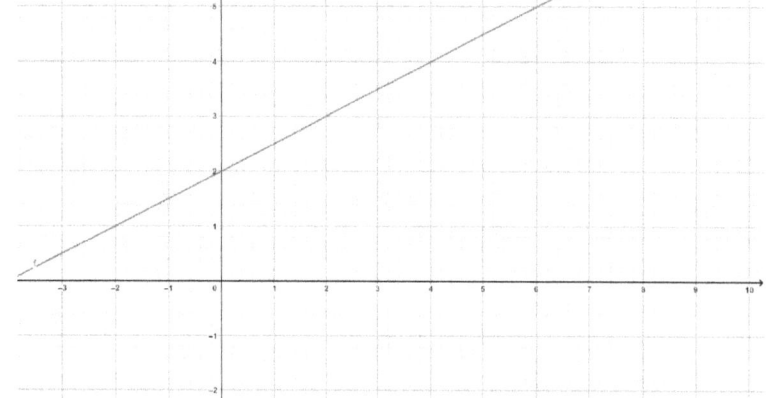

- (A) $y = \frac{1}{2}x + 2$
- (B) $y = \frac{1}{2}x$
- (C) $y = \frac{1}{2}x + 1$
- (D) $y = \frac{1}{2}x - 1$

8 Write the equation in slope–intercept form given the graph.

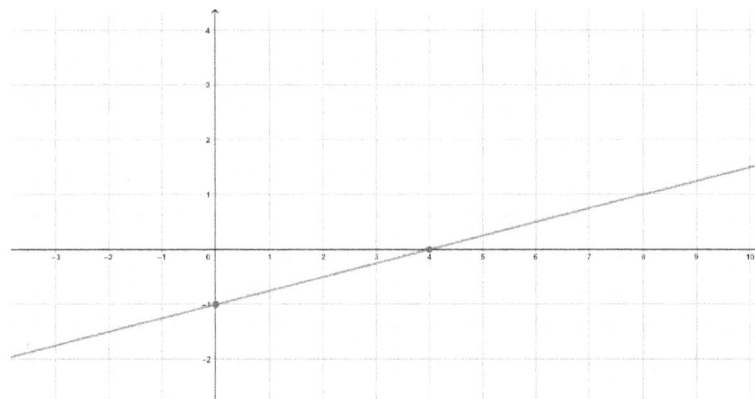

A $y = \frac{1}{4}x + 1$

B $y = -\frac{1}{4}x - 1$

C $y = \frac{1}{4}x - 1$

D $y = -\frac{1}{4}x + 1$

9 Write the equation in slope–intercept form given the graph.

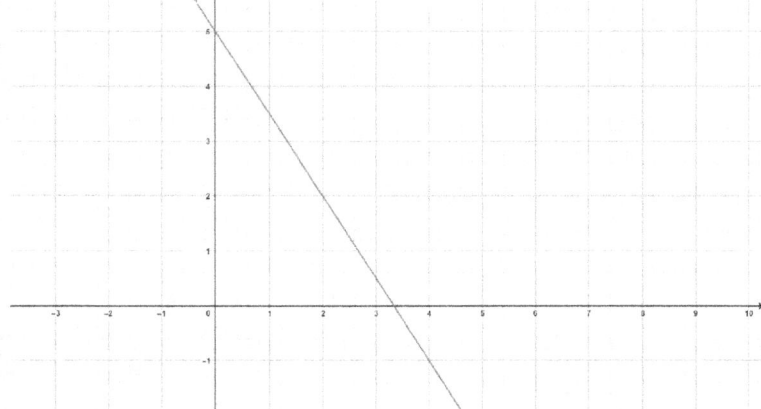

A $y = \frac{3}{2}x + 5$

B $y = -\frac{3}{2}x - 5$

C $y = -\frac{3}{2}x$

D $y = -\frac{3}{2}x + 5$

2.3 Identify and Rewrite Equations in Slope-Intercept Form

10 Determine the y-intercept from the graph.

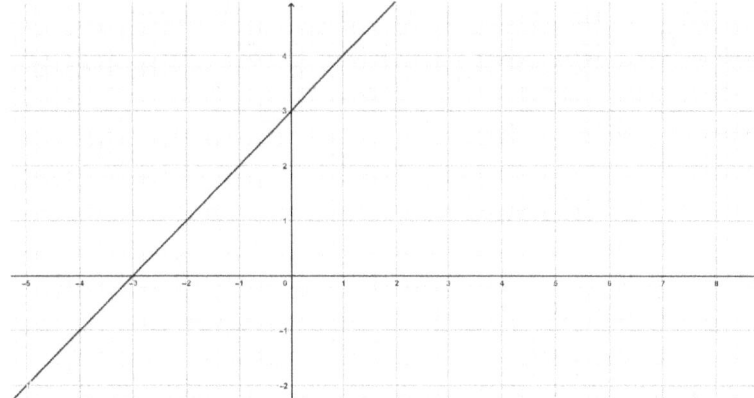

- (A) -3
- (B) 3
- (C) 0
- (D) 1

11 Determine the y-intercept from the graph.

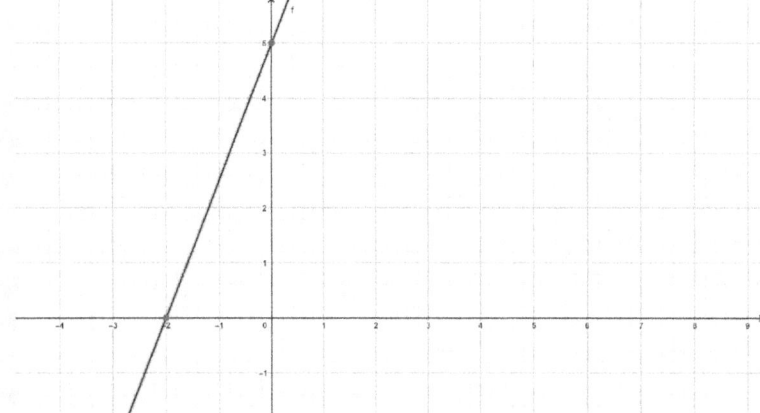

- (A) -2
- (B) 2
- (C) 5
- (D) -5

12 Determine the y–intercept from the graph.

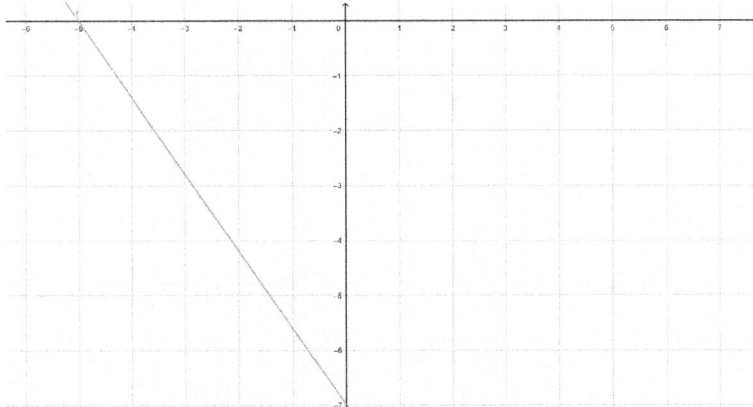

A) -5

B) 5

C) 7

D) -7

13 The level of the water is 8 inches and it increases 2 inches per hour. Write an equation that represents the level of water, y, depending on the number of hours, x.

A) $y = 2x + 8$

B) $y = -2x + 8$

C) $y = 2x - 8$

D) $y = -2x - 8$

14 Neha has $500 in her bank account and she saves $100 each week. Write an equation that represents the balance, y, depending on the number of weeks, x.

A) $y = 500x + 100$

B) $y = 500x - 100$

C) $y = 100x + 500$

D) $y = 100x - 500$

2.3 Identify and Rewrite Equations in Slope-Intercept Form

15 The height of the balloon is 40 yards, and it increases 4 yards per minute. Write an equation that represents the height of the balloon, y, depending on the number of minutes, x.

(A) $y = 40x + 4$

(B) $y = 4x + 40$

(C) $y = 4x - 40$

(D) $y = 40x - 4$

16 Ava weighs 90 kg, and she gains weight 4 kg each month. Write an equation that represents Mia's weight, y, depending on the number of months, x.

(A) $y = 4x + 90$

(B) $y = 4x - 90$

(C) $y = 90x + 4$

(D) $y = 90x - 4$

17 The level of the water is 16 inches, and it decreases 2 inches per hour. Write an equation that represents the level of water, y, depending on the number of hours, x.

(A) $y = 2x + 16$

(B) $y = -2x - 16$

(C) $y = 2x - 16$

(D) $y = -2x + 16$

18 Jack has 300 bottles of Soda in the store, and he sells bottles in six-packs. Write an equation that represents the total number of bottles, y, depending on the number of six-packs sold, x.

(A) $y = 6x + 300$

(B) $y = -6x + 300$

(C) $y = -6x - 300$

(D) $y = 6x - 300$

19 Write the following equations in slope–intercept form.

$$\frac{x}{2} + \frac{y}{3} = 1$$

20 Write an equation in slope–intercept form for the given graph.

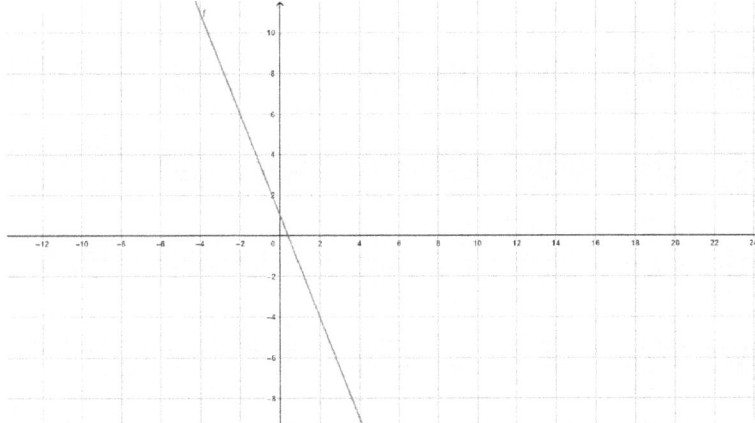

Next Section: Analyzing Graph

ANALYZING GRAPH

Analyzing a graph involves examining the various features of a plotted set of data points, lines, or curves on a graph in order to gain insights into the relationship between the variables being studied.

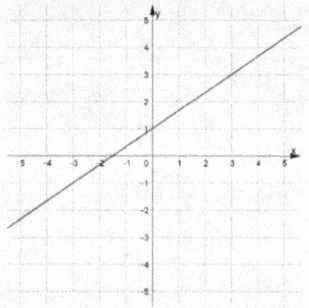

A graph is increasing if a line goes up from left to right. A graph increases if the slope of a line is positive.

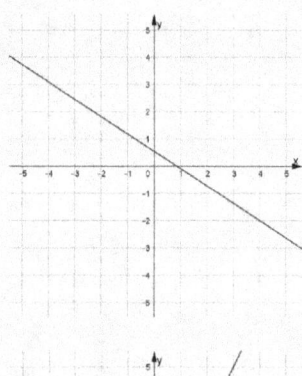

A graph is decreasing if a line goes down from left to right. A graph decreases when the slope of a line is negative.

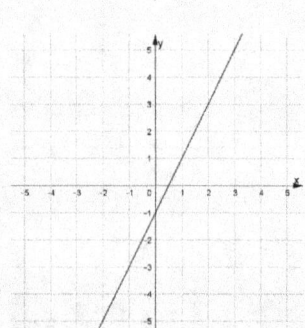

A graph is linear if it is represented by a straight line.

ANALYZING GRAPH

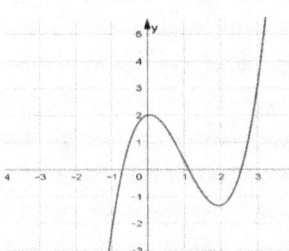

A graph is non-linear if it is represented by a curve.

The domain of the function $y=f(x)$ is the set of all the values of x.

The range of the function $y=f(x)$ is the set of all the values of y.

Example: Find the domain and range of the function $y=f(x)$ given by the table below.

x	0	2	4
y	7	5	3

Domain: $\{0,2,4\}$; **Range:** $\{7,5,3\}$.

2.4   **Analyzing Graph**

1   Determine whether the graph is increasing or decreasing.

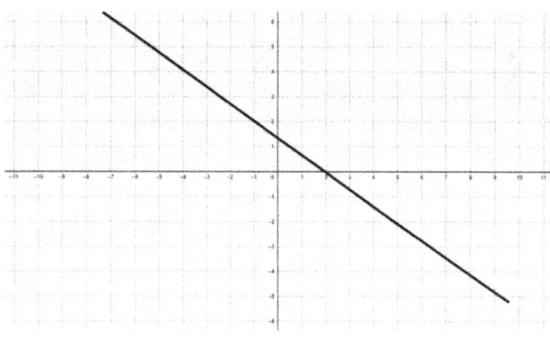

(A) Increasing

(B) Decreasing

2   Determine whether the graph is increasing or decreasing.

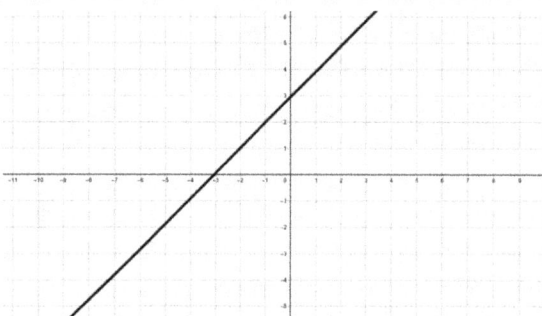

(A) Increasing

(B) Decreasing

3   Determine whether a graph is linear or non-linear.

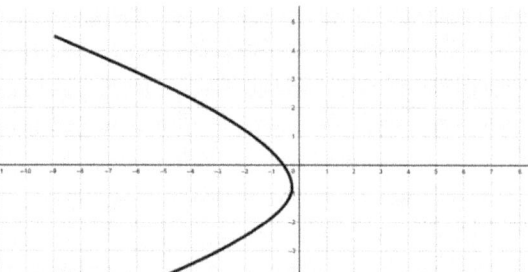

(A) Linear

(B) Non-linear

4   Determine whether a graph is linear or non-linear.

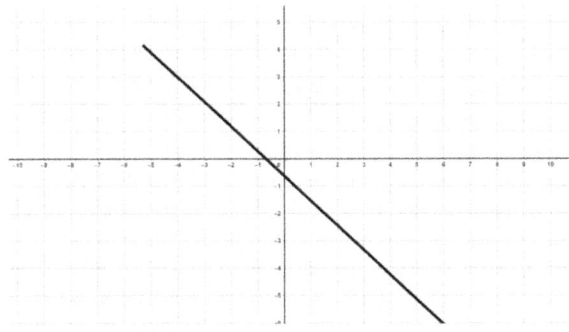

(A)   Linear

(B)   Non-linear

5   Identify the domain of the function.

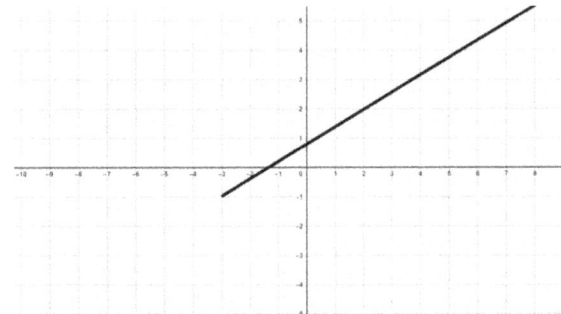

(A) $x \in (-3, \infty)$

(B) $x \in (-3, 1)$

(C) $x \in [-3, \infty)$

(D) $x \in [3, \infty)$

6   Identify the domain of the function.

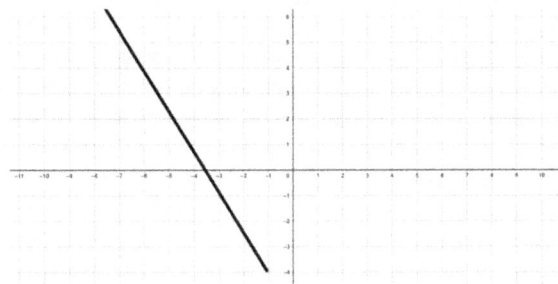

(A) $x \in (4, \infty)$

(B) $x \in [-4, \infty)$

(C) $x \in (-\infty, -1)$

(D) $x \in (-\infty, -1]$

2.4   **Analyzing Graph**

7   Identify the range of the function.

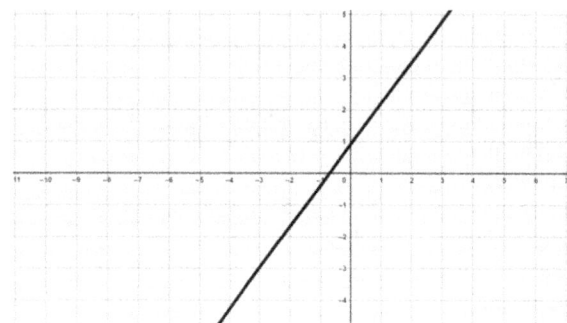

(A) $x \in (-\infty, \infty)$

(B) $x \in (-\infty, 1)$

(C) $x \in (-\infty, -1)$

(D) $x \in (-\infty, 1]$

8   Identify the range of the function.

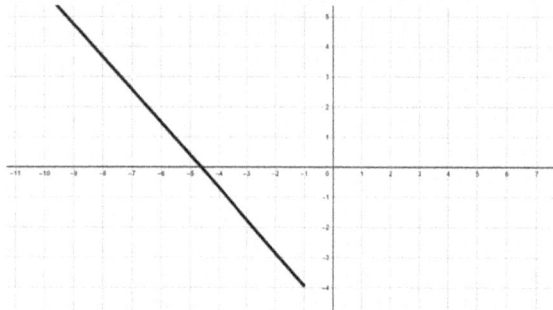

(A) $x \in (-\infty, \infty)$

(B) $x \in (-\infty, -4)$

(C) $x \in [-4, \infty)$

(D) $x \in (-4, \infty)$

9   Mercy has 16 cakes and bakes 4 cakes every minute for 20 minutes. Create a linear function that represents this situation and determine the range and domain of the function.

10 Michael has 40 books and sells 2 books every day. Create a linear function that represents this situation and determine the range and domain of the function.

_____

11 The table below shows a relationship between the side length of a square and its area. Is $y = f(x)$ a linear or non-linear function?

x	0	2	4
y	3	6	12

(A) Linear   (B) Non-linear

12 The table below shows a relationship between the side length of a square and its area. Is $y = f(x)$ a linear or non-linear function?

x	3	4	5
y	7	14	21

(A) Linear   (B) Non-linear

13 The table below shows a relationship between the number of packages sold and the number of bottles of Coke left. Is the $y = f(x)$ function increasing or decreasing?

x	0	5	10
y	64	52	40

(A) Increasing   (B) Decreasing

2.4 **Analyzing Graph**

14 The table below shows a relationship between the number of packages sold and the number of bottles of Soda left. Is the function $y = f(x)$ increasing or decreasing?

x	4	8	12
y	35	42	49

(A) Increasing (B) Decreasing

15 The table below shows a relationship between the number of triangles and the number of their sides. Determine the range of the function.

x	2	5	8
y			

16 The wind speed, y, which changes at a constant rate depending on the number of hours, x, is represented by the equation $y = 100 + 5x$. Is this function increasing or decreasing?

(A) Increasing (B) Decreasing

Analyzing Graph | 2.4

17 Emily walks toward the lake at a constant rate. The distance from the lake, y, depending on the number of hours, x, is represented by the equation $y = 19 - 4x$. Is this function increasing or decreasing?

(A) Increasing (B) Decreasing

18 Which function represents a line?

(A) $y = x^2 + 3$

(B) $y = x^2 + 4x + 2$

(C) $y = \frac{x^2}{3} + \frac{1}{2}$

(D) $y = \frac{4}{2}x + \frac{1}{5}$

19 How can the function $y = x^2 + 8$ be described?

(A) It is a nonlinear function because it involves an exponential form of x.

(B) is a linear function that intersects the x-axis at $(8, 0)$.

(C) is a nonlinear function because it is a positive function.

(D) is a linear function that intersects the y-axis at $(0, 8)$.

2.4   Analyzing Graph

20   Is this function linear?

$$y = -\frac{x}{4} - 14$$

(A)   Yes, because it involves multiples of 4.

(B)   Yes, it would be graphed as a line.

(C)   No, because it contains negative values.

(D)   No, because it would be graphed as a curve.

Next Section:
Chapter Review

1 Determine the range of the function in the graph.

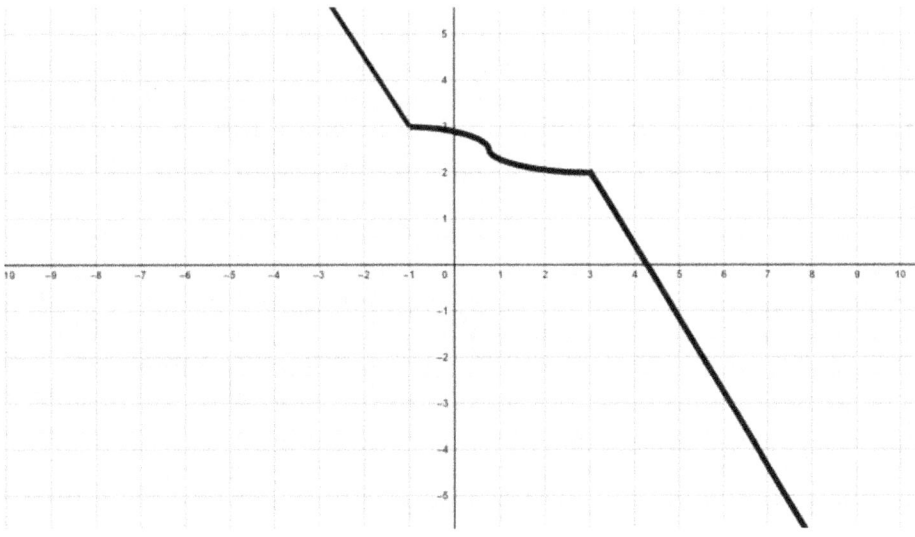

(A) $-6 \leq y \leq 6$ (B) $-3 \leq y \leq 3$ (C) $-6 < y < 6$ (D) $-3 \leq y \leq 6$

2 Evaluate the function $y = 4x + 2$, when $x = -1$.

(A) 1 (B) -1 (C) -2 (D) 2

3 What is the value of y in this function when $x = -4$?

$$y = \frac{x - 8}{4 - x}$$

(A) $\frac{4}{5}$ (B) $\frac{8}{3}$ (C) 0 (D) $-\frac{12}{8}$

2.5 | **Chapter Review**

4 Apples are sold at $2 per pound. Which table shows the relationship between the number of pounds x and the cost y?

A)

x	1	2	3
y	4	6	8

B)

x	2	4	6
y	2	4	6

C)

x	1	2	3
y	2	4	6

D)

x	2	4	6
y	1	2	3

5 Which table is a correct representation of the graph?

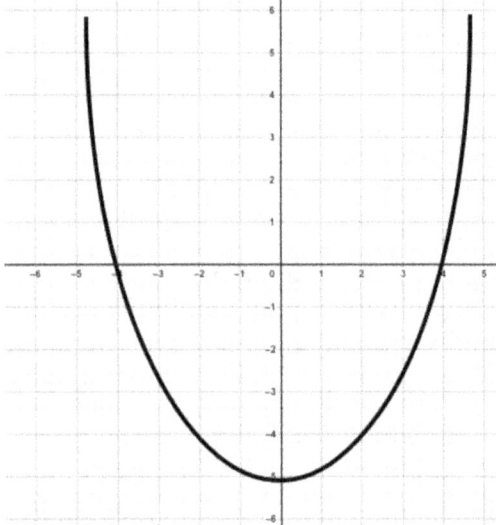

A)

x	-4	0	4
y	5	0	5

B)

x	-4	0	4
y	0	-5	0

C)

x	0	-5	0
y	-4	0	4

D)

x	5	0	5
y	-4	0	4

6 Which statement could represent information in the graph?

(A) A bike is stopped at a stop light for a set amount of time.

(B) A bike accelerates after stopping at a stop sign.

(C) A bike decelerates as it approaches a stop sign.

(D) A bike leaves its location at a constant speed.

7 Eric said when given the equation $y = 5x + 3$, the 5 represents the rate of change for this function. Was Eric correct?

(A) Yes, he was correct.

(B) No, he was incorrect.

(C) There is not enough information to determine whether he was correct.

(D) He was neither correct nor incorrect, there is another way to look at this problem.

2.5 Chapter Review

8 Function A is defined as $y = \frac{x}{8} - 9$ and Function B is defined as $y = -\frac{x}{8} - 9$. How are these functions different?

(A) Function A has a decreasing slope and function B has an increasing slope.

(B) Function A intercepts y at $\frac{9}{8}$ and Function B intercepts y at $\frac{8}{9}$.

(C) Function B intercepts y at -9 and Function A intercepts y at -9.

(D) Function B has a decreasing slope and Function A has an increasing slope.

9 Which value in this expression represents the y-intercept?

$$y = 6x + 4$$

(A) 6   (B) 4   (C) $-\frac{3}{2}$ (D) $-\frac{2}{3}$

10 Mia says this relation is not a function. $y = |x + 5|$

She believes it will not pass the vertical line test if represented on a graph. Is Mia correct?

(A) Yes, he was correct.

(B) No, he was incorrect.

(C) There is not enough information to determine whether he was correct.

(D) She was neither correct nor incorrect, there is another way to look at this problem.

11 Which equation represents a linear function?

(A) $\frac{3}{4}x \cdot 2$

(B) $x = 6$

(C) $y = |x + 4|$

(D) $y = 6x + 7$

12 What is the difference between the slope of Function A and the slope of Function B?

Function A: $y = 6x$ **Function B:** $y = \frac{1}{6}x$

(A) Function B will be a steeper line.

(B) Function A will be a steeper line.

(C) Function B is non-linear.

(D) Function A will be a horizontal line.

13 What is the y-intercept of this function?

$$y = 4x - 16$$

(A) $(4, -16)$

(B) $(-16, 4)$

(C) $(0, -16)$

(D) $(4, 0)$

14 Which function shows a nonlinear relationship?

(A) $y = 4x + \frac{1}{2}$

(B) $y = \frac{1}{2}x - 12$

(C) $y = x^3 + 2x$

(D) $y = \frac{3}{7}x$

2.5 Chapter Review

15 How would you describe the relationship shown in this table?

x	y
3	9
4	16
5	25

(A) Linear increasing.

(B) Nonlinear increasing.

(C) Linear decreasing.

(D) Constant.

16 Which strategy can you use to determine whether this function is linear?

$$y = |x - 5|$$

_____

17 Ryan stated that the function below is a decreasing function. Was he correct?

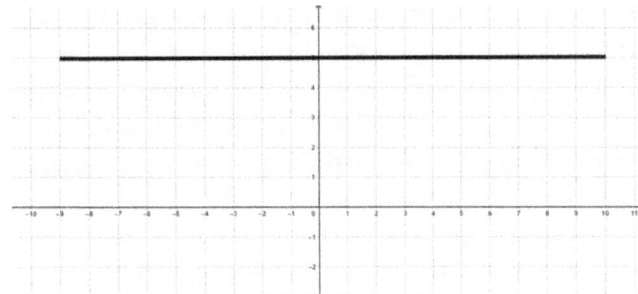

_____

18 Which response describes this function?

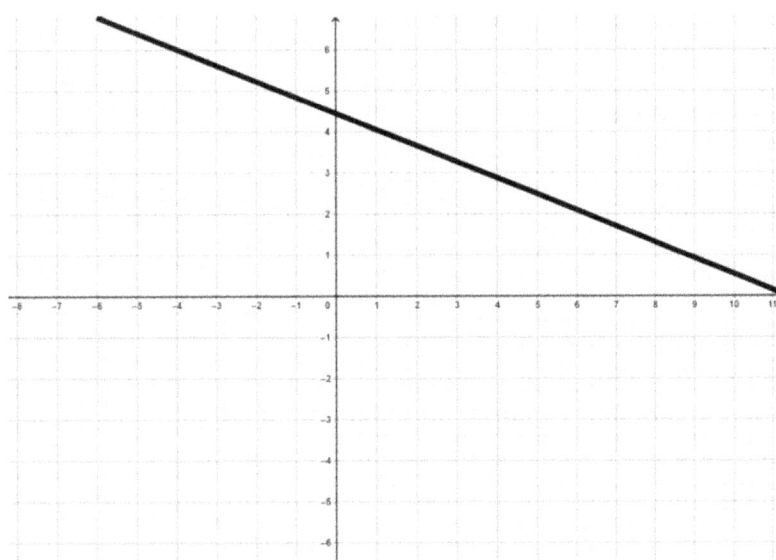

(A) Function is decreasing.   (B) Function is increasing.

(C) Function is nonlinear.   (D) Line is not a function.

19 How many ordered pairs from a graph are needed to create a table of values from a function?

(A) One   (B) Two

(C) Three   (D) Pattern of the function.

2.5 Chapter Review

20 How to determine if a factor is a function linear.

(A) contains a slope.

(B) Intersects the y-axis at some point on the graph.

(C) It is a line.

(D) points not connected.

Next Chapter: Fractions >>

CHAPTER 3

EQUATIONS AND INEQUALITIES

		2	8	7	1	5		
	1						2	
3				9				1
6			3		7			4
5		7				1		2
1			5		2			7
7				8		2		5
	8				3		1	
		1	6	2	4	3		8

PROPORTIONAL RELATIONSHIPS

Proportional relationships are often represented using the equation $y = kx$, where x and y are the variables, and k is the constant of proportionality.

If the two amounts x and y, rise or fall uniformly together, they are proportional.

This relationship is represented by the equation:

$$y=kx$$

Where k is the **constant of proportionality**.

Example:

You read 20 pages every hour.

The constant of proportionality is 20, because

$$\{Pages\ read\} = 20\times \{Hours\ read\}$$

The relationship between the two proportional amounts can be represented by the graph of the straight line. The line must pass through the origin, and its slope is equal to the constant of proportionality.

EQUATIONS AND INEQUALITIES

3.1 **Proportional Relationships**

1 Given the equation of a graph $y = mx$, what does m represent?

(A) m is the x- intercept value.

(B) m is the y- intercept value.

(C) m is the solution of the line.

(D) m is the slope of the line.

2 When a line has the form $y = mx$, where does the line intersect the x-axis?

(A) At the value of $-m$

(B) At the origin

(C) At the b value of the equation

(D) At the value of m

3 In the form $y = mx$, what is the proper way to refer to m?

(A) m is the constant of variation.

(B) m is the unit rate.

(C) m is the slope of the line.

(D) All these definitions correctly refer to m

4 When a line is in form, $y = mx$, what value does the m have?

(A) m increases as x decreases

(B) m increases as x increases.

(C) m is a constant number.

(D) m decreases as y decreases

5 When a line has the form $y = mx$, where does the line intersect the y – axis?

(A) At the value of $-m$ (B) At the origin

(C) At the b value of the equation   (D) At the value of m

6 The table shows the amount of juice in the different numbers of bottles. How many liters of juice are in one bottle?

Packs	0	1	2	3
Liters of juice	0		2.5	3.75

3.1 Proportional Relationships

7 The graph shows the distance Amy passed depending on the time elapsed. What is Amy's average speed?

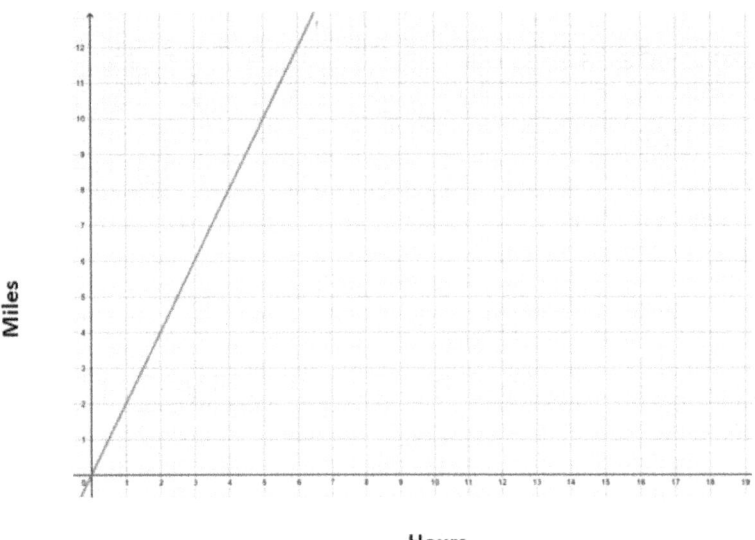

Miles

Hours

(A) 2 mph

(B) 4 mph

(C) 6 mph

(D) 8 mph

8 Given the equation $y = \dfrac{1}{6}x$, what is the constant of variation?

(A) 6

(B) $\dfrac{1}{6}x$

(C) $\dfrac{1}{6}$

(D) $6y$

9 Given the equation, $y = 9x$, what is the slope?

(A) $9x$

(B) $\dfrac{1}{9}$

(C) $\dfrac{9}{y}$

(D) 9

Proportional Relationships 3.1

10 Given the values in this table, what is the unit rate?

x	1	2	3
y	20	40	60

(A) 10   (B) 20   (C) 40   (D) 60

11 What is the slope of the line represented by this table of values?

x	1	2	3
y	$\frac{1}{2}$	1	$1\frac{1}{2}$

(A) $\frac{1}{2}$ (B) 1   (C) 2   (D) 3

12 Sarah draws similar rectangles. The table shows the relationship between the width and length of the rectangles. What is the constant of proportionality between the dimensions of the rectangles?

Length	0	1	2	3
Width	0		0.6	0.9

3.1   **Proportional Relationships**

13   What is the constant of variation of the following graph?

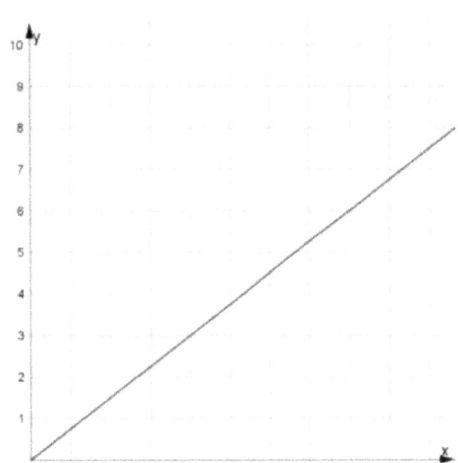

(A) 3

(B) 4

(C) $\dfrac{3}{4}$

(D) $\dfrac{4}{3}$

14   What is the constant of variation of the following graph?

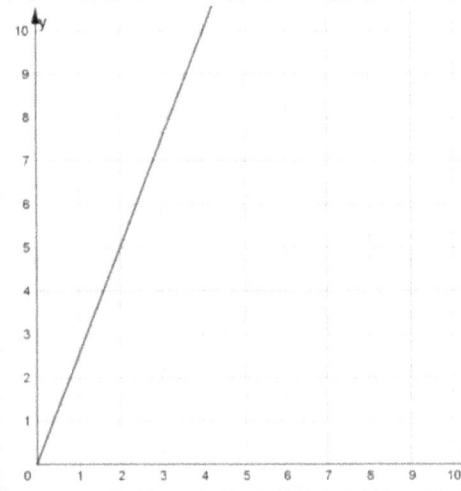

(A) $\dfrac{2}{5}$

(B) $\dfrac{1}{5}$

(C) 5

(D) $\dfrac{5}{2}$

Proportional Relationships   3.1

15 Which two sets of ordered pairs could be used to find the slope of this line using similar triangles?

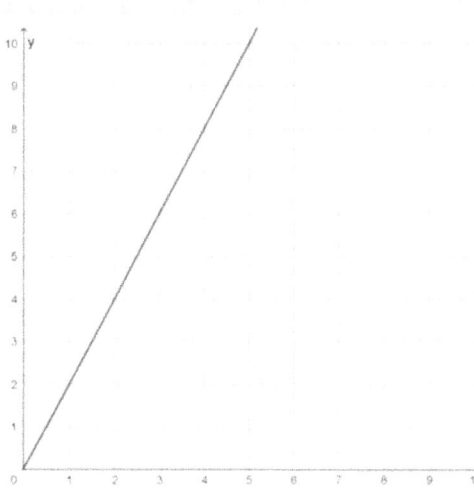

A) {(0,0), (2,2)} and {(6,4), (4,6)}

B) {(2,3), (4,6)} and {(4,6), (6,9)}

C) {(1,4), (3,2)} and {(0,0), (9,6)}

D) {(0,0), (1,2)} and {(1,2), (4,8)}

16 Which two sets of ordered pairs could be used to find the slope of this line using similar triangles?

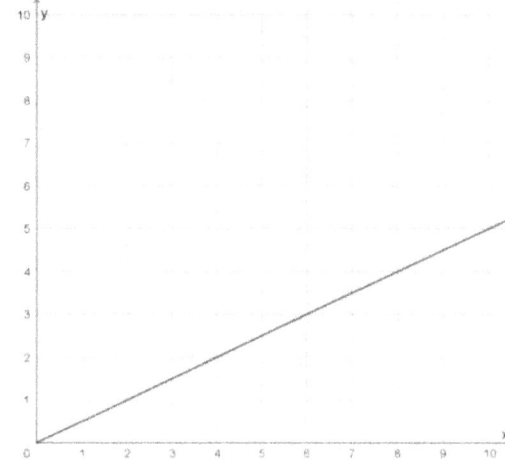

A) {(0,0), (2,4)} and {(4,2), (8,4)}

B) {(2,1), (4,2)} and {(2,0), (4,8)}

C) {(1,2), (3,4)} and {(0,0), (4,8)}

D) {(0,0), (2,4)} and {(1,2), (8,4)}

3.1 **Proportional Relationships**

17 Which equation represents the line shown on this graph?

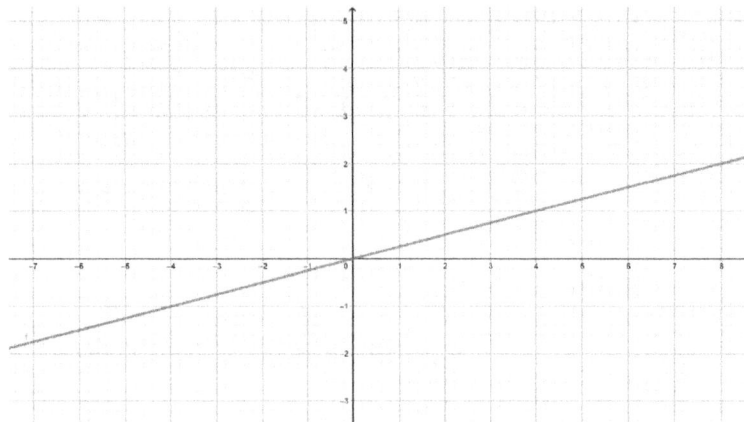

A) $y = 4x$

B) $y = x + 4$

C) $y = \frac{1}{4}x$

D) $y = 4 - x$

18 Which equation represents the line shown on this graph?

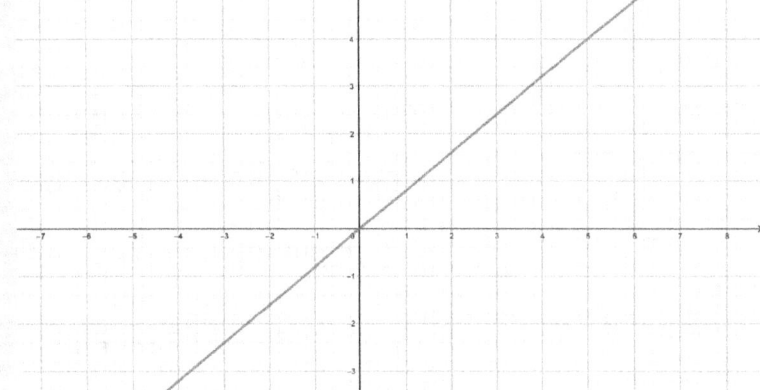

A) $y = -\frac{4}{5}$

B) $y = \frac{4}{5}$

C) $y = \frac{5}{4}$

D) $y = -\frac{5}{4}$

19   Write an equation to represent the line shown on this graph.

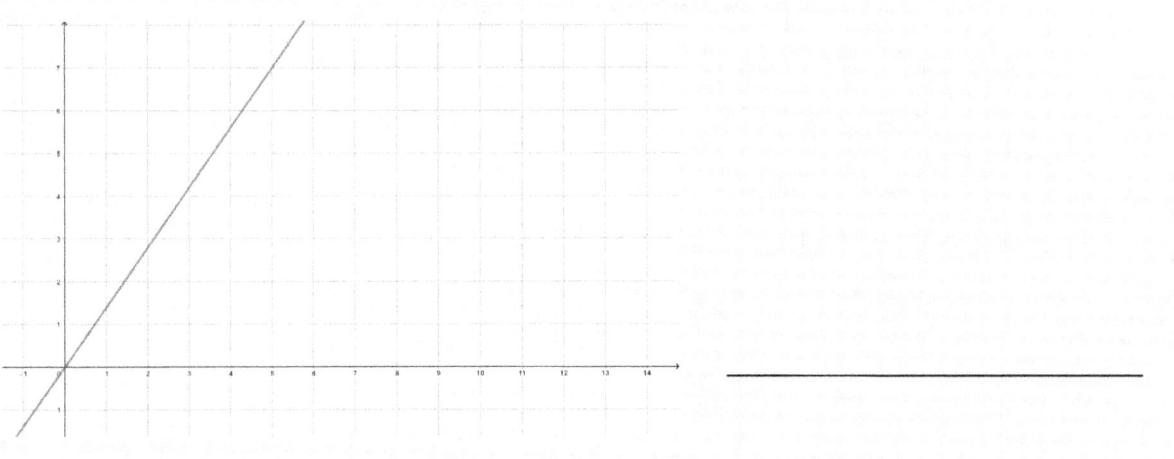

_____

20   Write an equation to represent the line shown on this graph.

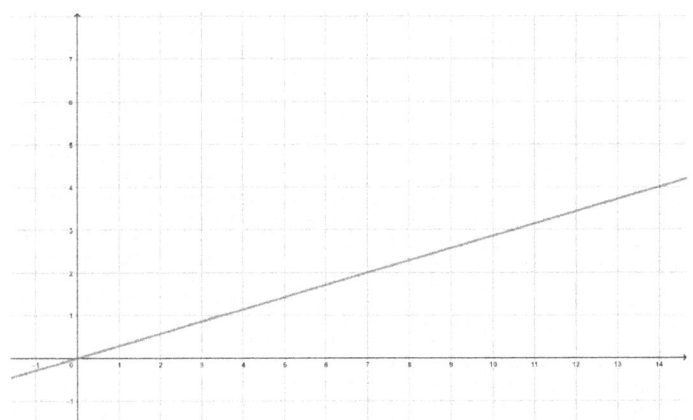

_____

Next Section: Finding Slope and Slope of a Graph

FINDING SLOPE AND SLOPE OF A GRAPH

Finding the slope of a line is an important concept in mathematics that describes the steepness of a line.

The slope of a line shows how steep a straight line is.

$$\text{Slope} = \frac{\text{change in } y}{\text{change in } x}$$

The slope can be positive or negative.

If the line goes up, then the slope is positive.

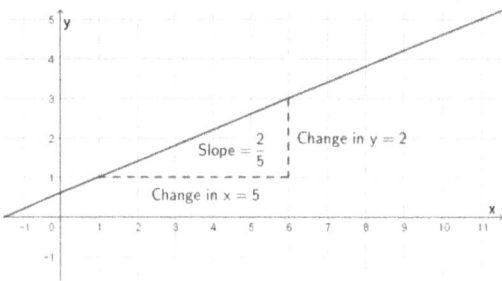

If the line goes down, then the slope is negative.

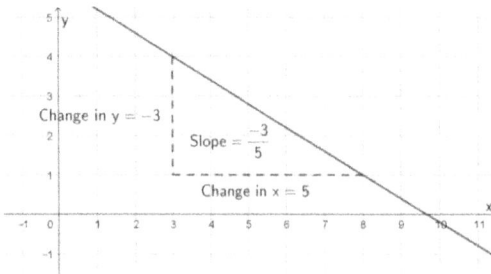

Example:

Find the slope of the line represented by the linear equation

$$y = -\frac{2}{3}x + 6 = m = -\frac{2}{3}$$

Finding Slope and Graph of a Slope 3.2

1 Find the slope of the graph below.

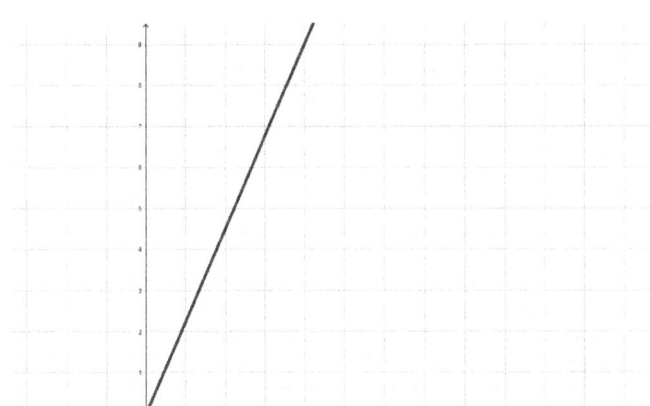

Ⓐ $\dfrac{7}{4}$ Ⓑ $\dfrac{4}{7}$

Ⓒ $\dfrac{9}{4}$ Ⓓ $\dfrac{4}{9}$

2 Find the slope of the graph below.

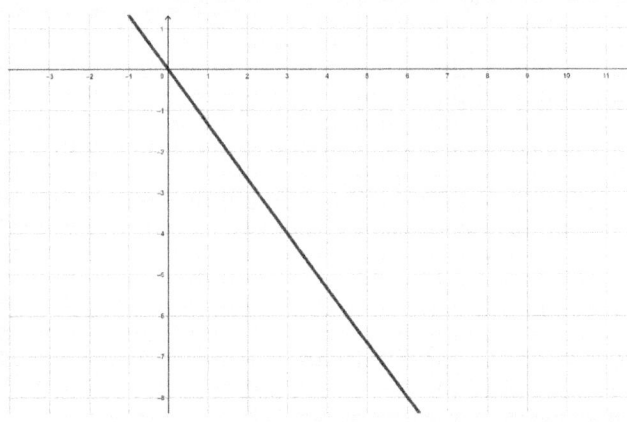

Ⓐ $-\dfrac{3}{4}$ Ⓑ $-\dfrac{4}{3}$

Ⓒ $\dfrac{4}{3}$ Ⓓ $\dfrac{3}{4}$

3.2   Finding Slope and Graph of a Slope

3   Graph a line for the given slope m, using the grid below.

$$m = \frac{1}{4}$$

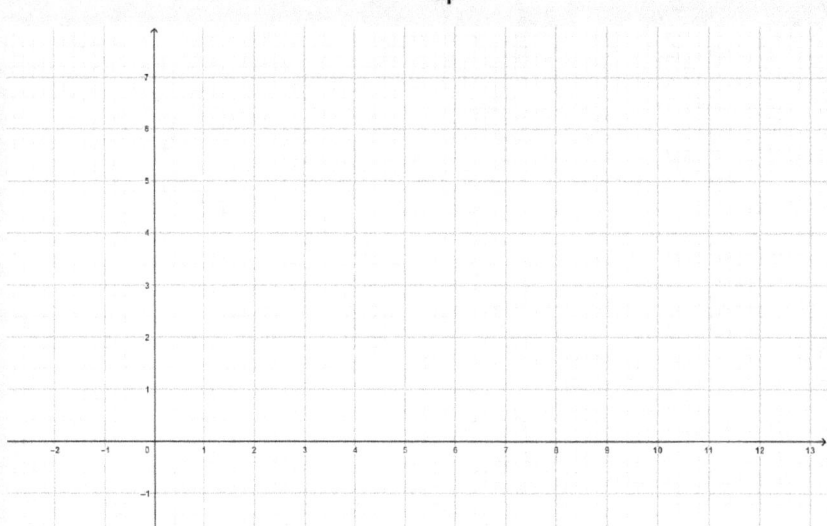

4   Graph a line for the given slope m, using the grid below.

$$m = 5$$

5 Graph a line given in slope–intercept form.

$$m = \frac{3}{2}x + 1$$

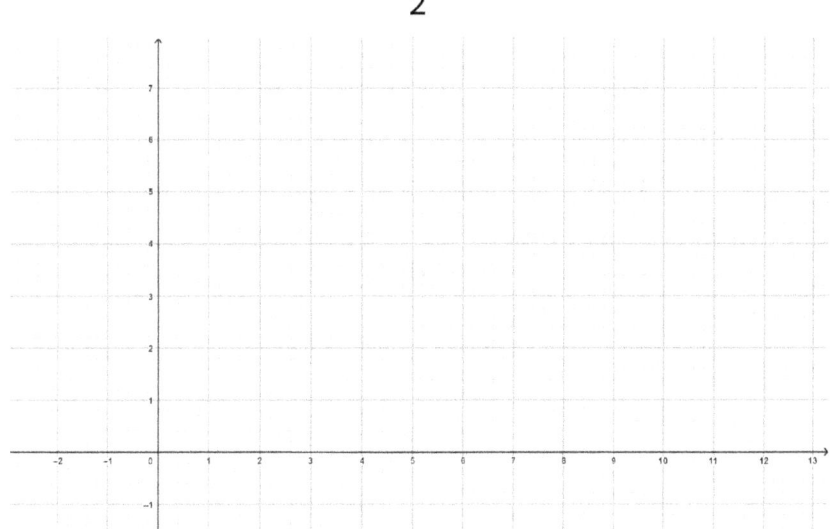

6 Graph a line for the given slope m, using the grid below.

$$m = \frac{5}{4}x - 2$$

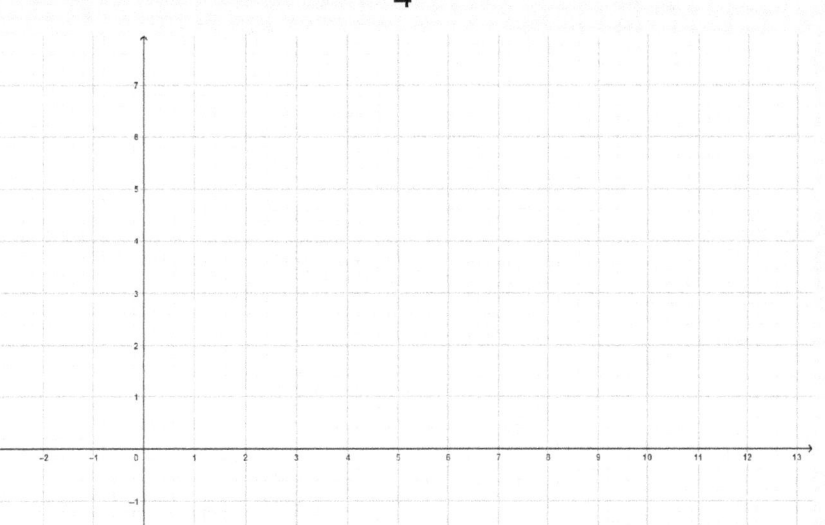

3.2 Finding Slope and Graph of a Slope

7 Find the slope of the line that passes through the points.

$$A(5,6), B(3,5).$$

(A) $\dfrac{1}{2}$ (B) $-\dfrac{1}{2}$ (C) 2 (D) -2

8 Find the slope of the line that passes through the points.

$$A(7,-3), B(4,-6).$$

(A) 2 (B) $\dfrac{4}{7}$ (C) -1 (D) 1

9 Find the slope of the line represented by the linear equation.

$$y = 5 - 7x$$

(A) 7 (B) -7 (C) 5 (D) -5

10 Find the slope of the line represented by the linear equation.

$$y = \dfrac{3x-5}{6}$$

(A) 2 (B) -2 (C) $\dfrac{1}{2}$ (D) $-\dfrac{1}{2}$

11 Plumber earns $200 after 4 hours, and $280 after 8 hours. How much money does a plumber earn per hour?

(A) Plumber earns $10 per hour   (B) Plumber earns $20 per hour

(C) Plumber earns $30 per hour   (D) Plumber earns $40 per hour

12 The equation shows the total number of chairs, y, depending on the number of tables, x. Not all chairs are around the tables. How many chairs are around a table?

$$-4x + \frac{1}{2}y - 10 = 0$$

(A) There are 8 chairs around a table

(B) There are 4 chairs around a table

(C) There are 6 chairs around a table

(D) There are 10 chairs around a table.

13 Babysitter earns $80 after 2 hours and $155 after 5 hours. How much money does a babysitter earn per hour?

(A) Babysitter earns $10 per hour   (B) Babysitter earns $15 per hour

(C) Babysitter earns $20 per hour   (D) Babysitter earns $25 per hour

3.2 Finding Slope and Graph of a Slope

---

14 Emily sold a total of 17 flowers after selling 2 bouquets, and 47 flowers after selling 7 bouquets. How many flowers are in a bouquet?

(A) There are 4 flowers in a bouquet

(B) There are 6 flowers in a bouquet

(C) There are 8 flowers in a bouque

(D) There are 10 flowers in a bouquet

---

15 The equation shows the total cost, y depending on the number of tickets bought, x. What is the cost of a single ticket?

$$-4x + \frac{1}{3}y - 10 = 0$$

---

16 The equation shows the total cost of a taxi ride, y, depending on the number of miles passed, x. How much does a taxi driver charge per mile?

$$8x - y + 5 = 0$$

17 There are 40 trees in 5 rows. Graph a line that represents the number of trees depending on the number of rows.

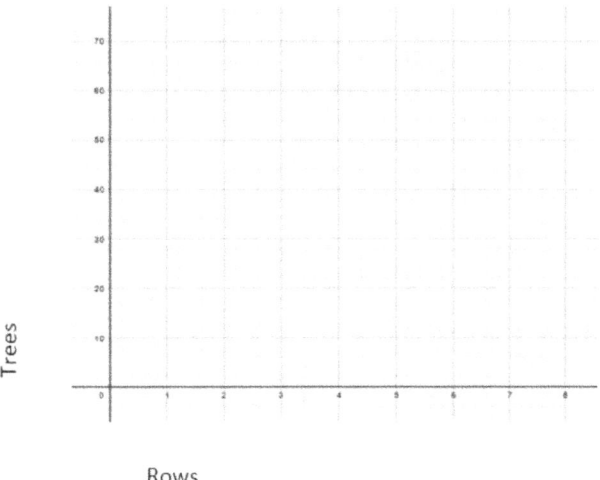

Rows

18 The cost of a pencil is $0.25, and the cost of delivery is $4. The total cost is represented by the equation $y = 0.25x + 4$. Graph a line that represents the total cost depending on the number of pencils ordered.

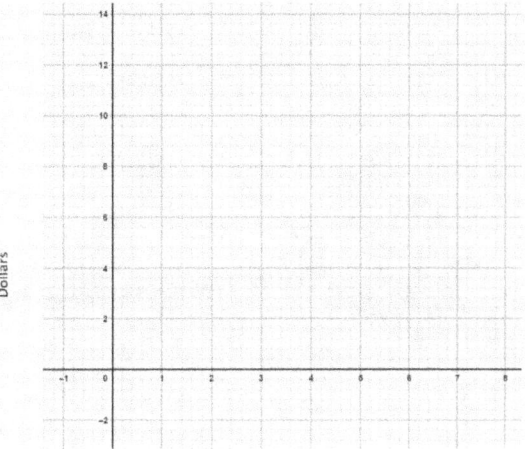

Pencils

3.2   **Finding Slope and Graph of a Slope**

19   Find the slope of a linear equation.

$$\frac{x}{3} + \frac{y}{4} = -1$$

_____

20   Find the slope of a linear equation.

$$\frac{x}{4} + 2y = -5$$

_____

Next Section: Solve Two-Step and Multi-Step Equations

SOLVE TWO-STEP AND MULTI - STEP EQUATIONS

Two-step and multi-step equations are mathematical equations that involve more than one operation to solve. In a two-step equation, two operations are required to isolate the variable, whereas multi-step equations require three or more operations to solve.

Solve Two-Step Equations (Like Terms and with Variables on Both Sides)

An equation contains an equal sign "=", an expression on the left-hand side of the equation, and an expression on the right-hand side of the equation.

Example: $x - 5 = 3$

Every equation also has a variable ($x, y, z,...$), and the solution of an equation is a value of the variable for which the equation is true.

$$x - 5 = 3$$
$$x = 8$$
$$8 - 5 = 3$$
$$3 = 3$$

True

A variable can appear on one side of the equation, like in the example above, or on both sides of the equation, like in the example below.

$$3x + 7 = 4 - 2x$$

When you solve an equation, you move all variables to the left-hand side of the equation, and all numbers to the right-hand side of the equation. When you move a variable or a number to the other side of the equation, its sign is changed.

$$3x + 2x = 4 - 7$$

Then you add similar terms.

$$5x = -3$$

Finally, isolate a variable on the left-hand side of the equation.

$$x = -\frac{3}{5}$$

EQUATIONS AND INEQUALITIES

3.3 Solve Two-Step and Multi-Step Equations

1 Solve $k + 8 = 18$, for k.

- (A) 9
- (B) 10
- (C) 11
- (D) 12

2 Given an equation with multiple operations without parentheses, which operations should be completed first?1

- (A) Addition and Subtraction
- (B) Multiplication and Division
- (C) Multiplication and Addition
- (D) Subtraction and Division

3 Solve for n. $3n + 8 = -10$.

- (A) 6
- (B) −6
- (C) −8
- (D) 8

4 Solving an equation without parentheses, what is the first step you should take before solving for a?

- (A) Combine like terms
- (B) Combine unlike terms
- (C) Simplify using order of operations
- (D) Adding variables

5 Solve for x. $\dfrac{7x + 2}{2} = 9$.

- (A) $\dfrac{1}{7}$
- (B) 7
- (C) $\dfrac{7}{6}$
- (D) $\dfrac{16}{7}$

Solve Two-Step and Multi-Step Equations | 3.3

6 Solve for u. $20u + 8(u - 6) = 32$.

A) $-\frac{20}{7}$ B) $\frac{20}{7}$ C) $\frac{10}{7}$ D) $-\frac{10}{7}$

7 Select a solution of the equation.

$$4x - 2 = 10$$

A) 1   B) 2   C) 3   D) 4

8 Solve for x. $6x - 2 - 4x = 6 + 2x - 4$.

A) 1   B) 2   C) 3   D) no solution

9 The cost of a pizza is $9 and the cost of delivery is $3. The total cost of x pizzas is represented by the equation $9x + 3 = 48$. How many pizzas are ordered?

_____

10 How many solutions does the equation have?

$$8x + 3x - 6 = 5 + 11x - 11$$

A) One   B) Two

C) No solution   D) Infinitely many solutions

EQUATIONS AND INEQUALITIES

3.3 Solve Two-Step and Multi-Step Equations

11 How many solutions does the equation have?

$$-8 - 4(x - 1) = 4x + 12.$$

(A) One
(B) Two
(C) No solution
(D) Infinitely many solutions

12 How many solutions does the equation have?

$$-5x + 8 - 3x = 3 - 8x - 11.$$

(A) One
(B) Two
(C) No solution
(D) Infinitely many solutions

13 The cost of a pencil is \$1 and the cost of delivery is \$4. The total cost of x pencils is represented by the equation $x + 4 = 15$. How many pencils are ordered?

_____

14 What must be the value of c if the equation $cx + 8 - 4x = 6 - 8x$ has no solution?

(A) -8
(B) 8
(C) 4
(D) -4

15 The cost of a pack of chewing gum is $6 and the cost of delivery is $5. The total cost of x packs of chewing gum is represented by the equation $6x + 5 = 41$. How many packs of chewing gums are ordered?

_____

16 There are 52 guests in the restaurant and 11 guests leave the restaurant every hour. The total number of guests left in the restaurant after x hours is represented by the equation $52 - 11x = 8$. How many hours elapsed?

_____

17 Complete the following.
$$6x - 4(3 - 5x) - 2 = 8 + 2(2x + 3).$$
$$x = \text{_____}$$

18 Complete the following.
$$(3 - 2x) - 4(x + 1) = -4x - 3(x - 5).$$
$$x = \text{_____}$$

3.3 **Solve Two-Step and Multi-Step Equations**

19 The cost of a donut is $2 and the cost of delivery is $4. The total cost of x donuts is represented by the equation $2x + 4 = 32$. How many donuts are ordered?

_____

20 There are 65 children in the park, and 7 children leave the park every hour. The total number of children left in the park after x hours is represented by the equation $65 - 7x = 2$. How many hours elapsed?

_____

Next Section:
Solve Two-Step Inequalities

SOLVE TWO-STEP INEQUALITIES

Two-step inequalities are mathematical inequalities that involve two operations to solve. Inequalities are mathematical expressions that compare two values, and they are commonly used to describe relationships between variables.

An inequality compares two or more values. Inequalities are described using the following symbols:

< - Less than

> - Greater than

< - Less than or equal to

> - Greater than or equal to

Every inequality has a variable, a symbol, and an expression.

Example: x - 5 < 3

The solution of an inequality is a set of values for the variable for which the inequality is true.

x - 5 < 3

x < 8

A solution of a linear inequality can be represented graphically. When graphing the inequality on a number line, you must use a circle and arrow to depict the solution to the inequality.

Inequality	Symbol	Representation on Number Line
Less Than	<	open circle, arrow moving to the left on the number line.
Greater Than	>	open circle, arrow moving to the right on the number line.
Less Than or Equal To	≤	closed circle, arrow moving to the left on the number line.
Greater Than or Equal To	≥	closed circle, arrow moving to the right on the number line.

Example: x < 8

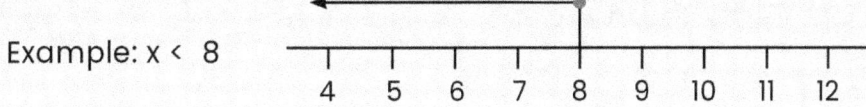

A open circle would be drawn above the 8 on the number line and a line would be drawn moving to the left.

3.4 **Solve Two-Step Inequalities**

1 Represent solution graphically.

$$15 \geq 3x$$

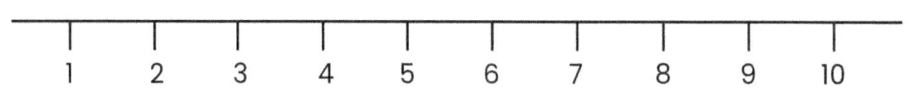

2 Select a solution of the inequality.

$$8 + 6x > 4x - 8$$

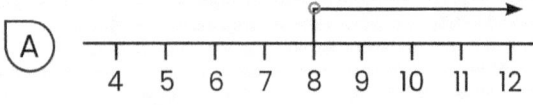

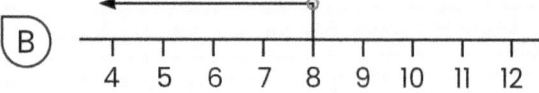

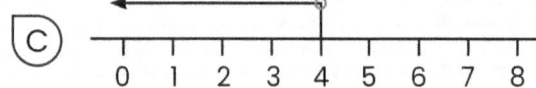

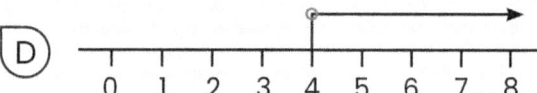

3 Sarah can spend at most $51 to order online. The cost of a cake is $7 and the cost of delivery is $2. The total cost of x cakes that Sarah can order is represented by the inequality $7x + 2 \leq 51$. At most, how many cakes can Sarah order?

4 Helen will spend at least $9 to order online. The cost of an Eraser is $1 and the cost of delivery is $5. The total cost of x pencils that Helen will order is represented by the inequality $x + 5 \geq 9$.nAt least how many pencils will Helen order?

(A) Helen will order at least 2 erasers

(B) Helen will order at least 3 erasers

(C) Helen will order at least 4 erasers

(D) Helen will order at least 5 erasers

5 Emily can spend at most $32 to order online. The cost of a cup of coffee is $3 and the cost for delivery is $2. The total cost of x cups of coffee that Emily can order is represented by the inequality $3x + 2 \leq 32$. At most how many cups of coffee can Ava order?

(A) Emily can order at most 10 cups of coffee

(B) Emily can order at most 8 cups of coffee

(C) Emily can order at most 12 cups of coffee

(D) Emily can order at most 3 cups of coffee

3.4 Solve Two-Step Inequalities

6 There are 26 apples in a bag and 4 apples are eaten every hour. The total number of apples left in a bag after x hours is greater than 2 and is represented by the inequality 26 − 4x > 2.
How many hours elapsed?

(A) Less than 6

(B) Less than 8

(C) More than 6

(D) More than 8

7 There are 49 candies in a bag and 5 candies are eaten every hour. The total number of candies left in a bag after x hours is less than 9 and is represented by the inequality 49 − 5x < 9.
How many hours elapsed?

(A) Less than 9

(B) Less than 8

(C) More than 9

(D) More than 8

8 Represent solution graphically.

$$6 - 3x > 3x - 8 + x$$

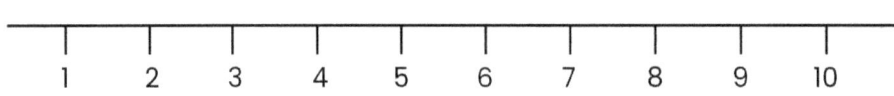

9   Represent the solution graphically.

$$6 - 3x > 4x - 12 + 2x$$

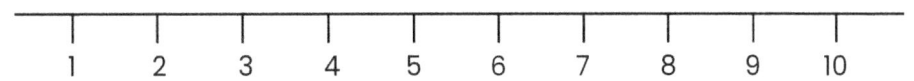

10   Represent the solution graphically.

$$7x - 3 - 8x + 1 \geq 8 - 3x + 6 - 2x$$

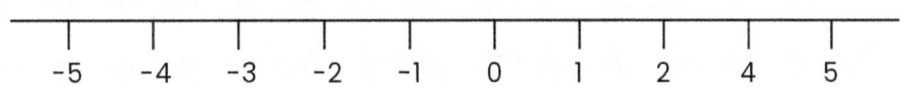

11   Represent the solution graphically.

$$5 < 6x - 13$$

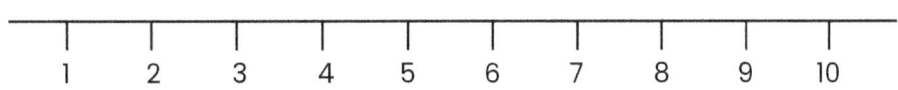

3.4   **Solve Two-Step Inequalities**

12 Solve graphically and select the correct answer.

There are 61 children in the zoo and 8 children leave the zoo every hour. The total number of children left in the zoo after x hours is greater than 5 and is represented by the inequality 61 - 8x > 5. How many hours elapsed?

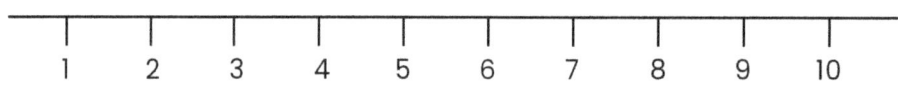

13 Solve graphically and complete the following.

Nancy spent more than $42 to order online. The cost of a pack of juice is $9 and the cost of delivery is $6. The total cost of x packs of Soda that Nancy ordered is represented by the inequality 9x + 6 > 42. At least how many packs of Soda did Nancy order?

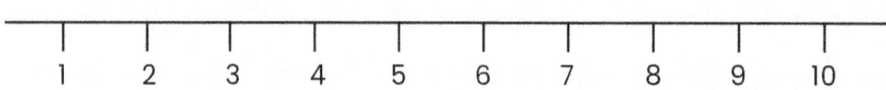

14 Solve graphically and complete the following.

Noah spent more than $18 to order online. The cost of a loaf of bread is $3 and the cost of delivery is $1. The total cost of x breads that Noah ordered is represented by the inequality, $3x + 1 > 18$. At least how many loaves breads of did Noah order?

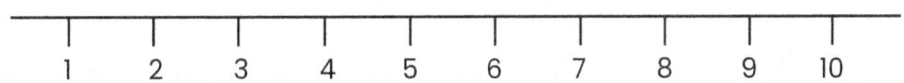

15 Solve graphically and select the correct answer.

There are 7 kg of sugar in a bag and 1 kg of sugar is used every hour. The total amount of sugar left in a bag after x hours is at least 2 and is represented by the inequality $7 - x \geq 2$. How many hours elapsed?

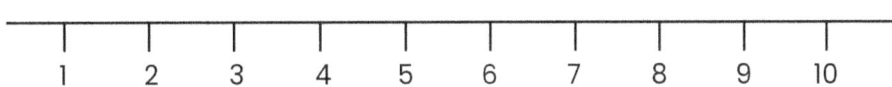

3.4 Solve Two-Step Inequalities

16 Select a solution to the inequality.

$$-4 + 3x > 4x - 8$$

(A)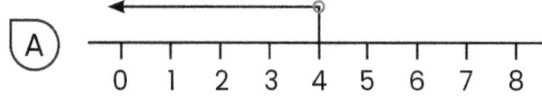

(B)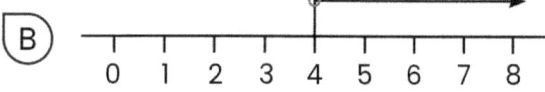

(C)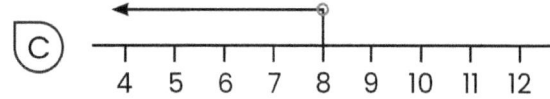

(D)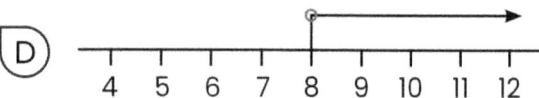

17 Select a solution to the inequality.

$$2x + 14 > 7x - 6$$

(A)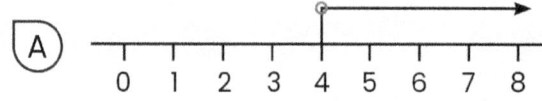

(B)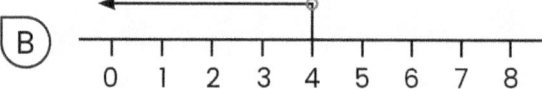

(C)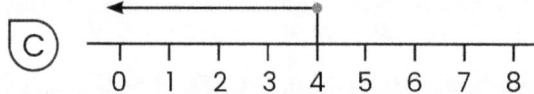

(D)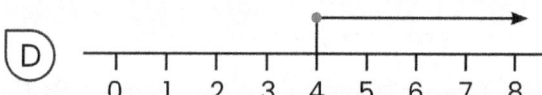

18 Select a solution to the inequality.

$$3x - 9 < -4x + 5$$

(A)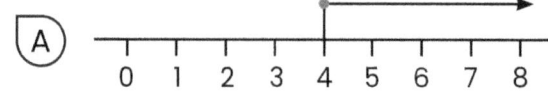

(B)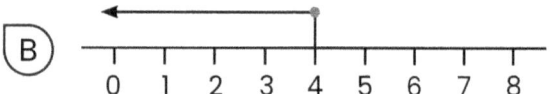

(C)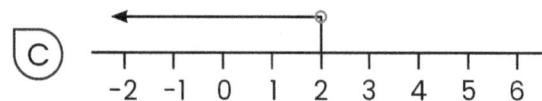

(D)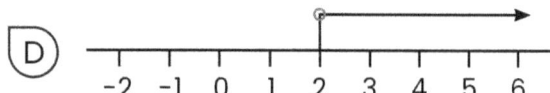

19 Select a solution to the inequality.

$$20 - 7x \geq 5 - 2x$$

(A)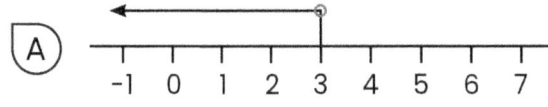

(B)

(C)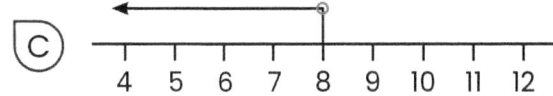

(D)

20 Select a solution to the inequality.

$$1 - 8x > -7$$

(A)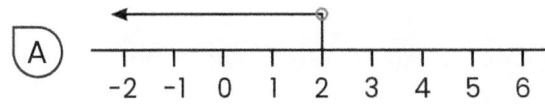

(B)

(C)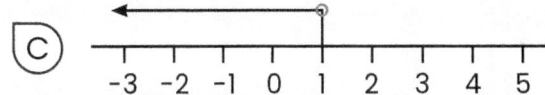

(D)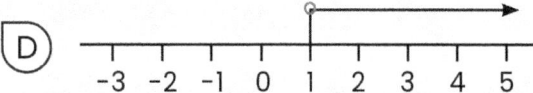

Next Section:
Solve a System of Equations

SOLVE A SYSTEM OF EQUATIONS

A system of equations is a set of two or more equations with multiple variables that are solved simultaneously to find the values of the variables that satisfy all the equations in the system. The solution to a system of equations is the set of values that make all the equations true at the same time.

A system of two linear equations can be represented graphically on a coordinate plane. Each equation can be represented by a straight line. The solution of the system of equations is the point of intersection.

Example:

Solve a system of equations.

$$x - y = 2$$
$$x + y = 4$$

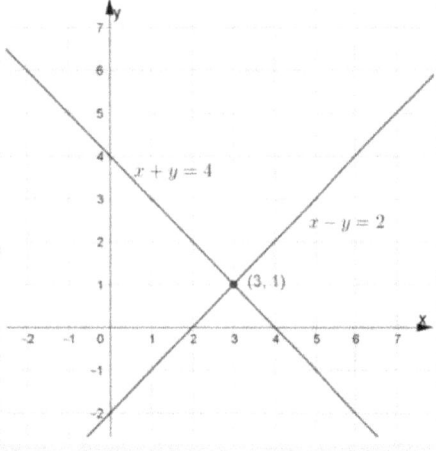

Solution:

Represent equations with straight lines.

The intersection point is $(3, 1)$. Therefore, the solution is

$x = 3$

$y = 1$.

Solve a System of Equations   **3.5**

1 How many solutions are impossible for a system of equations?

(A) 1   (B) 2

(C) Infinite many solutions   (D) None of the above

2 How do you express the solution to a system of equations?

(A) A line of the equation   (B) A triangle equation

(C) Ordered pair   (D) A solution of equations

3 When graphing a system of two equations, where do the graphs intersect?

(A) One equation starts and another equation ends.

(B) First equation is true, and the second is false.

(C) Solution to equations one and two.

(D) Equations 1 and 2 are false.

4 What is the significance of graphed lines being parallel in a linear system of equations?

(A) One solution   (B) Unsolved

(C) Infinitely many solutions   (D) No solution

3.5 Solve a System of Equations

5 What is the first step when solving a system of equations by substitution?

(A) Solve the first equation.

(B) Solve the second equation.

(C) Substitute zero for the y variable.

(D) Solve both of the equations.

6 How many solutions to a given system of two linear equations are represented graphically?

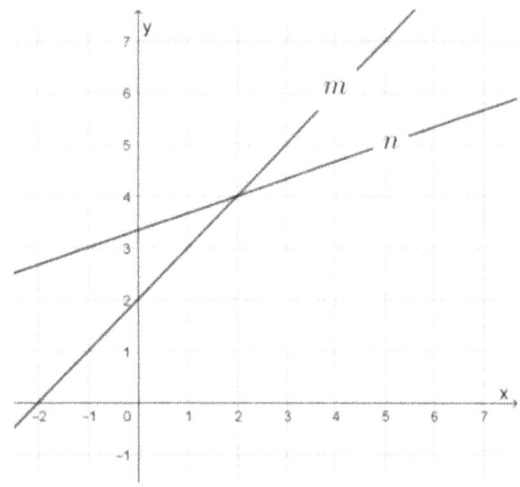

(A) One

(B) Two

(C) No solutions

(D) Infinitely many solutions

7 How many solutions to a given system of two linear equations are represented graphically?

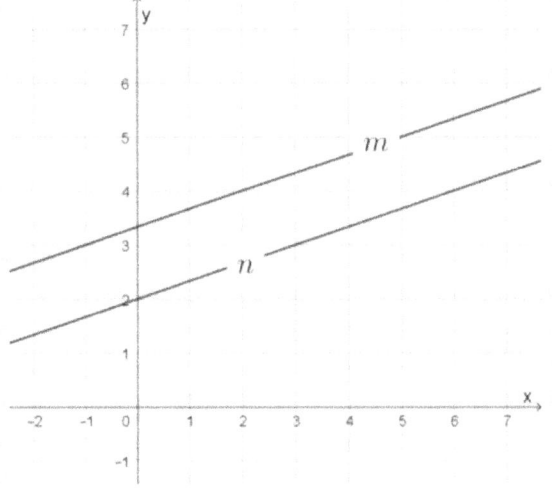

(A) Zero

(B) One

(C) Two

(D) Infinitely many solutions

8 How many solutions to a given system of two linear equations are represented graphically?

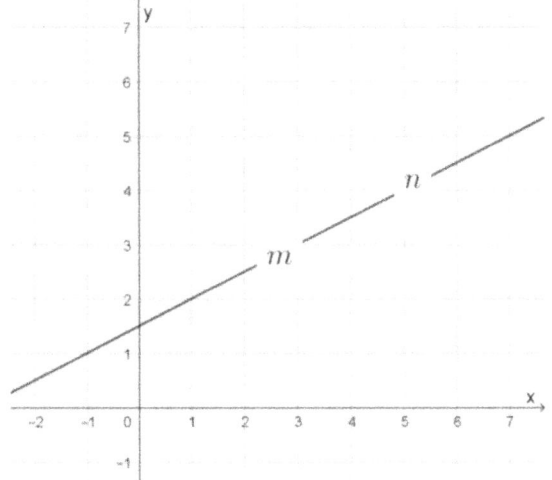

(A) Zero

(B) One

(C) Two

(D) Infinitely many solutions

3.5 Solve a System of Equations

9 Which line forms a system of equations with no solution with line n?

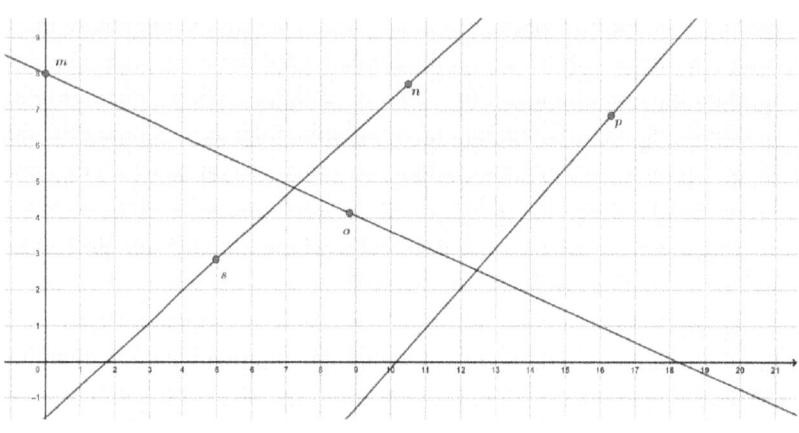

Ⓐ *o*   Ⓑ *p*   Ⓒ *s*   Ⓓ *m*

10 The profits of the two companies are represented in the graph below. Is there a moment when both profits are equal?

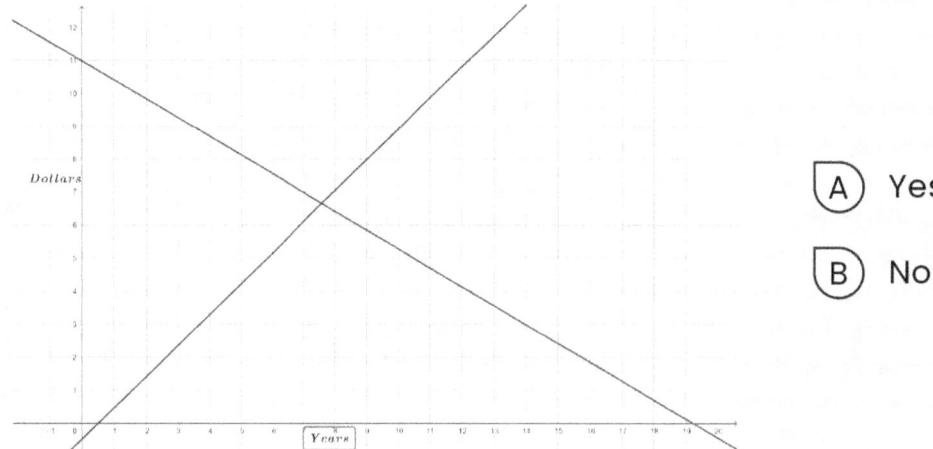

Ⓐ Yes

Ⓑ No

Solve a System of Equations   3.5

11 The distances of the two cars from the city are represented by the graph below. Is there a moment when the cars are at the same distance from the city?

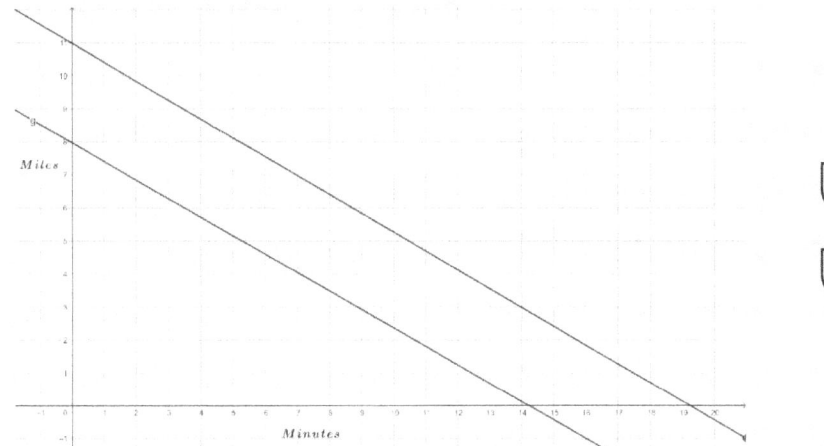

(A) Yes

(B) No

12 The heights of the two kites are represented by the same line in the graph below. Is there a moment when the heights of the kites are different?

(A) Yes   (B) No

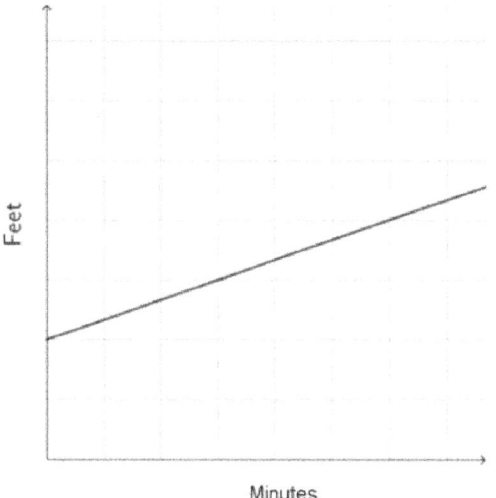

3.5 Solve a System of Equations

13 Ava and Merlin are reading the same book. Ava is on page 24 and reads 4 pages every night. Merlin is on the page 9 and reads 5 pages every night. The variable y represents the number of pages to read, and the variable x is the number of nights.

Which system can be used to determine the total number of pages they read?

A) $y = 24x + 5; x = 9y + 4$

B) $y = 24x + 9; y = 4x + 5$

C) $y = 4x + 24; y = 5x + 9$

D) $x = 24y + 5; y = 9x + 5$

14 What is the solution to this system of equations?

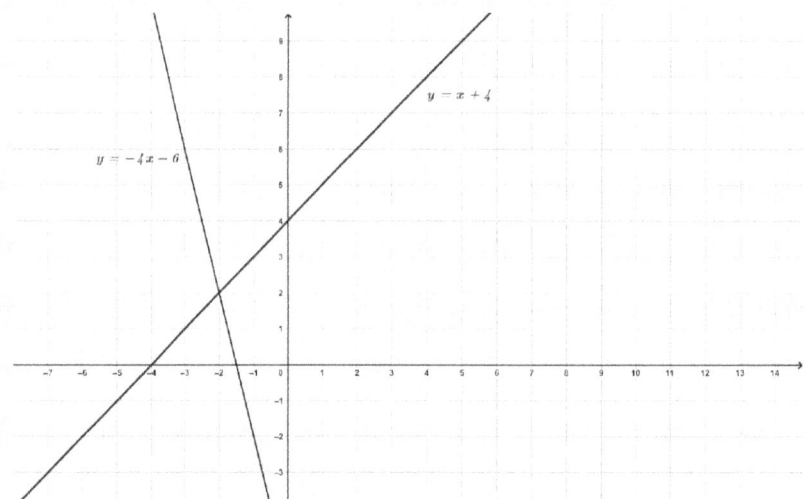

A) $(-2, 2)$ B) $(2, 2)$ C) $(2, -2)$ D) $(-2, -2)$

15 What is the solution to this system of equations?

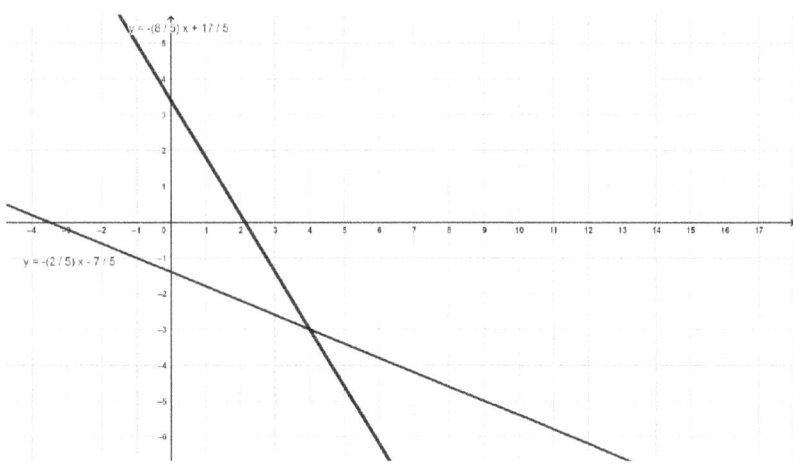

(A) (−4,3)   (B) (4,3)   (C) (4,−3)   (D) (−4,−3)

16 What is the solution to this system of equations?

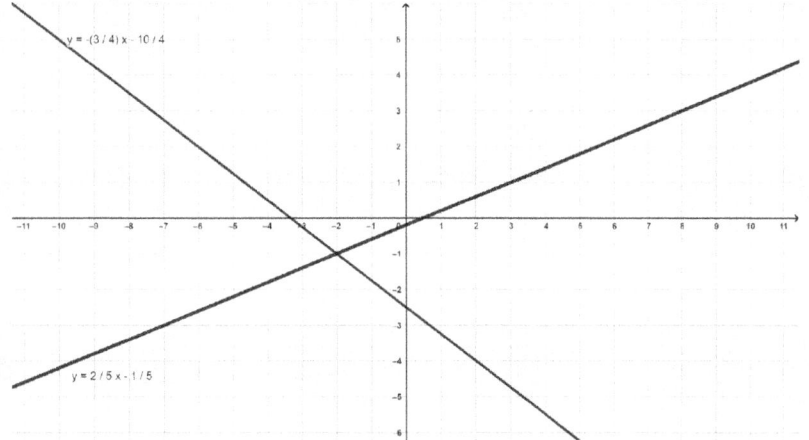

(A) (−1,−2)   (B) (2,1)   (C) (1,−2)   (D) (−2,−1)

3.5   Solve a System of Equations

17 The sum of the two numbers is 24, and their difference 16. Find the numbers.

_____

18 The perimeter of an isosceles triangle is 12, and the difference between the lateral side and a base is 3. Find the side lengths.

_____

19 One number is twice the other number, and their difference is 18. Find the numbers.

_____

Solve a System of Equations   3.5

20 The sum of the two numbers is thrice as its difference. The difference of the two numbers is 40. Find the numbers.

_____

Next Section: Chapter Review ≫

3.6   Chapter Review

1 What is the unit rate of the following graph?

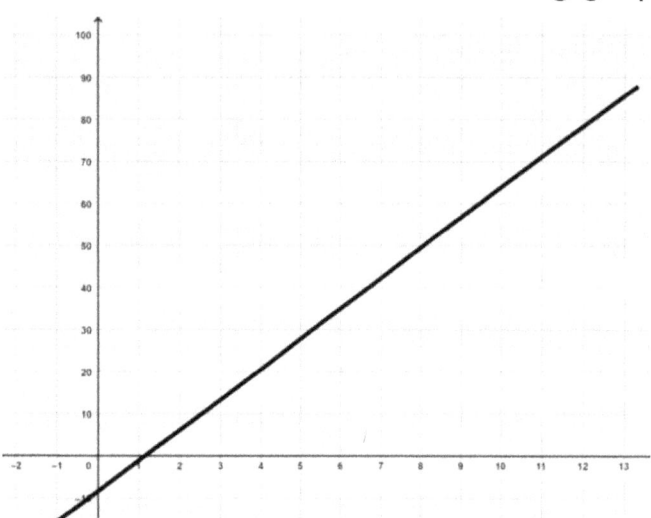

(A) $\dfrac{1}{2}$ (B) 10   (C) 5   (D) 20

2 Which equation contains a larger slope than the function shown in the table?

x	1	2	3
y	6	12	18

(A) y=2x   (B) y=6x   (C) y=12x   (D) y=$\dfrac{1}{12}$x

3 Which equation represents the line shown on this graph?

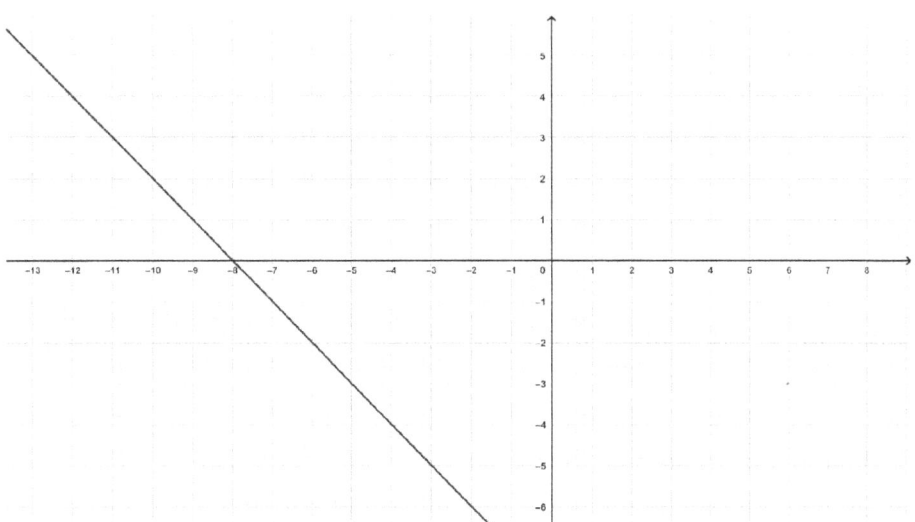

(A) y= -x - 8   (B) y = 8 - x   (C) y = x - 8   (D) y = x + 8

4 If given the equation, $\dfrac{1}{4} + \dfrac{y}{2} = 3$, which is the equivalent simplified equation?

(A) 4 +2y = 12   (B) 4 + 2y = 12

(C) 1 +4y = 12   (D) 1 + 2y = 12

5 If given the equation, 5.6 = 2.3y - 6.8, which is the equivalent simplified equation?

(A) 5.6 = 2.3y − 68   (B) 56 = 2.3y - 6.8

(C) 5.6 = 23y − 68   (D) 56 = 23y - 68

EQUATIONS AND INEQUALITIES

6 Evan has $8 and Emma has $12. Evan is saving $2 per week and Emma is saving $1 per week. After how many weeks will Evan and Emma have the same amount of money?

(A) 3   (B) 4   (C) 5   (D) 6

7 Kate and Emily start a lawn mowing business and purchase the mowers and equipment for $600. They charge $10 for each lawn and use $1.5 the worth of gas for each job. How many lawns must Kate and Emily mow before breaking even?

_____

8 Is the ordered pair is a solution to the system of equations?

$$(2,2)$$
$$x+y=4$$
$$x-y=-4$$

(A) Yes   (B) No

9 Create a system of equations and check whether the ordered pair is a solution to the system of equations.

The sum of the two numbers is 8 and their difference is 4.

Are these numbers represented by the ordered pair (6,2)?

(A) Yes   (B) No

10 Create a system of equations and check whether the ordered pair is a solution to the system of equations.

The sum of the two numbers is 24 and their difference 14.

Are these numbers represented by the ordered pair (18,6)?

(A) Yes

(B) No

11 The system of two linear equations is represented graphically. How many solutions does the system of equations have?

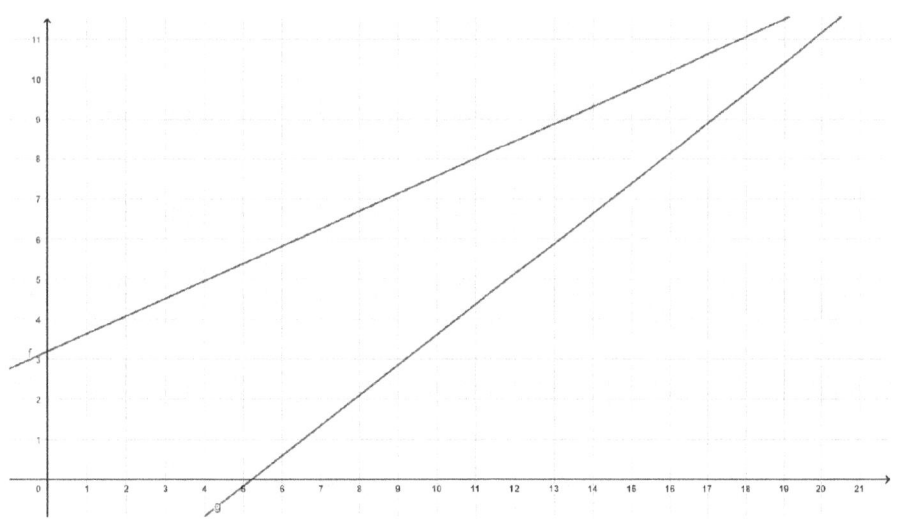

(A) 0

(B) 1

(C) 2

(D) ∞

3.6   Chapter Review

12 There are 50 matches in a matchbox. Graph a proportional relationship between the number of matches and the total number of matchboxes.

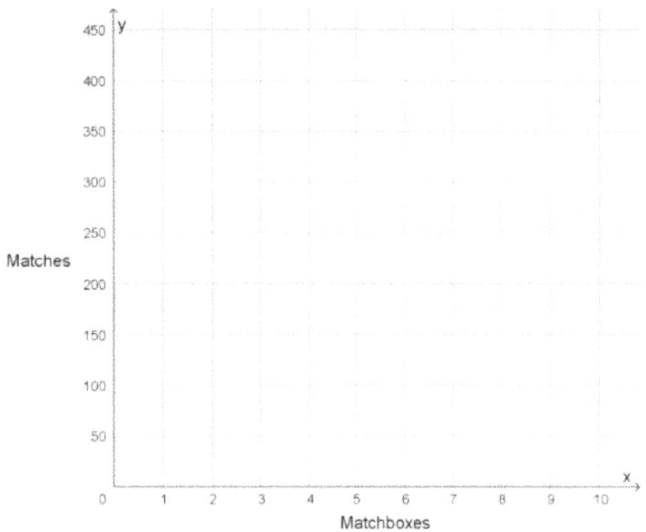

13 The cost of scissors is $8 and the cost of delivery is $3. The total cost of x scissors is represented by the equation $8x + 3 = 67$. How many scissors are ordered?

x = _____ scissors

14 Find the slope of a linear equation $\frac{x}{2} - \frac{y}{4} = 1$.

(A) 2   (B) -2   (C) $\frac{1}{2}$ (D) $-\frac{1}{2}$

15 Solve for x.

$$3x + 8 = 29$$

x = _____.

16 How many solutions does the equation have?

$$4x - 9x = 4 - 5x + 13$$

(A) 1   (B) 2   (C) No solution   (D) ∞

17 The perimeter of a parallelogram is 64 and the difference of its sides is 6. Find the side lengths. Create a system of equations and solve by the method of elimination.

_____

18 The salaries of the two drivers are represented by the graph below. Is there a moment when both salaries are equal?

(A) Yes   (B) No

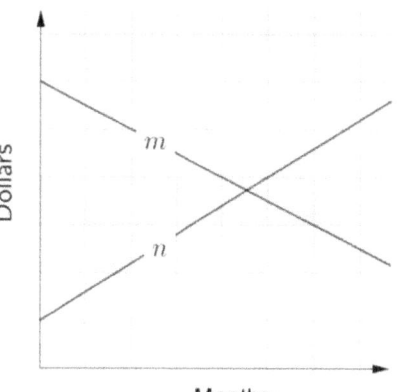

3.6 Chapter Review

19 Parker is deciding between two cell phone plans. Plan A has a $35 signup fee and a monthly cost of $30. Plan B has a $50 signup fee and costs $19 per month. Which equations represent the two cell phone plans?

(A) Plan A = 30m + 35 and Plan B = 19m + 50

(B) Plan A = 19m + 50 and Plan B = 30m + 35

(C) Plan A = 30m + 50 and Plan B = 19m + 35

(D) Plan A = 35m + 50 and Plan B = 30m + 19m

20 Write an equation to represent the line shown on this graph.

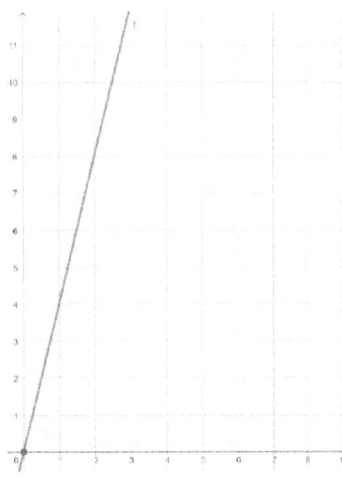

_____

Next Chapter:
Transformations

CHAPTER 4

TRANSFORMATIONS

9	7	8	2	6	1			5
	1					6		
	6		8	4			2	
	8					4		
3	9	6	4	7	2			8
	4			9			7	
	5		1		4			3
	2					7		
4	3	1		8			6	2

ROTATIONS AND DILATIONS

Lesson Introduction:

Rotation is defined by the center of rotation and the angle of rotation. The center of rotation is the point, and the angle of rotation can be clockwise or counterclockwise.

Example: Rotate △ABC around point D , 60° clockwise.

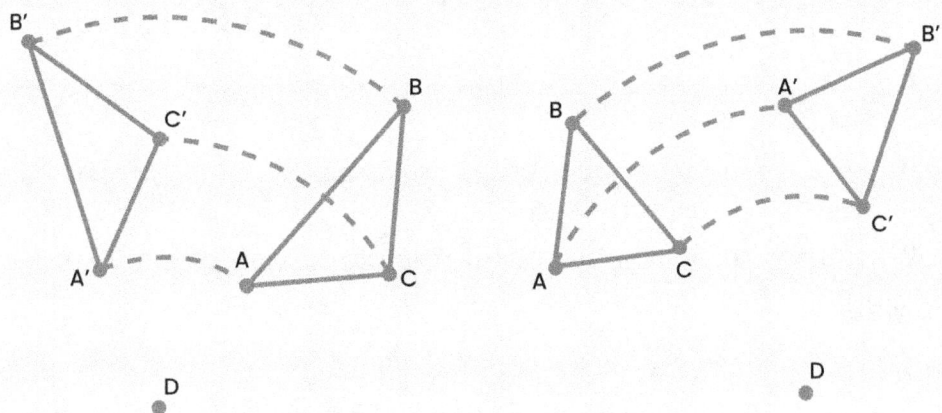

Dilation is defined by the center of dilation and the scale factor. The center of dilation is the point, and the scale factor can be positive or negative.

k – scale factor

|k|>1 – the figure is enlarged.

|k| < 1, k ≠ 0 – the figure is reduced.

Example: Dilation of △ABC with the center of dilation D and the scale factor 2.

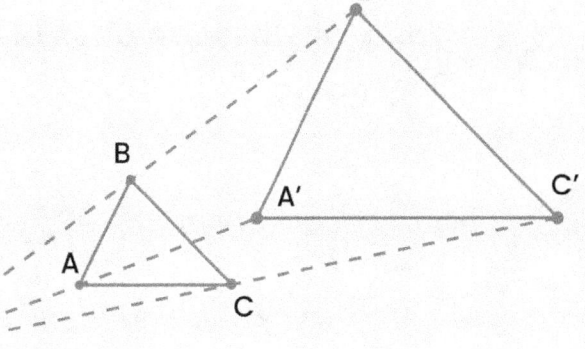

4.1   **Rotations and Dilations**

1   Check whether a rotation of point A is clockwise or counter clockwise.

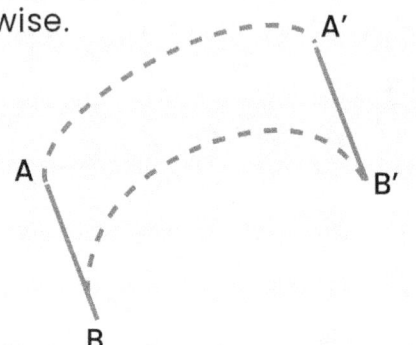

A) Clockwise

B) Counter clockwise

2   Check whether a rotation of point A is clockwise or counter clockwise.

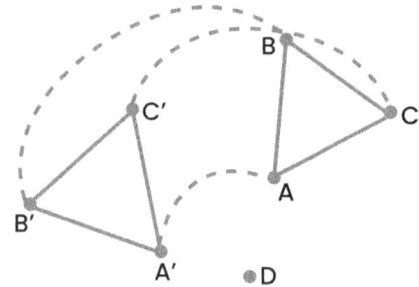

A) Clockwise

B) Counter clockwise

3   Check whether a rotation of point A is clockwise or counter clockwise.

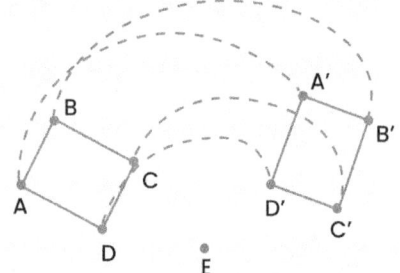

A) Clockwise

B) Counter clockwise

4 Check whether a rotation of point A is clockwise or counter clockwise.

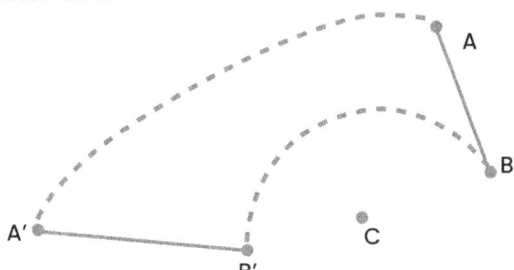

(A) Clockwise

(B) Counter clockwise

5 Determine the center of rotation.

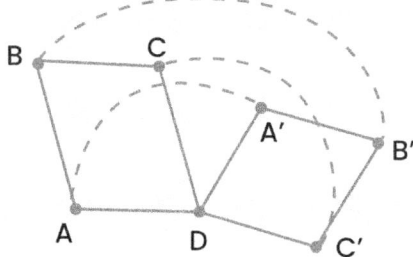

(A) Point A

(B) Point B

(C) Point C

(D) Point D

6 Determine the center of rotation.

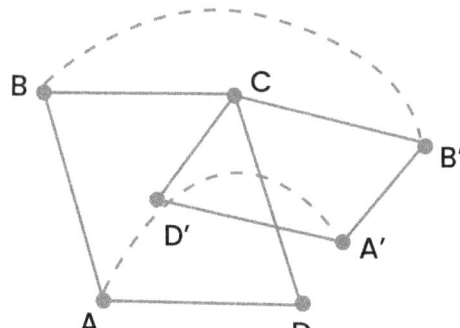

(A) Point A

(B) Point B

(C) Point C

(D) Point D

4.1 Rotations and Dilations

7 Determine the transformation.

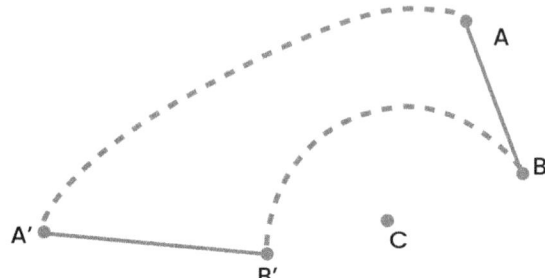

(A) Dilation

(B) Rotation

8 Determine the transformation.

(A) Dilation

(B) Rotation

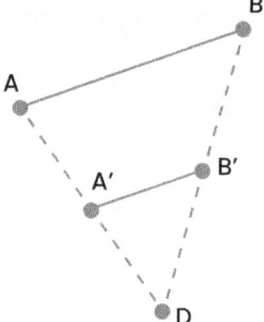

9 Determine the sign of the scale factor in the dilation shown below.

(A) Positive

(B) Negative

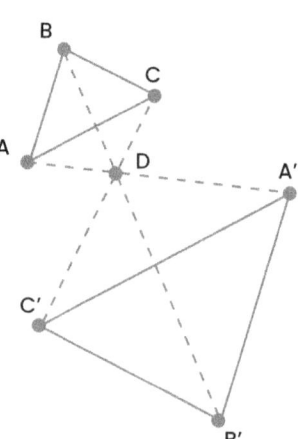

Rotations and Dilations  4.1

10 Determine the sign of the scale factor in the dilation shown below.

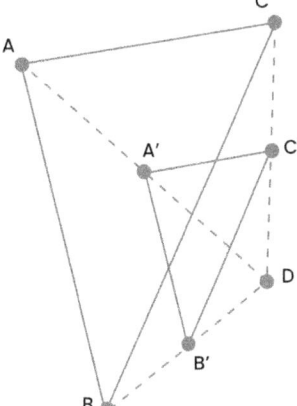

(A) Positive

(B) Negative

11 Parker is turned toward East. He turns right toward South. What is the angle of rotation?

(A) 90° clockwise   (B) 180° clockwise

(C) 270° clockwise   (D) 360° clockwise

12 Nancy–Go–Round turns a full turn. What is the angle of rotation?

(A) 90°   (B) 180°   (C) 270°   (D) 360°

13 The periscope turns $\frac{3}{4}$ of a full turn. What is the angle of rotation?

(A) 110°   (B) 180°   (C) 270°   (D) 290°

4.1 **Rotations and Dilations**

---

14 The arm of a clock points to 12. After 20 minutes it points to 4. What is the angle of rotation?

(A) 100°   (B) 140°   (C) 220°   (D) 120°

---

15 Mercury, Venus, Earth orbits around the Sun. What is the center of rotation?

_____

---

16 The wheel turns $\frac{1}{5}$ of a full turn. What is the angle of rotation?

(A) 72°   (B) 40°   (C) 86°   (D) 90°

---

17 One centimeter on a map represents an actual distance of 4 kilometers. What is the scale factor?

_____

18 One inch of the width of the model of a swimming pool represents an actual width of 3 feet. What is the scale factor?

(A) 12   (B) 36   (C) 30   (D) 18

19 The tree in the drawing is 25 centimeters high. The actual height of the tree is 5.5 meters. What is the scale factor?

_____

20 One foot of length of the model of a courtyard represents an actual length of 6 yards. What is the scale factor?

_____

Next Section: Reflections and Translations

REFLECTIONS AND TRANSLATIONS

Lesson Introduction:

Reflection is defined by the central or mirror line. Every pair of the corresponding points in the reflection is the same distance from the mirror line.

Example: Reflection of △ABC around the line m.

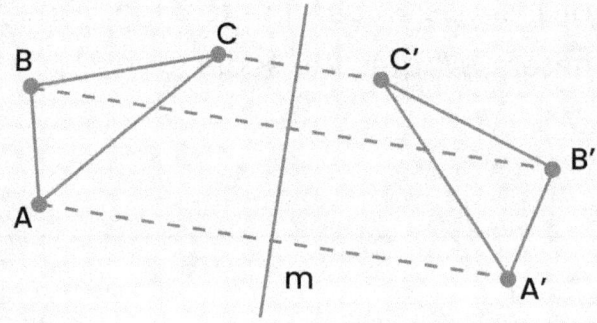

Translation is defined by the vector of translation. Every point in the translation is moved the same distance and in the same direction.

Example: Translation of △ABC by the vector $\vec{v}$.

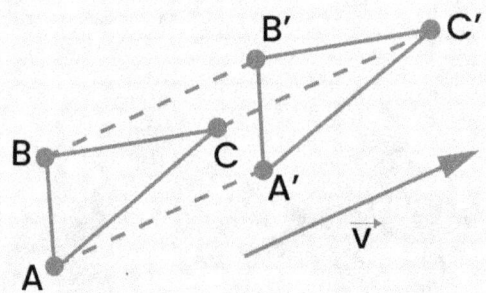

1   Determine the type of transformation in the image below.

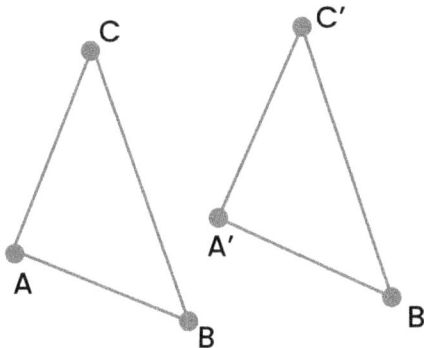

(A) Reflection

(B) Translation

2   Determine the type of transformation in the image below.

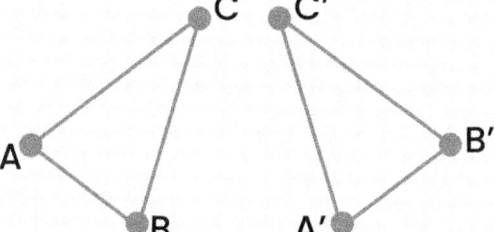

(A) Reflection

(B) Translation

3   Determine the type of transformation in the image below.

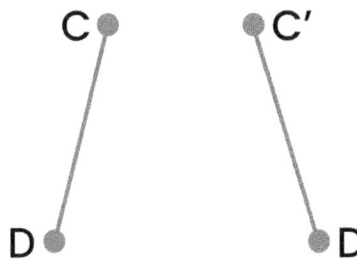

(A) Reflection

(B) Translation

4.2   Reflections and Translations

4   Determine the type of transformation in the image below.

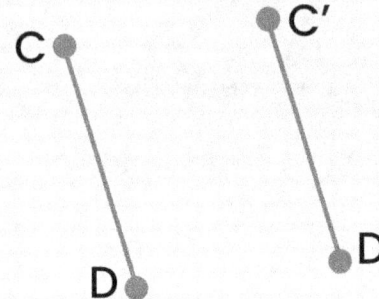

(A) Reflection

(B) Translation

5   Determine the type of transformation in the image below.

(A) Reflection

(B) Translation

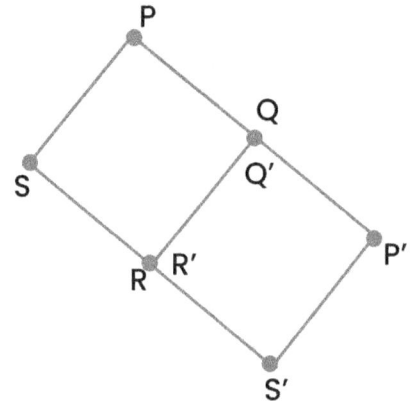

6   Determine the type of transformation in the image below.

(A) Reflection

(B) Translation

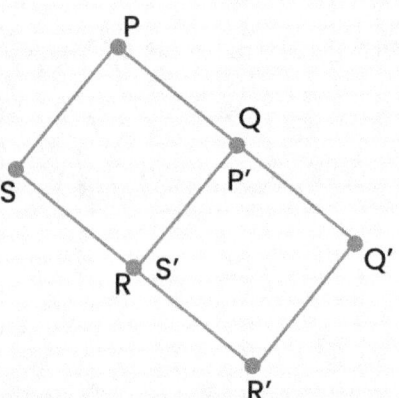

7 Determine the type of transformation in the image below.

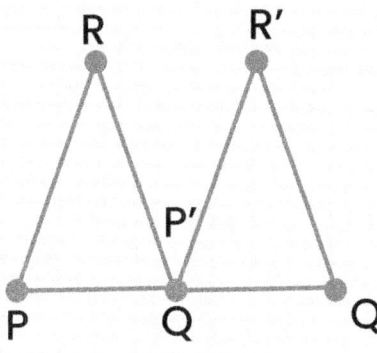

(A) Reflection

(B) Translation

8 Determine the type of transformation in the image below.

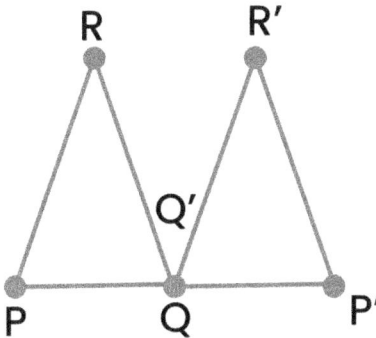

(A) Reflection

(B) Translation

9 Determine whether the transformation is a translation.
Mars orbits around the Sun.

(A) Yes   (B) No

4.2   **Reflections and Translations**

10 Determine whether the following transformation is a translation.
The car is moving along the road.

(A) Yes   (B) No

11 Determine whether the following transformation is a translation.
A coconut is falling from the tree.

(A) Yes   (B) No

12 Determine whether the following transformation is a translation.
Ryan is looking in the mirror.

(A) Yes   (B) No

13 Determine the type of transformation.
The elevator is moving in the showroom.

(A) Reflection   (B) Translation

14 Determine the type of transformation.
Noah is looking at the surface of the water pot.

(A) Reflection   (B) Translation

15 Determine the type of transformation.
The ball is dropped from the hand.

   (A) Reflection   (B) Translation

16 Write the vector of translation in the following translations of PQRS.

   (A) PP'   (B) QQ'

   (C) RR'   (D) SS'

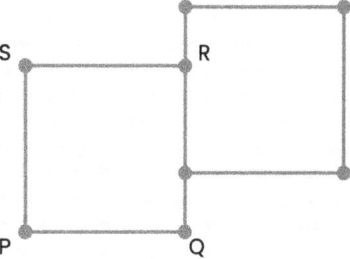

17 Write the vector of translation in the following translations of PQRS.

   (A) PP'   (B) QQ'

   (C) RR'   (D) SS'

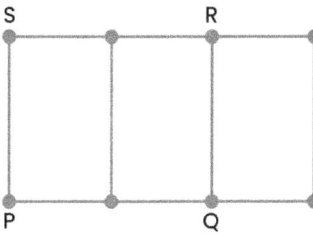

18 Write the vector of translation in the following translations of PQRS.

   (A) PQ   (B) RS

   (C) SR   (D) SQ

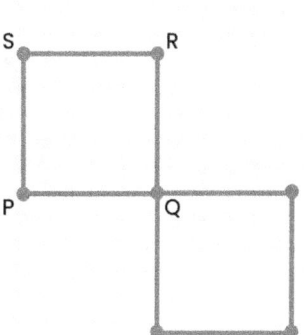

4.2   **Reflections and Translations**

19 How many lines of symmetry do the following figures have?
Regular decagon

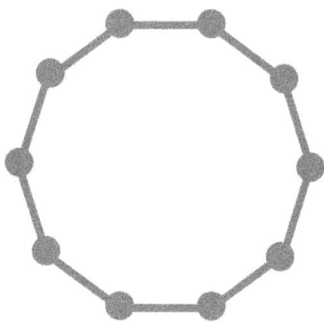

_____

20 How many lines of symmetry do the following figures have?
Regular octagon

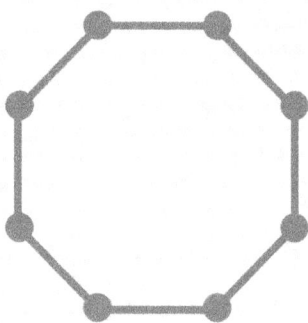

_____

Next Section: Similar Figures and Congruent Figures

SIMILAR FIGURES AND CONGRUENT FIGURES

Lesson Introduction:

Similar Figures

If one figure can be made into another using resizing, then the two figures are similar. The similarity of the two figures is defined by the scale factor, k.

Example: Similar triangles using resizing $(k > 1)$.

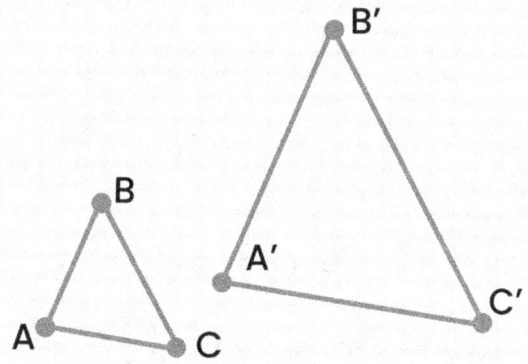

Congruent Figures

If one figure can become another using translation, rotation, and/or reflection, then the two figures are congruent.

Example: Congruent triangles using translation.

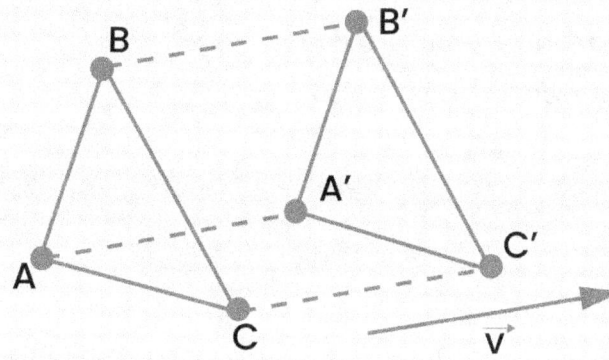

4.3 Similar Figures and Congruent Figures

1 Which transformation exhibits the congruence between the two triangles?

(A) Reflection   (B) Translation

(C) Rotation   (D) Dilation

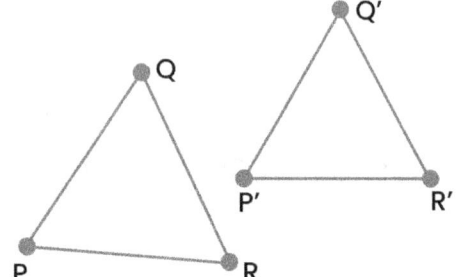

2 Which transformation exhibits the congruence between the two triangles?

(A) Reflection   (B) Translation

(C) Rotation   (D) Dilation

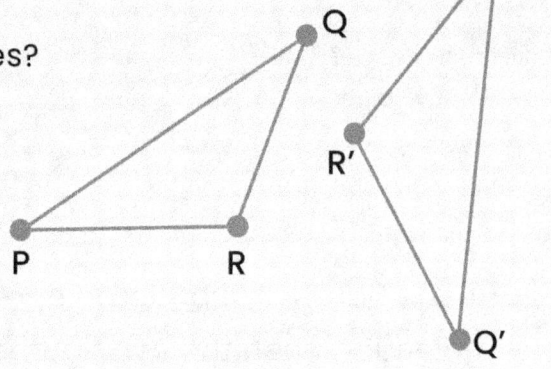

3 Which transformation exhibits the congruence between the two hexagons?

(A) Reflection   (B) Translation

(C) Rotation   (D) Dilation

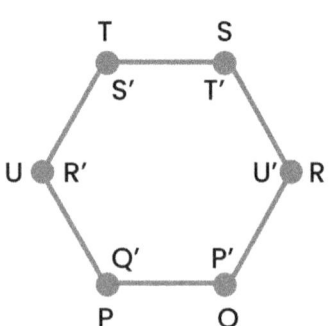

4 Describe a sequence of events that exhibits the congruence between ΔPQR and ΔP"Q"R"?

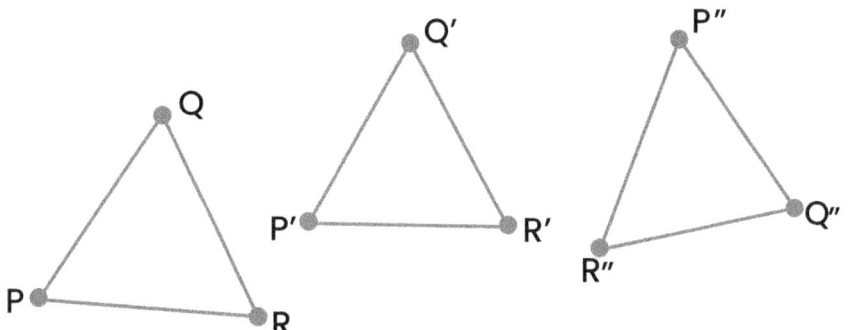

(A) Reflection + Rotation

(B) Rotation + Translation

(C) Translation + Reflection

(D) Translation + Rotation

5 Describe a sequence of events that exhibits the congruence between ΔPQR and ΔP"Q"R"?

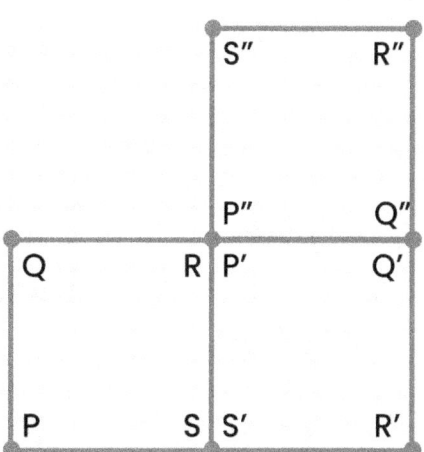

(A) Reflection + Rotation

(B) Rotation + Translation

(C) Translation + Reflection

(D) Translation + Rotation

4.3 Similar Figures and Congruent Figures

6 Find the coordinates of the point A', which is the image in the translation of the point A by the vector $\vec{v}$.

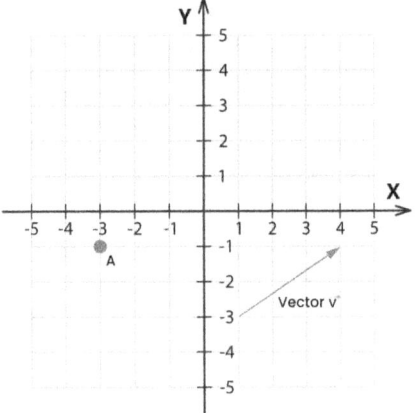

(A) A'(0,1)

(B) A'(1,1)

(C) A'(-1,1)

(D) A'(1,-1)

7 Find the coordinates of the point A', which is the image in the translation of the point A by the vector $\vec{v}$.

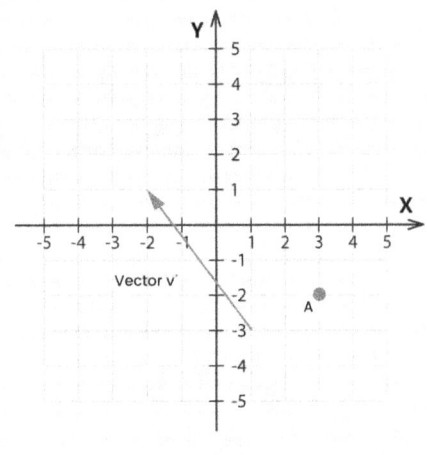

(A) A'(0,0)

(B) A'(0,1)

(C) A'(0,)

(D) A'(0,3)

8 Find the coordinates of the point A', which is the image in the translation of the point A by the vector $\vec{v}$.

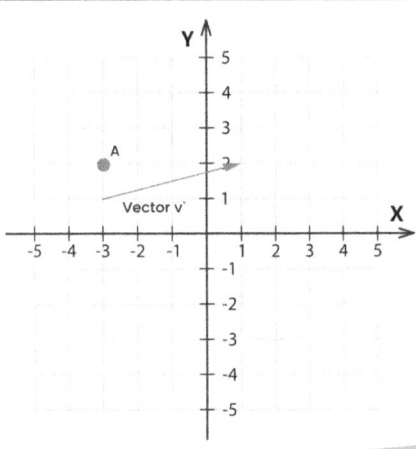

(A) A'(0,3)

(B) A'(1,3)

(C) A'(2,3)

(D) A'(-2,3)

Similar Figures and Congruent Figures **4.3**

9 Find the coordinates of the point A', which is the image in the rotation of the point A around the origin 90° clockwise.

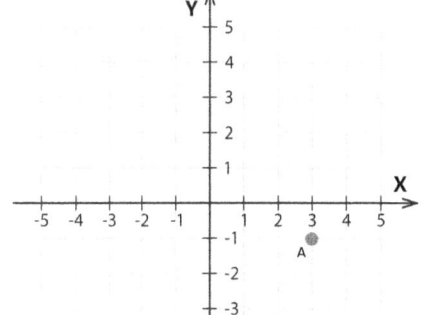

(A) A'(1,−3)

(B) A'(−1,3)

(C) A'(1,3)

(D) A'(−1,−3)

---

10 Find the coordinates of the point A', which is the image in the rotation of the point A around the origin 90° clockwise.

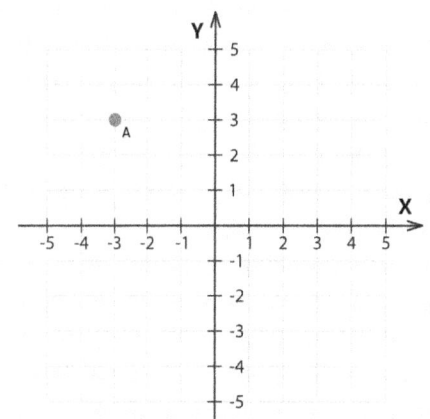

(A) A'(3,3)

(B) A'(−3,3)

(C) A'(3,−3)

(D) A'(−3,−3)

---

11 Find the coordinates of the point A', which is the image in the reflection of the point A around the x-axis.

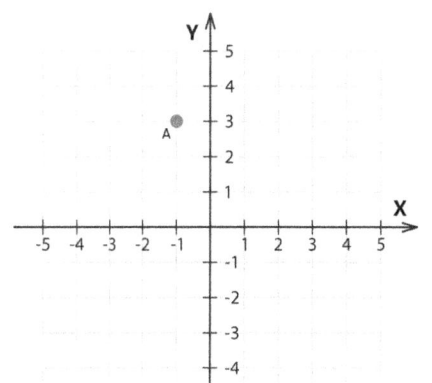

(A) A'(1,−3)

(B) A'(−1,−3)

(C) A'(−1,3)

(D) A'(1,3)

4.3   **Similar Figures and Congruent Figures**

11 Find the coordinates of the point A', which is the image in the reflection of the point A around the x-axis.

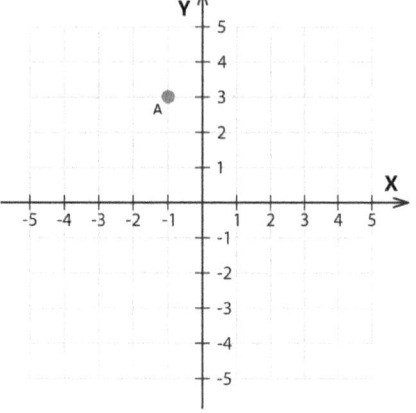

A) A'(1,–3)

B) A'(–1,–3)

C) A'(–1,3)

D) A'(1,3)

12 Find the coordinates of point A', which is the image in the reflection of point A around the y-axis.

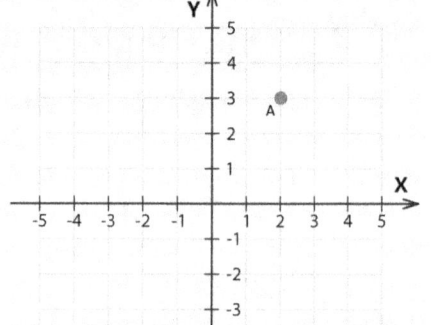

A) A'(1,–3)

B) A'(–1,–3)

C) A'(–1,3)

D) A'(1,3)

13 The coordinates of the marble are $(4,2)$. The trajectory of the marble is defined by the vector $\overrightarrow{AB}$, where $A(-2,-1)$ and $B(1,-4)$. What are the coordinates of the marble at the destination point?

A) (7,–1)   B) (1,–1)   C) (7,1)   D) (–1,–1)

14 The coordinates of the boat are $(-5,-2)$. The trajectory of the boat is a circle in which center is at the origin. What are the coordinates of the boat after rotation of $90°$ counter clockwise around the center?

(A) $(2,5)$ (B) $(2,-5)$ (C) $(-2,-5)$ (D) $(-2,5)$

15 The coordinates of the point on a circle are $(-4,1)$. The center of the circle is at the origin. What are the coordinates of the point after rotation of the circle $90°$ clockwise around the center?

(A) $(-4,1)$ (B) $(4,1)$ (C) $(4,-1)$ (D) $(-4,-1)$

16 The coordinates of the globe are $(6,2)$. The movement of the globe is defined by the vector $\vec{AB}$, where $A(-2,-4)$ and $B(-4,3)$. What are the coordinates of the globe at the destination point?

(A) $(4,8)$ (B) $(3,9)$ (C) $(4,9)$ (D) $(4,5)$

17 The coordinates of the asteroid are $(4,-1)$. The asteroid orbits around the planet which is at the origin. What are the coordinates of the asteroid after rotation of $90°$ counter clockwise around the sun?

(A) $(1,-4)$ (B) $(1,4)$ (C) $(-1,4)$ (D) $(-1,-4)$

4.3 Similar Figures and Congruent Figures

18 The coordinates of the particle are (–6,3). The particle is reflected across the mirror located along the x-axis. What are the new coordinates of the particle?

(A) (6,–3) (B) (–6,3) (C) (6,3) (D) (–6,–3)

19 Which transformation exhibits the congruence between the two rectangles?

(A) Translation (B) Reflection

(C) Rotation

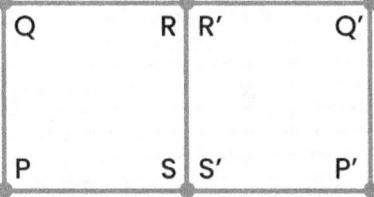

20 Which transformation exhibits the congruence between the two rectangles?

(A) Translation (B) Reflection

(C) Rotation

Next Section: Chapter Review ≫

1 Noah describes the transformation that transforms Figure A to Figure B as shown on this graph. What is the transformation shown below?

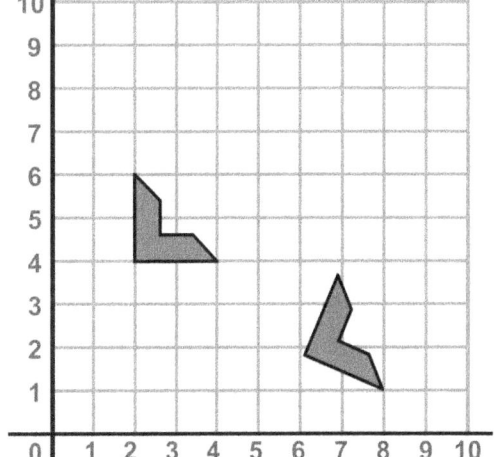

(A) Figure A is reflected twice.

(B) Figure A is reflected and rotated.

(C) Figure A is translated and rotated.

(D) Figure A is rotated 90 degrees.

2 Ava describes the transformation that transforms Figure P to Figure Q as shown on this graph. Which description matches the transformation?

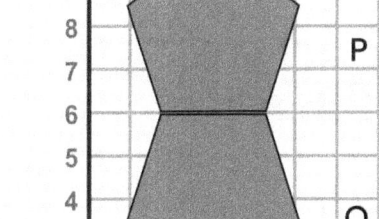

(A) Figure P is translated along the y - axis in the negative direction to create Figure Q.

(B) Figure P is reflected across the line y = 6 to create Figure Q.

(C) Figure P is translated across the linex = 6 to create Figure Q.

(D) Figure P is rotated about one vertex to create Figure Q.

4.4   **Chapter Review**

3 Triangles J and K are shown on the graph. Which sequence is used to transform Triangle A to Triangle B?

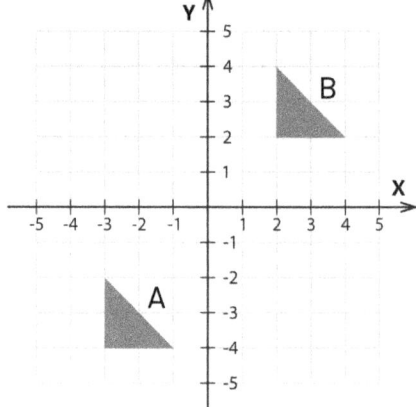

Ⓐ Translate Triangle A up 6 units and to the right 5 units.

Ⓑ Translate Triangle A up 5 units and to the right 6 units.

Ⓒ Translate Triangle A down 6 units and to the left 5 units.

Ⓓ Translate Triangle J down 5 units and to the right 6 units.

4 Which sequence is used to transform Quadrilateral ABCD to Quadrilateral PQRS?

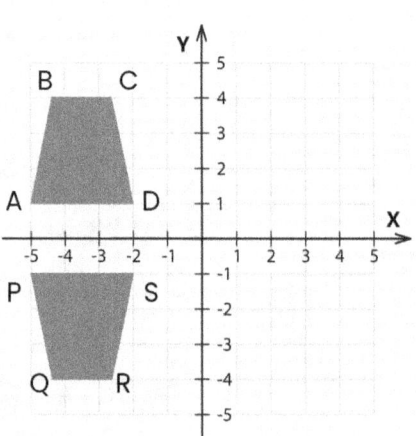

Ⓐ Quadrilateral ABCDis rotated about the origin.

Ⓑ Quadrilateral ABCD is reflected across the x – axis.

Ⓒ Quadrilateral ABCD is translated across the x – axis.

Ⓓ Quadrilateral ABCD is reflected across the y – axis.

5 The triangle PQR is shown on this graph. Triangle P'Q'R' is created by rotating Triangle PQR 180 degrees about the origin and then translating it 1 unit down.

What are the coordinates of the triangle P'Q'R'?

_____

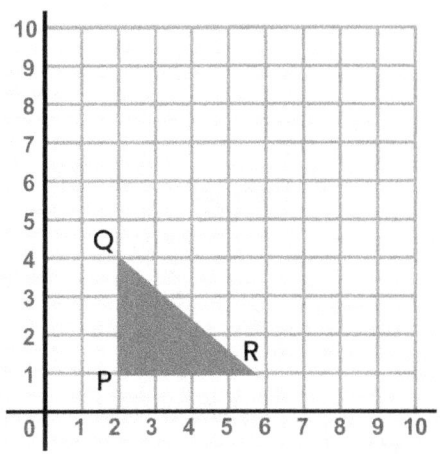

6 Quadrilateral PQRS is shown on this graph. Quadrilateral P'Q'R'S' is created by reflecting Quadrilateral PQRS across the y - axis and then reflecting it across the x - axis

What are the coordinates of Quadrilateral P'Q'R'S'?

_____

4.4 Chapter Review

7 The point Z (0, − 4) is translated 3 units right. What are the coordinates of the resulting point Z'?

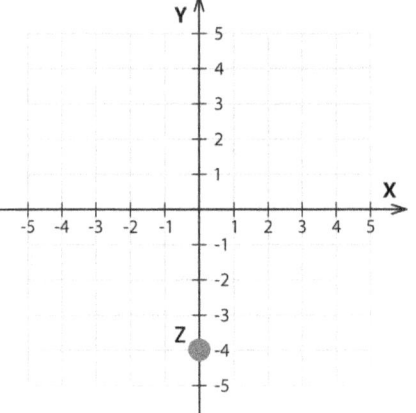

(A) (3,−4) (B) (3,4)

(C) (−3,−4) (D) (−3,4)

8 Point R (− 4, 0) is translated 6 units right. What are the coordinates of the resulting point R'?

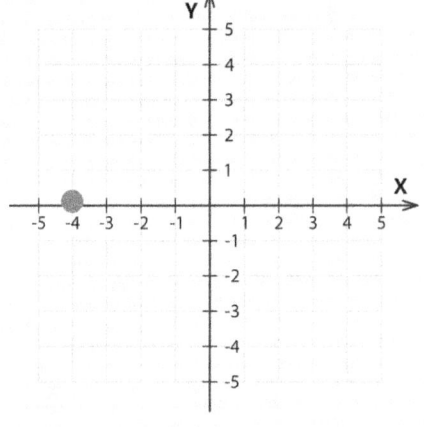

(A) (1,0) (B) (2,0)

(C) (3,0) (D) (4,0)

9 Point P (− 3, − 4) is translated 1 unit up. What are the coordinates of the resulting point, P'?

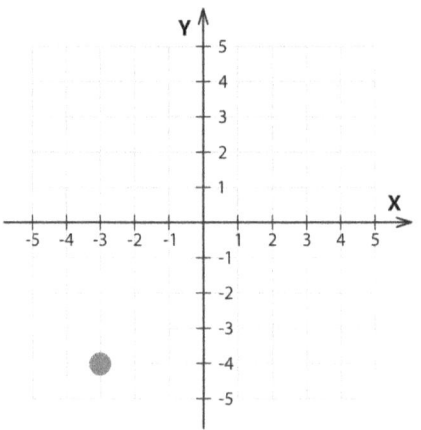

(A) (3,3) (B) (−3,−3)

(C) (3,−3) (D) (−3,3)

10 Point S (- 3, 0) is translated 1 unit right. What are the coordinates of the resulting point S'?

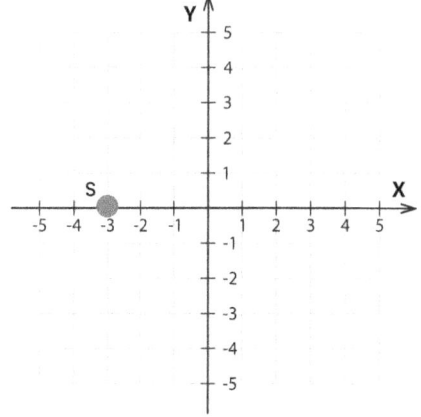

(A) (2,0)

(B) (−2,−1)

(C) (−2,0)

(D) (−2,2)

11 The triangle XYZ is shown on the graph below. Triangle X'Y'Z' is created by dilating the Triangle XYZ by a scale factor of 2 about the origin and translating the shape up 1 units. What are the coordinates of the Triangle X'Y'Z'?

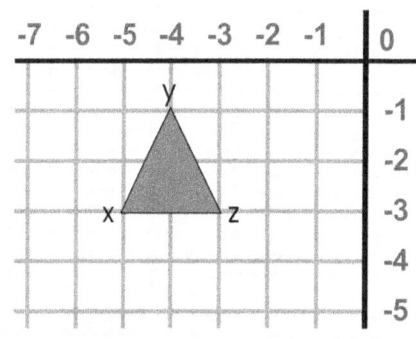

_____

12 The triangle ABC is shown on the graph below. Triangle A'B'C' is created by dilating Triangle DEF by a scale factor of 4 about the origin and reflecting the shape across the y - axis. What are the coordinates of the Triangle XYZ?

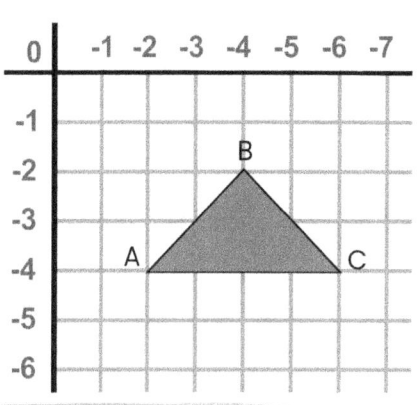

_____

13 Quadrilateral ABCD is shown on the graph. Quadrilateral A'B'C'D' is created by dilating Quadrilateral ABCD by a scale factor of $\frac{1}{3}$ about the origin.
What are the coordinates of Quadrilateral A'B'C'D'?

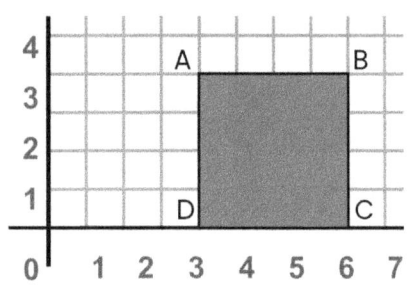

_____

14 Trapezoid JKLM is shown on the graph. Trapezoid J'K'L'M' is created by dilating Trapezoid JKLM by a scale factor of 2 about the origin. What are the coordinates of Trapezoid J'K'L'M'?

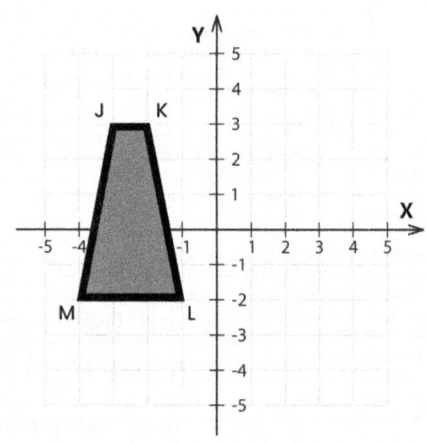

_____

15 Ron describes the transformation that takes Figure P to Figure Q as shown on this graph. Which description matches the transformation?

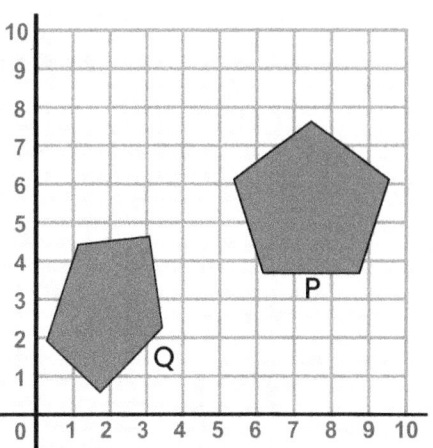

(A) Figure P is reflected across the y-axis.

(B) Figure P is reflected across the line x = 4.

(C) Figure P is rotated clockwise.

(D) Figure P is rotated counter clockwise.

16 **True or False:** If Point S (3, 0) is translated 2 units up, then the coordinates of the resulting coordinates of Point S' are (3,3).

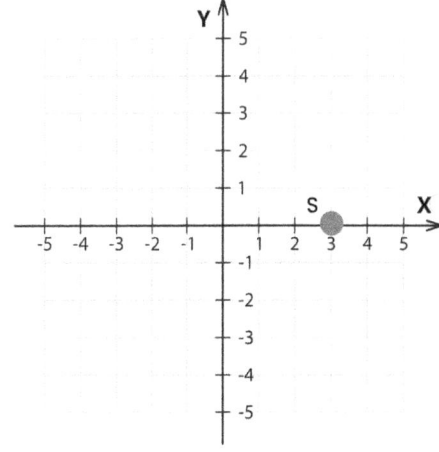

(A) True

(B) False

17 Rabbit turns his head $\frac{3}{20}$ of a full turn. What is the angle of rotation?

(A) 44°

(B) 54°

(C) 55°

(D) 18°

4.4   Chapter Review

18 Translate △PQR by the vector $\vec{PQR}$ into △P'Q'R and determine the coordinates of the vertices.

P' (_____ , _____), Q'(_____ , _____), R'(_____ , _____).

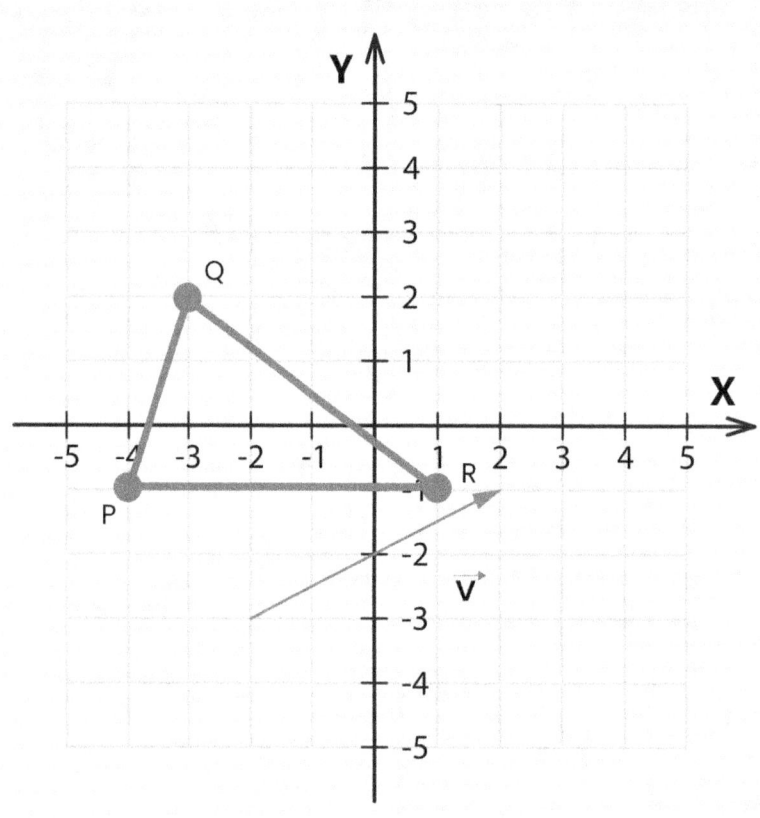

19 Translate ΔPQR by the vector $\overrightarrow{PQR}$ into ΔP'Q'R and determine the coordinates of the vertices.

P' (_____ , _____), Q'(_____ , _____), R'(_____ , _____).

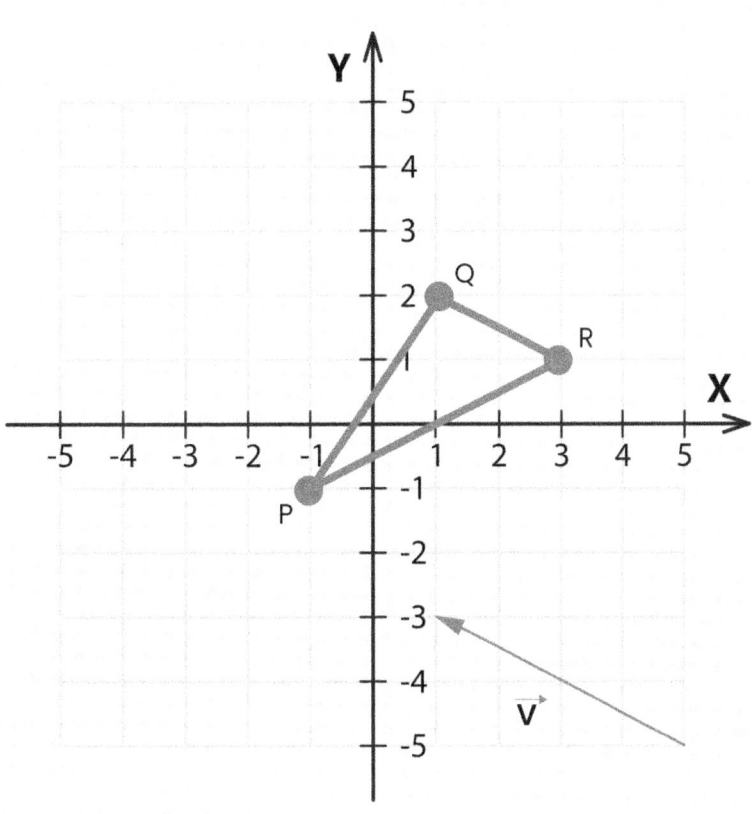

4.4   Chapter Review

20 Translate ΔPQR by the vector $\overrightarrow{PQR}$ into ΔP'Q'R and determine the coordinates of the vertices.

P' (_____ , _____), Q'(_____ , _____), R'(_____ , _____).

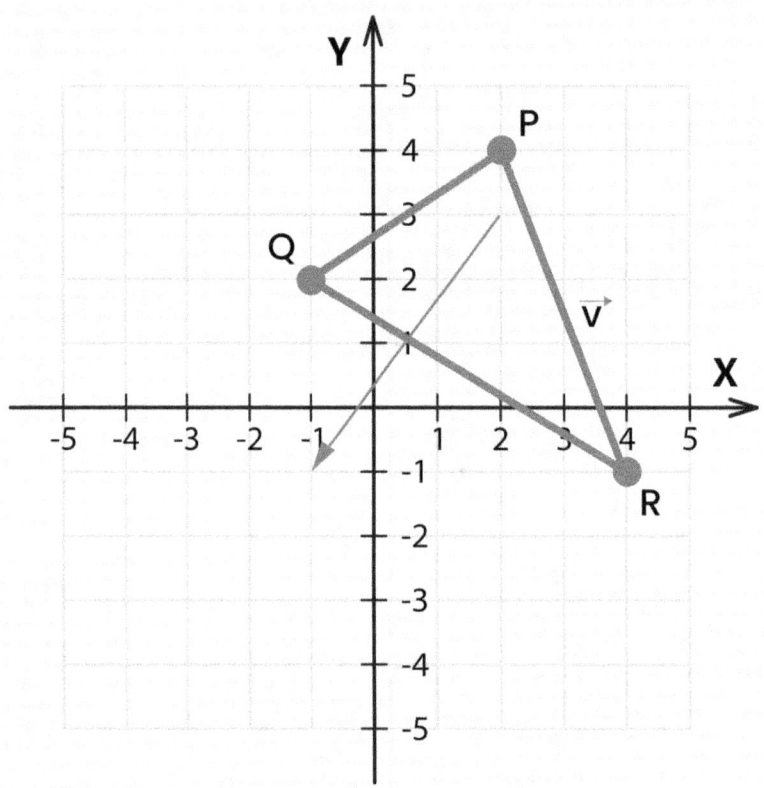

Next Chapter: Angles & Sides

CHAPTER 5

ANGLES & SIDES

		3	4	1	9	8		
	4						1	
	1		8	2	3			7
	9	8				5		
1	5		9	4	7			8
		7				2	9	4
7			1				6	
	8			6			2	
3		4	2	7	5	1		

MISSING ANGLES IN TRIANGLES AND EXTERIOR ANGLE THEOREM

Missing angles in triangles refer to the angles that are not explicitly given in a triangle but can be determined through the relationships between the known angles and sides of the triangle.

The exterior angle theorem states that the measure of an exterior angle of a triangle is equal to the sum of the measures of the two remote interior angles.

The sum of the interior angles of a triangle is 180°.

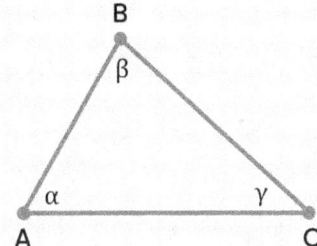

$$\alpha + \beta + \gamma = 180°$$

The sum of the exterior angles of a triangle is 360°

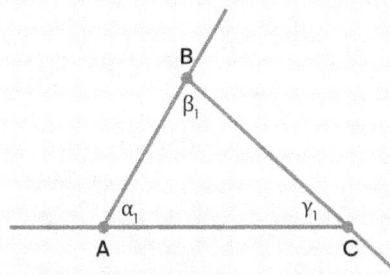

$$\alpha_1 + \beta_1 + \gamma_1 = 360°$$

The measure of an exterior angle of a triangle is equal to the sum of measures of the two opposite interior angles.

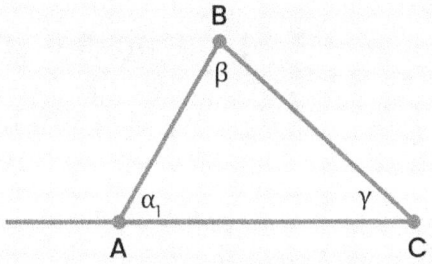

$$\alpha_1 = \beta + \gamma$$

5.1

Missing Angles in Triangles and Exterior Angle Theorem

1 Each subsequent interior angle of a triangle is three times as large as the previous one, beginning with the first. Find the measurements of the interior angles of the triangle.

_____

2 Starting from the first interior angle of a triangle each next interior angle is 20° greater than the previous one. Find the measures of the interior angles of the triangle.

(A) 20°, 40°, 60°

(B) 40°, 60°, 80°

(C) 60°, 80°, 100°

(D) 80°, 100°, 120°

3 Starting from the first interior angle of a triangle each next interior angle is 20° lower than the previous one. Find the measures of the interior angles of the triangle.

(A) 80°,60°,40°

(B) 20°,40°,60°

(C) 60°,40°,20°

(D) 40°,60°,80°

Missing Angles in Triangles and
Exterior Angle Theorem

5.1

4 Is it a right angle if the exterior angle of the triangle is 90°?

(A) True   (B) False

5 Match the following. Connect the corresponding interior and exterior angles of a triangle.

(A) 133°   (a) 93°

(B) 65°   (b) 47°

(C) 87°   (c) 115°

6 Match the following. Connect the corresponding interior and exterior angles of a triangle.

(A) 108°   (a) 85°

(B) 95°   (b) 27°

(C) 153°   (c) 72°

7 Match the following. Connect the corresponding interior and exterior angles of a triangle.

(A) 103°   (a) 75°

(B) 105°   (b) 103°

(C) 77°   (c) 77°

5.1 Missing Angles in Triangles and Exterior Angle Theorem

8 The exterior angle of a triangle is θ. Which of the following could be the opposite interior angles of the same triangle?

$$\theta = 148°$$

(A) 92° and 56°   (B) 70° and 88°

(C) 78° and 80°   (D) 91° and 47°

9 The exterior angle of a triangle is θ. Which of the following could be the opposite interior angles of the same triangle?

$$\theta = 156°$$

(A) 82° and 76°   (B) 45° and 51°

(C) 93° and 63°   (D) 97° and 52°

10 The exterior angle of a triangle is θ. Which of the following could be the opposite interior angles of the same triangle?

$$\theta = 162°$$

(A) 99° and 36°   (B) 77° and 85°

(C) 72° and 45°   (D) 71° and 67°

Missing Angles in Triangles and
Exterior Angle Theorem

5.1

11 One of the interior angles of the triangle is the mean of the other two interior angles. The measure of the greatest interior angle is 90°. Find the measures of the remaining two interior angles of the triangle

(A) 20°, 30°, 90°

(B) 25°, 45°, 90°

(C) 30°, 45°, 90°

(D) 30°, 60°, 90°

12 One of the interior angles of the triangle is the mean of the other two interior angles. The measure of the lowest interior angle is 40°. Find the measures of the remaining two interior angles of the triangle.

(A) 20°, 40°, 60°

(B) 40°, 60°, 80°

(C) 60°, 80°, 100°

(D) 80°, 100°, 120°

13 One of the interior angles of the triangle is equal to the sum of the other two interior angles. The measure of the middle interior angle is 55°. Find the measures of the remaining two interior angles of the triangle.

(A) 30°, 55°, 90°

(B) 45°, 55°, 90°

(C) 35°, 55°, 90°

(D) 50°, 55°, 75°

5.1 Missing Angles in Triangles and
Exterior Angle Theorem

14 One of the interior angles of the triangle is equal to one-third of the sum of the other two interior angles. The measure of the greatest interior angle is 85°. Find the measures of the remaining two interior angles of the triangle.

(A) 45°, 50°, 85°

(B) 40°, 50°, 85°

(C) 45°, 55°, 85°

(D) 30°, 60°, 85°

15 One of the interior angles of the triangle is equal to one-fourth of the sum of the other two interior angles. The measure of the greatest interior angle is 110°. Find the measures of the remaining two interior angles of the triangle.

(A) 30°, 50°, 110°

(B) 36°, 36°, 110°

(C) 44°, 46°, 110°

(D) 34°, 36°, 110°

16 The exterior angle of a triangle is 3 times an opposite interior angle of the same triangle. If the measure of the greatest interior angle is 90°, what is the measure of the smallest interior angle?

(A) 45° or 30°

(B) 55° or 30°

(C) 55° or 50°

(D) 50° or 20°

17 The exterior angle of a triangle is 4 times the opposite interior angle of the same triangle. If the measure of the smallest interior angle is 40°, what is the measure of the greatest interior angle?

(A) 110° or 70°

(B) 115° or 45°

(C) 111° or 99°

(D) 120° or 105°

18 The interior angles of a triangle are shown. What is the value of x?

$$\frac{x°}{3}, x° + 10°, 2x° - 10°.$$

(A) 60

(B) 70

(C) 54

(D) 64

19 The interior angles of a triangle are shown. What is the value of x?

$$x°, 3x° + 20°, 2x° - 20°.$$

(A) 10

(B) 20

(C) 30

(D) 40

5.1 **Missing Angles in Triangles and Exterior Angle Theorem**

20 The exterior angles of a triangle are shown. What is the value of x?

$$x° + 40°, x° - 20°, x° - 20°.$$

(A) 120   (B) 110   (C) 100   (D) 130

Next Section: Angles Formed by a Transversal

ANGLES FORMED BY A TRANSVERSAL

A transversal is a line that intersects two or more other lines at different points. The lines that the transversal intersects are called the transverse lines.

In the figure below, transversal t cuts parallel lines m and n and forms angles a, b, c, d, e, f, g and h.

There are 4 types of angles formed by a transversal:

- **Corresponding angles** are equal.
$$a = e, b = f, c = g, d = h$$
- **Alternate interior angles** are equal.
$$c = f, d = e$$
- **Alternate exterior angles** are equal.
$$a = h, b = g$$
- **Consecutive interior angles** add up to 180°.
$$c + e = 180, d + f = 180$$

5.2   Angles Formed by a Transversal

1 In the figures below, transversal w cuts parallel lines x and y. Determine the type of angles α and β.

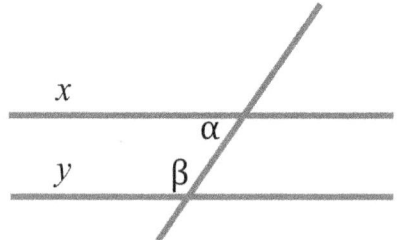

(A) Alternate interior angles

(B) Alternate exterior angles

(C) Consecutive interior angles

(D) Corresponding angles

2 In the figures below, transversal w cuts parallel lines x and y. Determine the type of angles α and β.

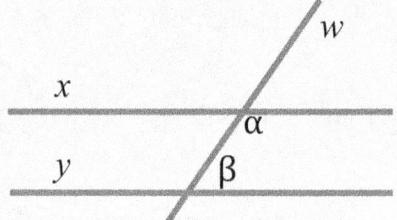

(A) Alternate interior angles

(B) Alternate exterior angles

(C) Consecutive interior angles

(D) Corresponding angles

3 In the figures below, transversal w cuts parallel lines x and y. Determine the type of angles α and β.

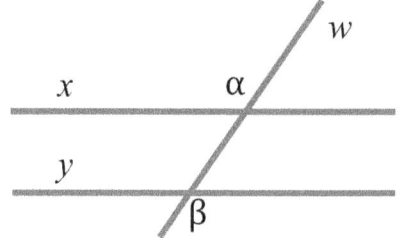

(A) Alternate interior angles

(B) Alternate exterior angles

(C) Consecutive interior angles

(D) Corresponding angles

Angles Formed by a Transversal   **5.2**

4 In the figures below, transversal w cuts parallel lines x and y. Determine the type of angles α and β.

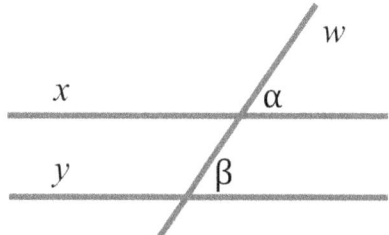

(A) Alternate interior angles

(B) Alternate exterior angles

(C) Consecutive interior angles

(D) Corresponding angles

5 In the figures below, transversal w cuts parallel lines x and y. Determine the type of angles α and β.

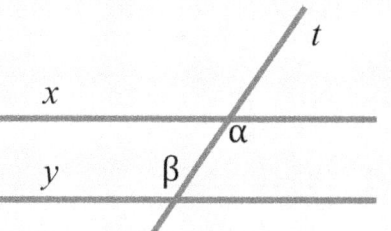

(A) Alternate interior angles

(B) Alternate exterior angles

(C) Consecutive interior angles

(D) Corresponding angles

6 Find the measure of angle α.

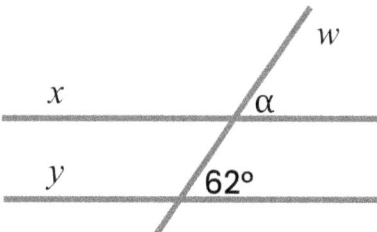

(A) 62°

(B) 128°

(C) 100°

(D) 80°

5.2 Angles Formed by a Transversal

7 Find the measure of angle α.

A) 88°   B) 38°

C) 142°   D) 132°

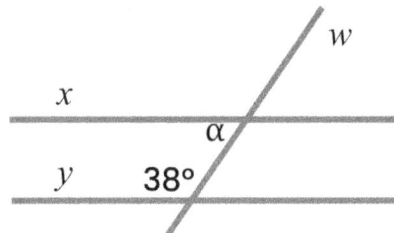

8 Write the measures of all the angles in the figures below.

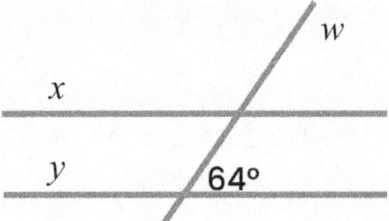

_____

9 Determine whether the lines x and y are parallel or not.

A) Lines are parallel.

B) Lines are not parallel.

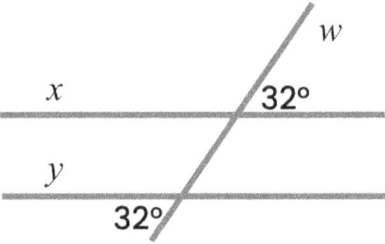

10 Determine whether the lines x and y are parallel or not.

A) Lines are parallel.

B) Lines are not parallel.

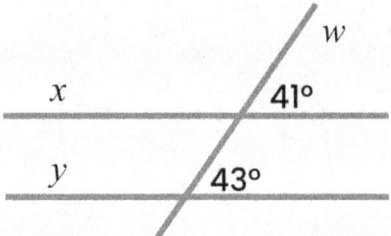

Angles Formed by a Transversal   **5.2**

11 Determine whether the lines x and y are parallel or not.

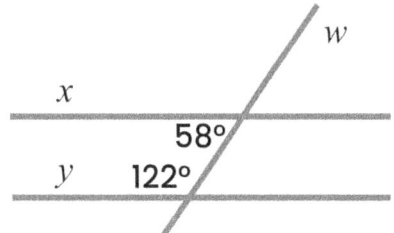

(A) Lines are parallel.

(B) Lines are not parallel.

12 Parallel lines x and y are cut by a transversal t. The measure of one exterior angle formed by a transversal and lines x and y is 82°. What is the measure of its alternate exterior angle?

_____

13 Parallel lines x and y are cut by a transversal t. The measure of one exterior angle formed by a transversal and lines x and y is 128°. What is the measure of its corresponding angle?

_____

14 Parallel lines x and y are cut by a transversal w. The measure of one interior angle formed by a transversal and lines x and y is 62°. What is the measure of its alternate exterior angle?

_____

5.2   Angles Formed by a Transversal

15 Parallel lines x and y are cut by a transversal w. The difference between the two consecutive interior angles is 64°. What is the measure of the smaller interior angle?

(A) 58°   (B) 64°   (C) 126°   (D) 54°

16 Parallel lines x and y are cut by a transversal w. The difference between the two consecutive interior angles is 42°. What is the measure of the smaller interior angle?

(A) 138°   (B) 111°   (C) 121°   (D) 69°

17 Parallel lines x and y are cut by a transversal w. The difference between the two consecutive interior angles is 46°, and their sum is 179°. Are lines x and n parallel?

(A) Yes   (B) No

18 Parallel lines x and y are cut by a transversal w. The difference between the two consecutive interior angles is 56°, and their sum is 180°. Are lines x and n parallel?

(A) Yes   (B) No

19 In the figures below, transversal w cuts parallel lines x and y. Find the measure of angle α.

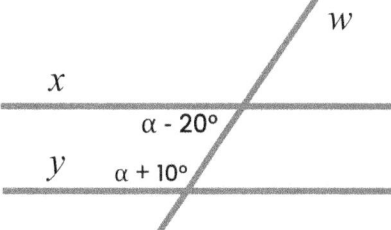

_____

20 In the figures below, transversal w cuts parallel lines x and y. Find the measure of angle α.

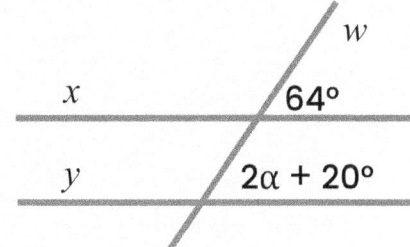

_____

Next Section:
Pythagorean Theorem

PYTHAGOREAN THEOREM

Pythagorean Theorem states that if the square of the length of the longest side of a triangle (hypotenuse) is equal to the sum of the squares of the other two sides (legs), then the triangle is a right triangle.

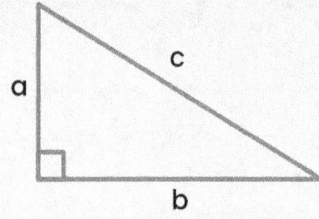

$$c^2 = a^2 + b^2$$

This means that if we know the side lengths of a triangle, we can determine whether the triangle is right or not.

Example: Check whether the triangle with side lengths 4,7, and 9 is a right triangle.

$$9^2 = 4^2 + 7^2$$
$$81 = 16 + 49$$
$$81 \neq 65$$

The triangle is not right.

If we know the side lengths of the triangle, we can also determine whether a triangle is acute or obtuse

$$c^2 < a^2 + b^2 \Rightarrow \text{acute triangle}$$
$$c^2 > a^2 + b^2 \Rightarrow \text{obtuse triangle}$$

Example: Check whether the triangle with side lengths 4,7, and 9 is an acute or an obtuse triangle.

$$9^2 = 4^2 + 7^2$$
$$81 = 16 + 49$$
$$81 > 65$$

The triangle is obtuse.

Pythagorean Theorem   **5.3**

1 Determine whether the following is a right triangle based on the side lengths given.

$$a = 6, b = 8, c = 10.$$

(A) True   (B) False

2 Determine whether the following is a right triangle based on the side lengths given.

$$a = 2, b = 3, c = 4.$$

(A) True   (B) False

3 Determine the type of triangle based on the side lengths given.

$$a = 3, b = 4, c = 5.$$

(A) Acute   (B) Obtuse   (C) Right

4 Determine the type of triangle based on the side lengths given.

$$a = 2, b = 5, c = 6.$$

(A) Acute   (B) Obtuse   (C) Right

5 Determine where the following is a right triangle based on the side lengths given.

$$a = 4, b = 6, c = 6.5.$$

(A) Acute   (B) Obtuse   (C) Right

5.3   Pythagorean Theorem

6   If the lengths of the legs of a right triangle are 5 centimeters and 6 centimeters, what is the length of a hypotenuse?

(A) $6\sqrt{5}$ cm   (B) $\sqrt{5}$ cm   (C) $\sqrt{51}$ cm   (D) $\sqrt{61}$ cm

7   If the lengths of the legs of a right triangle are 9 centimeters and 10 centimeters, what is the length of a hypotenuse?

(A) $10\sqrt{81}$ cm   (B) $\sqrt{181}$ cm   (C) $\sqrt{90}$ cm   (D) $\sqrt{111}$ cm

8   If the lengths of the legs of a right triangle are 11 centimeters and 12 centimeters, what is the length of a hypotenuse?

(A) $\sqrt{265}$ cm   (B) 21 cm   (C) 23 cm   (D) $\sqrt{144}$ cm

9   If the lengths of the legs of a right triangle are 8 centimeters and 10 centimeters, what is the length of a hypotenuse?

(A) 25 cm   (B) $\sqrt{164}$ cm   (C) 26 cm   (D) $\sqrt{154}$ cm

10   **True or False:** A triangle with side lengths of 10 kilometers, 11 kilometers, and 15 kilometers is a right triangle.

(A) True   (B) False

11 **True or False:** A triangle with side lengths of 8 kilometers, 15 kilometers, and 17 kilometers is a right triangle.

(A) True   (B) False

12 **True or False:** A triangle with side lengths of 7 kilometers, 9 kilometers, and 11 kilometers is a right triangle.

(A) True   (B) False

13 In a right triangle, the length of the hypotenuse is 10 mm and the length of one leg is 6 mm. What is the length of the other leg?

(A) 5 mm   (B) 7 mm   (C) 8 mm   (D) 9 mm

14 In a right triangle, the hypotenuse is 15 km and the other leg is 12 km. What is the length of the other leg?

(A) 6 km   (B) 7 km   (C) 7.5 km   (D) 9 km

15 In a right triangle, the hypotenuse is 20 in and the other leg is 16 in. What is the length of the other leg?

(A) 11 in   (B) 12 in   (C) 13 in   (D) 14 in

5.3   **Pythagorean Theorem**

16 What is the length of the hypotenuse of the triangle below?

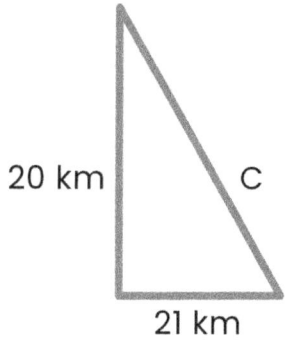

20 km   C

21 km

_____

17 What is the length of the hypotenuse in the triangle below?

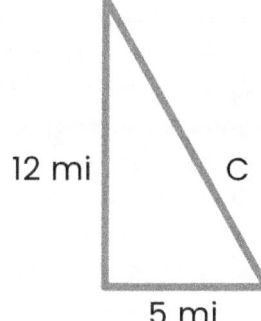

12 mi   C

5 mi

_____

18 What is the length of the hypotenuse in the triangle below?

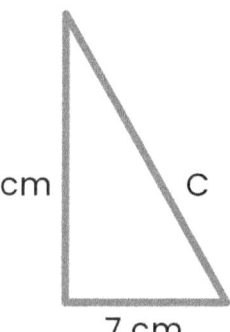

8 cm   C

7 cm

_____

19 What is the approximate distance between Point B and Point C?

- (A) 4 units
- (B) 11 units
- (C) 2.4 units
- (D) 5.6 units

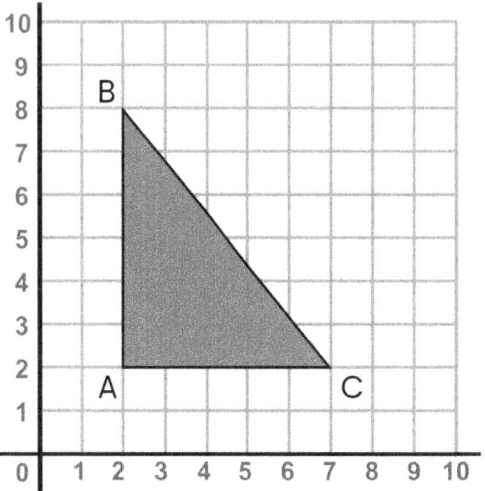

20 What is the approximate distance between Point B and Point C?

- (A) 6.4 units
- (B) 2.7 units
- (C) 5.4 units
- (D) 4.42 units

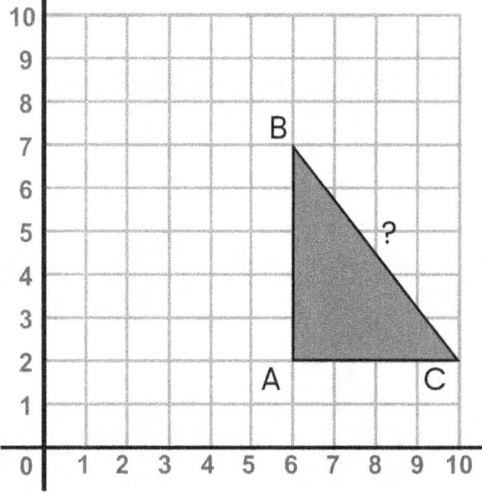

Next Section: Chapter Review ❯❯

5.4 Chapter Review

1 Ryan rearranges the angles of a triangle so the angles connect to form a straight angle. Which set of angles could be the three angles?

(A) 46°, 84°, 60°

(B) 52°, 98°, 30°

(C) 50°, 90°, 50°

(D) 100°, 44°, 16°

2 Emily uses this drawing to prove the triangle sum theorem. What conclusions can be made from her drawing?

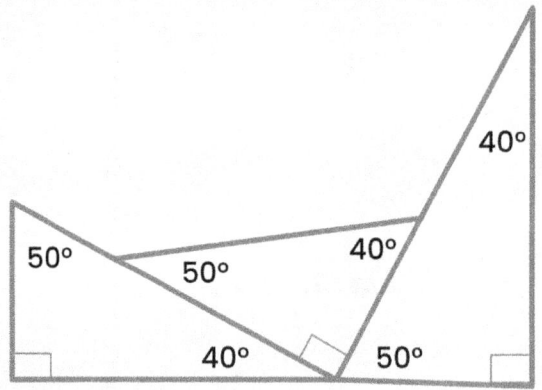

(A) The exterior angles of a triangle have a sum of 360 degrees

(B) A right angle is a complementary angle

(C) A right triangle will always have 40, 50, and 90 degree angles

(D) The interior angles of a triangle have a sum of 180 degrees

3   Lines MO || PQ. Which statement can be justified by the diagram

(A) Angle M is congruent to Angle D because Triangle MNO is similar to Triangle PNQ

(B) Angle N is congruent to Angle D because Triangle MNO is an equilateral triangle.

(C) Angle M is congruent to Angle Q because they are adjacent angles.

(D) Angle N is congruent to Angle P because Triangle MNO is similar to Triangle NPQ.

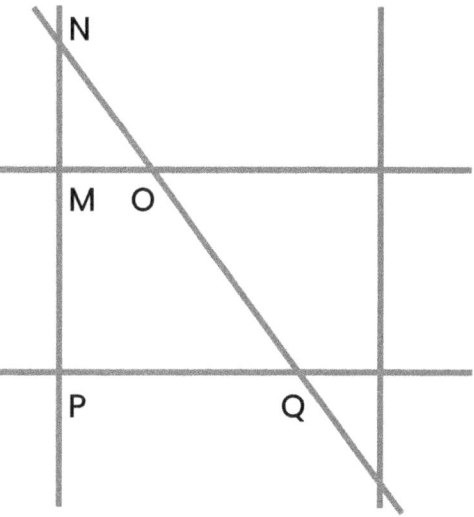

4   The parallel lines in this diagram are cut by a transversal. What is the measure of Angle N?

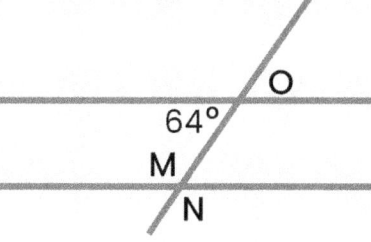

_____

5.4　　**Chapter Review**

5 Lines A and B are parallel. Angle x has a measure of 92 degrees. What are the measures of Angles o and w?

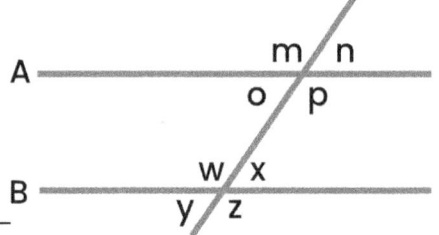

_____

6 If the lengths of the legs of a right triangle are 8 centimeters and 11 centimeters, what is the length of the hypotenuse?

(A) $\sqrt{185}$ cm　　(B) 15 cm　　(C) $5\sqrt{37}$ cm　　(D) 5 cm

7 If the lengths of the legs of a right triangle are 7 centimeters and 24 centimeters, what is the length of the hypotenuse?

(A) $4\sqrt{23}$ cm　　(B) 25 cm　　(C) $2\sqrt{17}$ cm　　(D) $3\sqrt{13}$ cm

8 What is the perimeter of a right triangle when the lengths of its legs are 9 m and 12 m? _____ m

9 What is the perimeter of a right triangle when the lengths of its legs are 6 yd and 8 yd? _____ yd

10 What is the approximate distance between Point M and Point N?

A) 3.4 units   B) 2.4 units

C) 6.6 units   D) 5.4 units

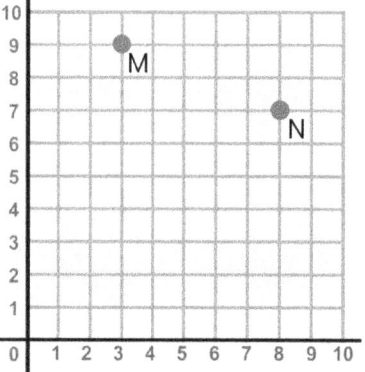

11 What is the approximate distance between Point M and Point N?

A) 4.8 units   B) 8.6 units

C) 9.0 units   D) 7.0 units

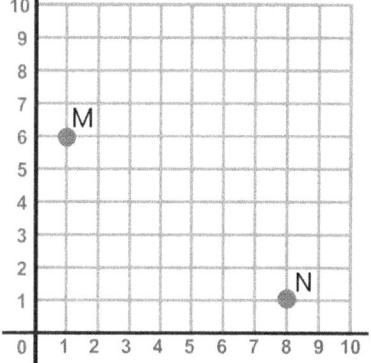

12 What is the approximate distance between the points (3, 4) and (8, 10)?

A) 5.2 units   B) 7.6 units

C) 7.7 units   D) 7.8 units

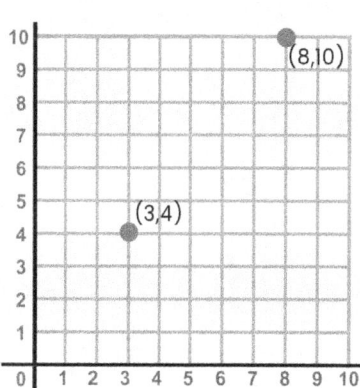

5.4 Chapter Review

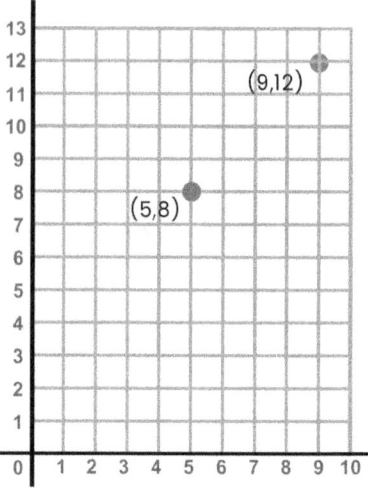

13 What is the approximate distance between the points $(5, 8)$ and $(9, 12)$?

(A) 5.6 units

(B) 6.6 units

(C) 7.2 units

(D) 16 units

14 What is the distance between the 2 points $(2, 11)$ and $(3,1)$ without using the graph?

_____

15 What is the distance between the 2 points $(3, 3)$ and $(3,9)$ without using the graph?

_____

16 Find x, x, ϵ N for which 4, $x + 2$ and $x + 4$ are the side lengths of a right triangle.

(A) 1

(B) 2

(C) 3

(D) 4

17 The longest side of the triangle is 20, and it is twice the shortest side. The third side is the mean of the other two sides. Determine whether this triangle is a right triangle.

(A) Yes

(B) No

18 The distances between the three towns on a map are 4, 7 and 9 inches. Do these towns form an obtuse triangle on the map?

(A) Yes

(B) No

19 Which of the following CANNOT be a pair of an exterior angle of a triangle and a corresponding interior opposite angle?

(A) Exterior angle: 120°, Interior angle: 60°

(B) Exterior angle: 70°, Interior angle: 110°

(C) Exterior angle: 100°, Interior angle: 80°

(D) Exterior angle: 70°, Interior angle: 104°

5.4

Chapter Review

20

Find the measure of the interior angle of a triangle.

$$\alpha = 44°, \beta = 72°, \gamma = ?$$

_____

Next Chapter: Volume of 3D

CHAPTER 6

VOLUME OF 3D

9	1	5	8	7	2	4	3	6
4				3				9
			4	9	5			
8		4		5		3		7
	3			8			5	
6		1		4		9		8
	9			2			6	
2		7		6		1		3
	6		9	1	3		4	

VOLUME OF CYLINDERS

A cylinder is a three-dimensional shape that consists of two parallel, congruent circular bases, and a curved surface that connects the bases. The axis of a cylinder is the line segment that connects the centers of the two circular bases.

h - height of a cylinder
r - radius of a base
V - volume of a cylinder

The formula for the volume of a cylinder: $V = \pi r^2 h$

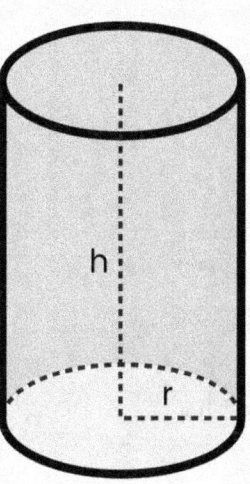

VOLUME OF 3D

6.1 Volume of Cylinders

1 What is the formula for the volume of a cylinder?

(A) πrh (B) πr^2h (C) πr^3h (D) $\frac{1}{3}\pi r^2h$

2 Find the volume of the cylinder given the radius and the height.
$$r = 2, h = 6.$$

(A) 10π (B) 8π (C) 24π (D) 36π

3 Find the volume of the cylinder given the radius and the height.
$$r = 7, h = 9.$$

(A) 441π (B) 288π (C) 657π (D) 231π

4 Find the height of a cylinder given the volume and the radius.
$$V = 64\pi, r = 4.$$

(A) 6 (B) 8 (C) 9 (D) 4

5 Find the height of a cylinder given the volume and the radius.
$$V = 150\pi, r = 5.$$

(A) 30 (B) 3 (C) 5 (D) 6

6 Find the radius of a cylinder given the volume and the height.

$V = 384\pi$, h = 6, r = _____.

7 Find the height of a cylinder given the volume and the radius.

$V = 180\pi$, h = 5, r = _____.

8 How many times does the volume of a cylinder increase if you double its height?

(A) Two times   (B) Three times

(C) Four times   (D) No change

9 How many times does the volume of a cylinder increase if you double its radius?

(A) Two times   (B) Three times

(C) Four times   (D) No change

10 A height of a cylindrical tank is 5 meters and the radius of its base is 1 meter. What is the volume of the cylindrical tank?

(A) 15.7 m³   (B) 12.5 m³   (C) 10.2 m³   (D) 25 m³

6.1 Volume of Cylinders

11 The circumference of a cylinder's base is 8π and its height is 4. What is the volume of the cylinder?

(A) 105.11   (B) 122.01   (C) 201.07   (D) 229.22

12 The area of a cylinder's base is 36π and its height is 6. What is the volume of the cylinder?

(A) 468.57   (B) 566.46   (C) 111.6   (D) 678.6

13 A diameter of a circular swimming pool is 14 meters and its depth is 2 meters. What is the volume of the swimming pool?

(A) 456.8 m³   (B) 307.9 m³   (C) 206.6 m³   (D) 458.6 m³

14 A diameter of a circular hole on the road is 20 centimeters and its depth is 6 centimeters. How much cubic centimeters of asphalt is needed to fill the hole?

(A) 1,345 m³   (B) 1,358 m³   (C) 1,567 m³   (D) 1,885 m³

Volume of Cylinders   **6.1**

15 A diameter of a cylindrical piece of cake is 8 inches and its thickness is 1 inch. What is the volume of the piece of cake?

(A) 40.4 in³   (B) 44.4 in³   (C) 50.3 in³   (D) 60.6 in³

16 What is the approximate volume of a cylinder whose radius is 10 ft and height is 8 ft? Use π = 3.14.

(A) 2,345 ft³   (B) 2,456 ft³   (C) 2,234 ft³   (D) 2,513 ft³

17 What is the approximate volume of a cylinder whose radius is 6 ft and height is 11 ft? Use π = 3.14.

(A) 1,456 ft³   (B) 1,244 ft³   (C) 1,658 ft³   (D) 1,498 ft³

18 What is the approximate volume of a cylinder whose radius is 4 m and height is 8 m? Use π = 3.14.

(A) 402 m³   (B) 468 m³   (C) 465 m³   (D) 356 m³

VOLUME OF 3D

6.1   Volume of Cylinders

19   Your parent's car has 5 cylinders in the engine. What is the approximate volume, to the nearest cubic cm, of one of those cylinders if the height is 5 cm and the radius is 4 cm?

Use π = 3.14.

= _____ m³.

---

20   **True or False:** The approximate volume of a cylinder that has a radius of 6 m and a height of 12m is 1,357.2 m³.

(A) True   (B) False

Next Section: Volume of Cone ≫

VOLUME OF CONE

A cone is a three-dimensional shape with a circular base that tapers smoothly to a point, called the apex.

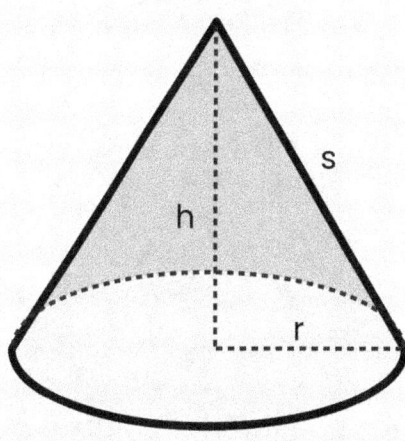

h - height of a cone

r - radius of a base

s - slant height

V - volume of a cone

The formula for the volume of a cone: $V = \frac{1}{3}\pi r^2 h$

VOLUME OF 3D

6.2 Volume of Cone

1 What is the formula for the volume of a cone?

(A) πrh (B) πr^2h (C) πr^3h (D) $\frac{1}{3}\pi r^2h$

2 Find the volume of the cone given the radius and the height.
$$r = 3, h = 6.$$

(A) 18π (B) 10π (C) 24π (D) 16π

3 Find the volume of the cone given the radius and the height.
$$r = 9, h = 5.$$

(A) 445π (B) 145π (C) 135π (D) 405π

4 Find the volume of the cone given the volume and the radius.
$$V = 18\pi, r = 3.$$

(A) 6   (B) 8   (C) 9   (D) 4

5 Find the volume of the cone given the radius and the height.
$$V = 20\pi, r = 2.$$

(A) 30   (B) 15   (C) 25   (D) 10

Volume of Cone | 6.2

6 Find the radius of the cone given the volume and the height.

$V = 108\pi$, $h = 4$, $r =$ _____.

7 Find the radius of the cone given the volume and the height.

$V = 96\pi$, $h = 8$, $r =$ _____.

8 How many times does the volume of a cone increase if you double its height?

(A) Two times   (B) Three times

(C) Four times   (D) No change

9 How many times does the volume of a cone increase if you double its radius?

(A) Two times   (B) Three times

(C) Four times   (D) No change

10 A slant height of a cone is 5 and the radius of its base is 3. What is the volume of the cone?

(A) 10π (B) 12π (C) 16π (D) 20π

6.2   Volume of Cone

11 A slant height of a cone is 10 and its height is 8. What is the volume of the cone?

(A) 88π (B) 112π (C) 168π (D) 96π

12 A slant height of a cone is 13 and the area of the base of the cone is 144π. What is the volume of the cone?

(A) 360π (B) 240π (C) 200π (D) 300π

13 The angle between the slant height of a cone and its base is 60°. The slant height is 16. What is the volume of the cone?

(A) $\frac{512\sqrt{3}}{3}\pi$ (B) $512\sqrt{3}\pi$ (C) $\frac{512}{3}\pi$ (D) 512π

14 The angle between the slant height of a cone and its base is 30°. The slant height is 12. What is the volume of the cone?

(A) $\frac{216\sqrt{3}}{3}\pi$ (B) $216\sqrt{3}\pi$ (C) $\frac{216}{3}\pi$ (D) 216π

15 The angle between the slant height of a cone and its base is 45°. The slant height is 4. What is the volume of the cone?

(A) $\dfrac{8\sqrt{3}}{3}\pi$ (B) $8\sqrt{3}\pi$ (C) $\dfrac{8}{3}\pi$ (D) 16π

16 What is the approximate volume of a cone with a radius of 5 m and a height of 6m? Use $\pi = 3.14$

(A) 157.1 m³ (B) 175.1 m³ (C) 145.1 m³ (D) 166.1 m³

17 What is the approximate volume of a cone with a radius of 4 yds and a height of 27 yds?

(A) 567.4 yd³ (B) 659.4 yd³ (C) 765.4 yd³ (D) 452.4 yd³

18 Mercy wants to know how much ice cream she can place in her ice cream cone. Her cone has a height of 17 cm and a radius of 6 cm. How much ice cream can it hold if the cone is filled to the top? Use $\pi = 3.14$.

= _____ cm³.

VOLUME OF 3D

6.2 Volume of Cone

19 Kate puts candy in some cones her friends made. What is the approximate volume, to the nearest whole number, of the candy one cone holds if the diameter of the cone is 12 cm and the height is 12 cm? Use π = 3.14.

= _____ cm³.

20 Allen found a large pine cone in a Park while on vacation with his family. The diameter of the pine cone (shaped like a cone) is 4 inches with a height of 15 inches? What is the approximate volume, to the nearest cubic inch, of the cone? Use π = 3.14.

= _____ in³.

Next Section: Volume of Sphere ›

VOLUME OF SPHERE

A sphere is a three-dimensional object that is perfectly round, with all points on its surface equidistant from the center. The surface of a sphere is called a sphere's surface area, and its volume is called its sphere's volume.

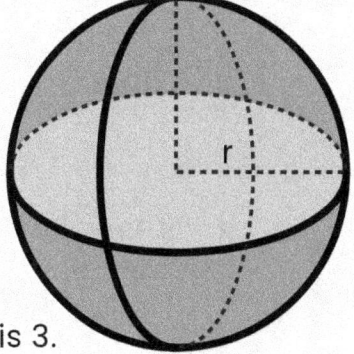

r- the radius of a sphere

V- volume of a sphere

The formula for the volume of a sphere: $V = \dfrac{4}{3}\pi r^3 h$

Example: Find the volume of a sphere whose radius is 3.

Solution:

$$r = 3$$
$$V = ?$$
$$V = 4333$$
$$V = 4 \times 9\pi$$
$$V = 36\pi.$$

6.3   **Volume of Sphere**

---

1 What is the formula for the volume of a cone?

(A) $3\pi r$ (B) $\frac{4}{3}\pi r^3$ (C) $\frac{2}{3}\pi r^3$ (D) $\frac{1}{3}\pi r^2$

---

2 Find the volume of a sphere.

$$r = 4.$$

(A) 256π (B) $\frac{246}{3}\pi$ (C) $\frac{256}{3}\pi$ (D) 143π

---

3 Find the volume of a sphere.

$$r = 6.$$

(A) 444π (B) 443π (C) 288π (D) 144π

---

4 Find the radius of the sphere given the volume.

$$V = 36\pi.$$

(A) 6   (B) 3   (C) 9   (D) 4

---

5 Find the radius of the sphere given the volume.

$$V = 4500\pi.$$

(A) 15   (B) 12   (C) 11   (D) 45

Volume of Sphere   6.3

6 Find the volume of the sphere given the radius.

$r = 24$, $V =$ _____.

7 Find the volume of the sphere given the radius.

$r = 18$, $V =$ _____.

8 How many times does the volume of a sphere increase if you double its radius?

(A) Two times

(B) Three times

(C) Four times

(D) No change

9 How many times does the volume of a sphere decrease if you halve its radius?

(A) Two times

(B) Three times

(C) Four times

(D) No change

10 The diameter of a soccer ball is 24 cm. What is the volume of the soccer ball? Use $\pi = 3.14$.

(A) 7,684 cm³   (B) 7,987.6 cm³   (C) 7,234.6 cm³   (D) 7,534 cm³

6.3   Volume of Sphere

11 The circumference of a volleyball ball is 18.02 in. What is the volume of the volleyball ball?

   (A) 111.1 in³   (B) 102.1 in³   (C) 135.1 in³   (D) 107.8 in³π

12 The edge of a cube is 8. What is the volume of a sphere inscribed in the cube?

   (A) $\dfrac{256}{3}\pi$ (B) $\dfrac{512\sqrt{2}}{3}\pi$ (C) $\dfrac{512\sqrt{3}}{3}\pi$ (D) $\dfrac{142\sqrt{3}}{3}\pi$

13 The edge of a cube is $4\sqrt{3}$. What is the volume of a sphere circumscribed around the cube?

   (A) $\dfrac{188\sqrt{3}}{3}\pi$ (B) $288\sqrt{3}\pi$ (C) $\dfrac{288}{3}\pi$ (D) 288π

14 A sphere is inscribed in a cylinder. The height of the cylinder is 6. What is the volume of a sphere?

   (A) 27π (B) 36π (C) 16π (D) 21π

15 The circumference of a sphere is 14π. What is the volume of the sphere?

(A) $\dfrac{1589}{3}\pi$ (B) $\dfrac{1372}{3}\pi$ (C) $\dfrac{1764}{3}\pi$ (D) $\dfrac{1987}{3}\pi$

16 What is the approximate volume of a sphere with a radius of 2 ft? Use $\pi = 3.14$

(A) 32.5 ft³   (B) 31.5 ft³   (C) 33.5 ft³   (D) 43.5 ft³

17 While Helen was on a field trip with her class, she saw an unusual sphere filled with a red liquid. What is the approximate volume, to the nearest tenth of a cubic yard, of the sphere if it has a radius of 20 yds?

Use $\pi = 3.14$.

= _____ yds³.

18 A group of guys from the school's varsity football team volunteered some time at a local youth center. They brought a large round, lightweight ball to play some push ball games. What is the approximate volume, to the nearest tenth of a cubic foot, of the ball they will be playing with if the diameter is 3 ft?

Use $\pi = 3.14$.

= _____ ft³.

6.3 Volume of Sphere

19 **True or False:** The approximate volume of a sphere that has a radius of 15 m is 14,137 m³.

(A) True   (B) False

20 **True or False:** The approximate volume of a sphere that has a radius of 11 m is 5,555 m³.

(A) True   (B) False

Next Section: Chapter Review

1 Find the volume of a cylinder.

$$r = 2, h = 4.$$

(A) 6π (B) 20π (C) 8π (D) 16π

2 Find the volume of a cone.

$$r = 3, h = 30.$$

(A) 18π (B) 90π (C) 27π (D) 30π

3 Find the volume of a sphere.

$$r = 30.$$

(A) $36{,}000\pi$ (B) 12000π (C) 42000π (D) 16000π

4 Find the height of the cylinder given the volume and radius.

$$V = 396\pi, r = 6.$$

(A) 9   (B) 11   (C) 13   (D) 14

5 Find the radius of the cylinder given the volume and the height.

$V = 1152\pi, h = 8, r = $ _____.

VOLUME OF 3D

6
Find the height of the cylinder given the volume and the radius.
$V = 192\pi$, r = 4.

(A) 12   (B) 16   (C) 32   (D) 36

7
Find the radius of the cone given the volume and height.
$V = 300\pi$, h = 4, r = _____.

8
Select the correct radius of a sphere.
$$V = 12, 348\pi.$$

(A) 18   (B) 21   (C) 19   (D) 29

9
Find the volume of the sphere given the radius.
r = 33, V = _____.

10
What is the approximate volume of a sphere with a radius of 21 ft?
Use $\pi = 3.14$.

(A) 38,792 ft³   (B) 38,569 ft³   (C) 38,983 ft³   (D) 38,888 ft³

11
What is the approximate volume of a cone with a radius of 7 m and a height of 12m? Use $\pi = 3.14$.

(A) 478 m³   (B) 616 m³   (C) 765 m³   (D) 556 m³

12 What is the approximate volume of a cylinder with a radius of 7 cm and a height of 10 cm? Use $\pi = 3.14$.

(A) 2344.44 cm³   (B) 1234.5 cm³   (C) 1539.4 cm³   (D) 1866.8 cm³

13 **True or False:** The approximate volume of a cone that has a radius of 13m and height 18 m is 3186 m³.

(A) True   (B) False

14 **True or False:** The approximate volume of a sphere that has a radius of 13 ft is 8181 ft³.

(A) True   (B) False

15 **True or False:** The approximate volume of a cylinder that has a radius of 13 cm and height 18 cm is 9556.7 cm³.

(A) True   (B) False

16 How many times does the volume of a cylinder increase if you triple its height?

(A) Two times   (B) Three times

(C) Four times   (D) No change

6.4 Chapter Review

17 How many times does the volume of a cone increase if you triple its radius?

(A) Two times   (B) Three times

(C) Four times   (D) No change

18 How many times does the volume of a sphere increase if you triple its radius?

(A) 21 times   (B) 15 times

(C) 27 times   (D) 18 times

19 What is the approximate volume, rounded to the nearest whole cubic meter, of a cone if the radius is 10.2 m and the height is 12.4 m? Use $\pi = 3.14$.

= _____ m³.

20 What is the approximate volume, rounded to the nearest whole cubic meter, of a cone if the radius is 2.22 m and the height is 3.33 m? Use $\pi = 3.14$.

= _____ m³.

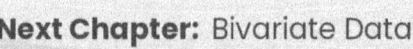

Next Chapter: Bivariate Data

CHAPTER 7

BIVARIATE DATA

		2	8	7	1	5		
	1						2	
3				9				1
6			3		7			4
5		7				1		2
1			5		2			7
7				8		2		5
	8				3		1	
		1	6	2	4	3		8

CONSTRUCT AND INTERPRET SCATTERPLOTS

A scatterplot is a graph of plotted points that shows the relationship between two sets of data.

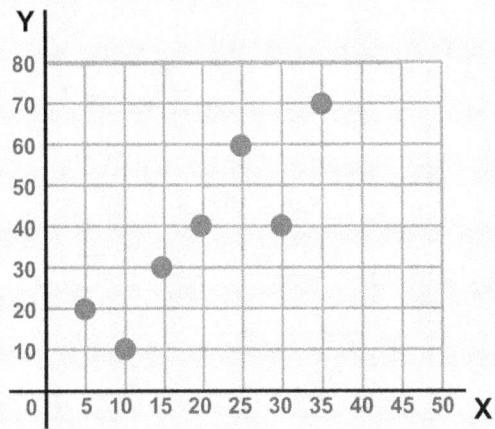

The scatterplot above shows a relationship between x and y. This relationship can also be represented by the table below.

x	5	10	15	20	25	30	35
y	20	10	30	40	60	40	70

A line of best fit is a line on a scatterplot that shows the direction that plotted points follow.

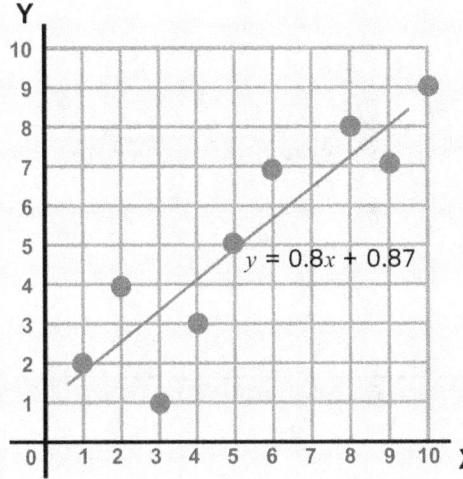

$y = 0.8x + 0.87$

The equation of line of best fit is

$y = mx + b$

m > 0 – positive correlation

m < 0 – negative correlation

7.1 **Construct and Interpret Scatterplots**

1 Which correlation does this scatter plot show?

- (A) Positive
- (B) Negative
- (C) No correlation
- (D) Discontinuous

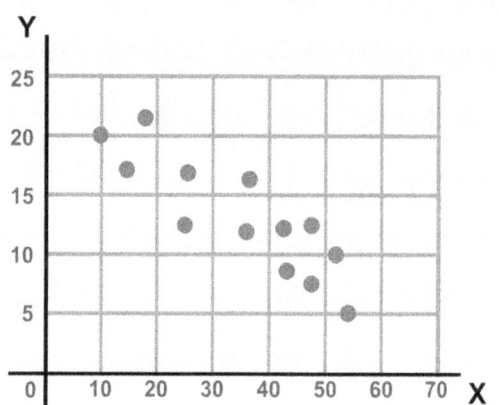

2 Which correlation does this scatter plot show?

- (A) Positive
- (B) Negative
- (C) No correlation
- (D) Discontinuous

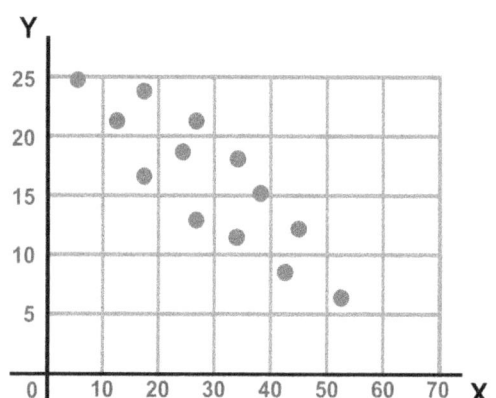

Construct and Interpret
Scatterplots

7.1

3 Which correlation does this scatter plot show?

(A) Positive

(B) Negative

(C) No correlation

(D) Discontinuous

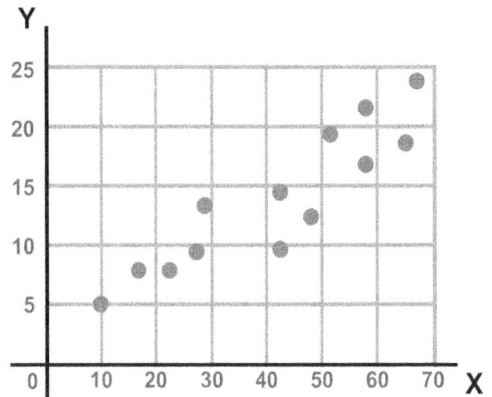

4 Which correlation does this scatter plot show?

(A) Positive

(B) Negative

(C) No correlation

(D) Discontinuous

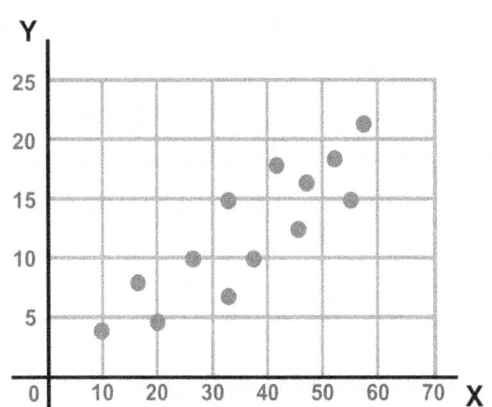

7.1 Construct and Interpret Scatterplots

5 Which correlation does this scatter plot show?

- (A) Positive
- (B) Negative
- (C) No correlation
- (D) Discontinuous

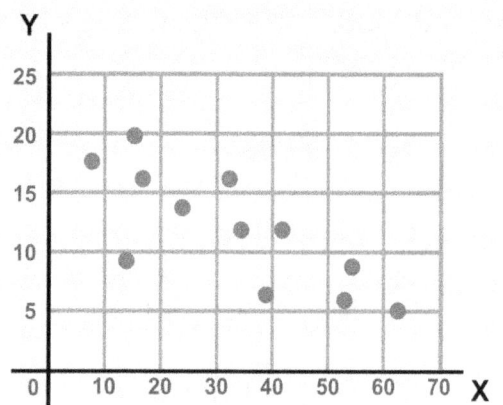

6 Which correlation does this scatter plot show?

- (A) Positive
- (B) Negative
- (C) No correlation
- (D) Discontinuous

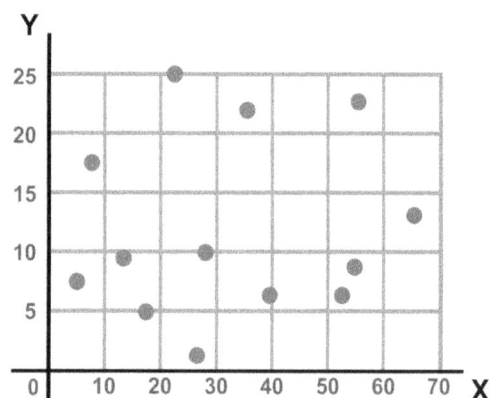

Construct and Interpret Scatterplots — 7.1

7 Which correlation does this scatter plot show?

(A) Positive

(B) Negative

(C) No correlation

(D) Discontinuous

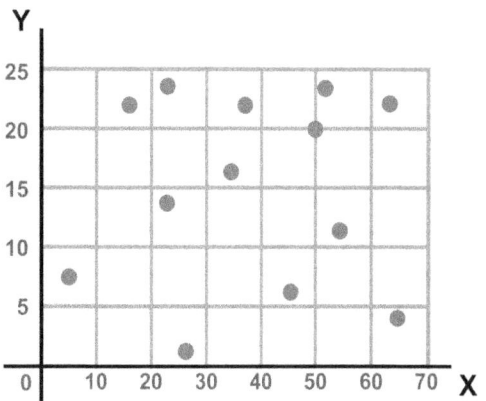

---

8 In which scatterplot does Point G appear to be an outlier?

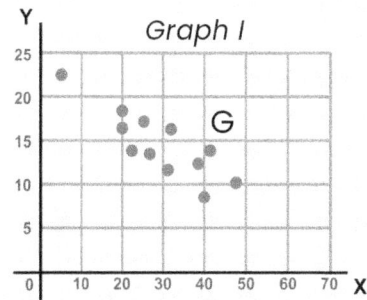

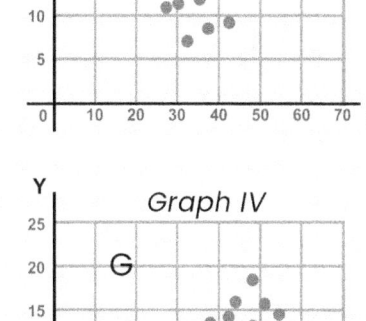

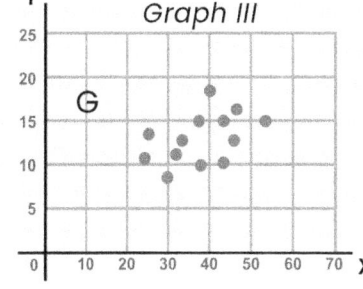

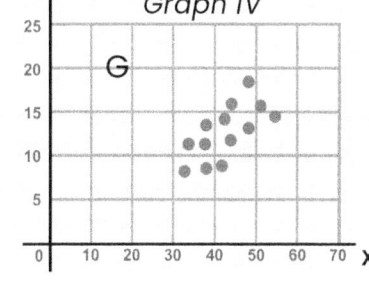

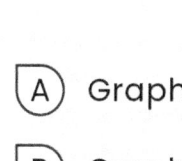
(A) Graph I

(B) Graph II

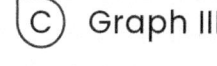
(C) Graph III

(D) Graph IV

7.1 Construct and Interpret Scatterplots

9 In which scatterplot does Point H appear to be an outlier?

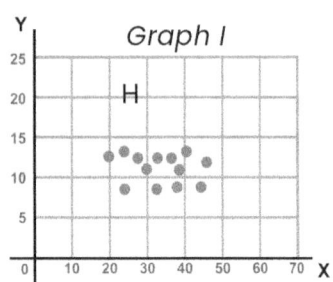

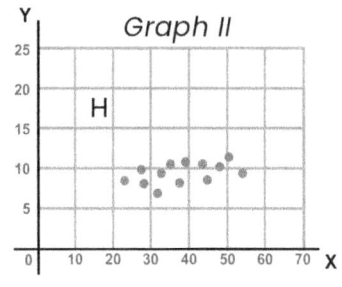

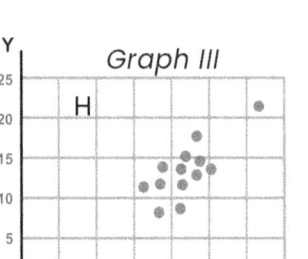

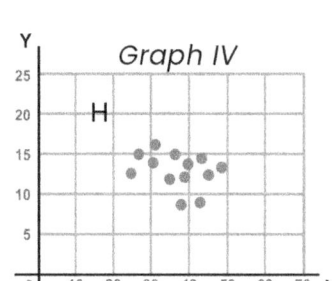

- (A) Graph I
- (B) Graph II
- (C) Graph III
- (D) Graph IV

10 In which scatterplot does Point B appear to be an outlier?

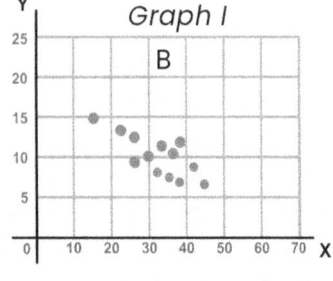

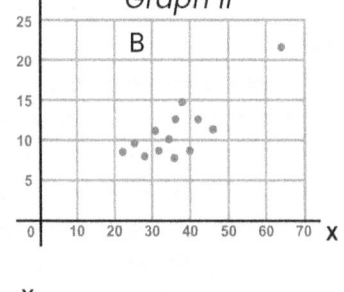

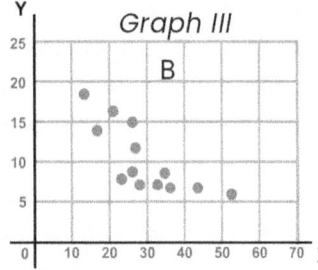

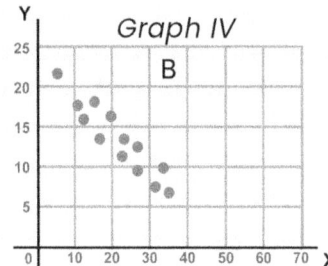

- (A) Graph I
- (B) Graph II
- (C) Graph III
- (D) Graph IV

11 What is the equation of the trend line in the scatter plot?

(A) $y = 3x + 12$

(B) $y = -3x - 12$

(C) $y = 3x - 12$

(D) $y = -3x + 12$

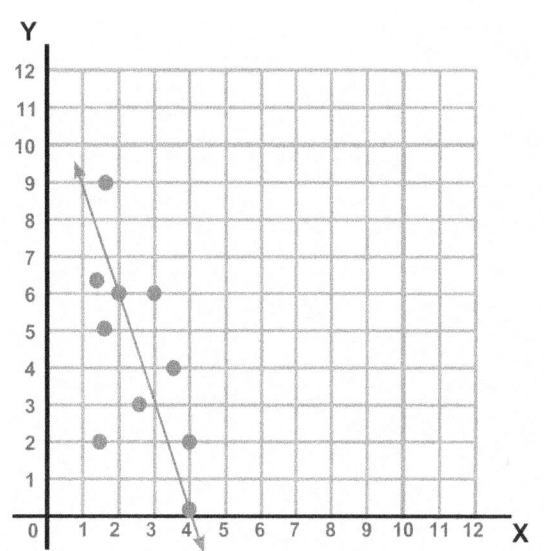

12 What is the equation of the trend line in the scatter plot?

(A) $y = -x + 10$

(B) $y = x + 10$

(C) $y = -x - 10$

(D) $y = x - 10$

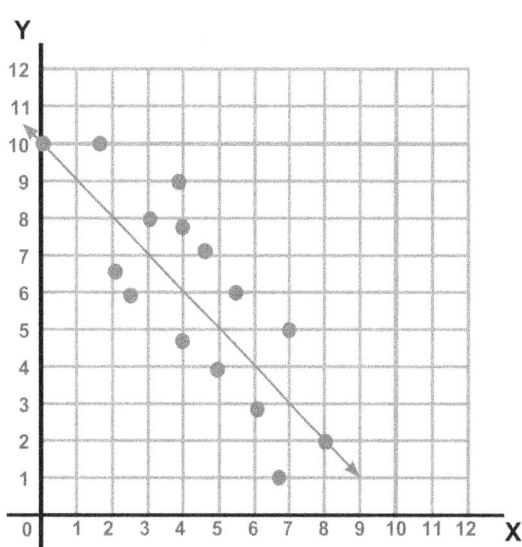

7.1 Construct and Interpret Scatterplots

13 What is the equation of the trend line in the scatter plot?

(A) $y = -\dfrac{10}{7}x - \dfrac{20}{7}$

(B) $y = \dfrac{10}{7}x - \dfrac{20}{7}$

(C) $y = \dfrac{10}{7}x + \dfrac{20}{7}$

(D) $y = -\dfrac{10}{7}x + \dfrac{20}{7}$

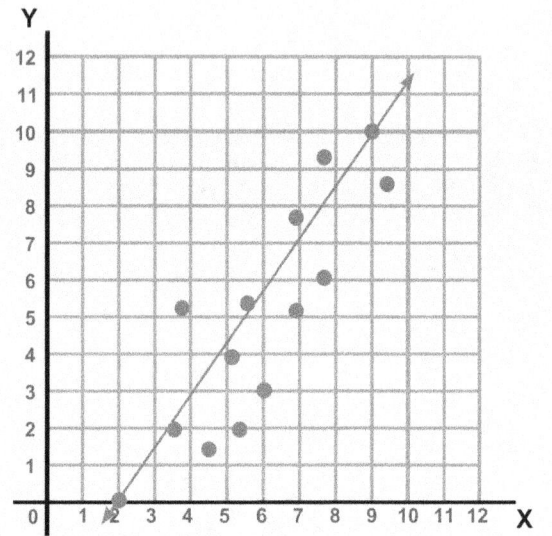

14 What is the equation of the trend line in the scatter plot?

(A) $\dfrac{4}{3}x - \dfrac{2}{3}$

(B) $\dfrac{4}{3}x + \dfrac{2}{3}$

(C) $-\dfrac{4}{3}x - \dfrac{2}{3}$

(D) $-\dfrac{4}{3}x + \dfrac{2}{3}$

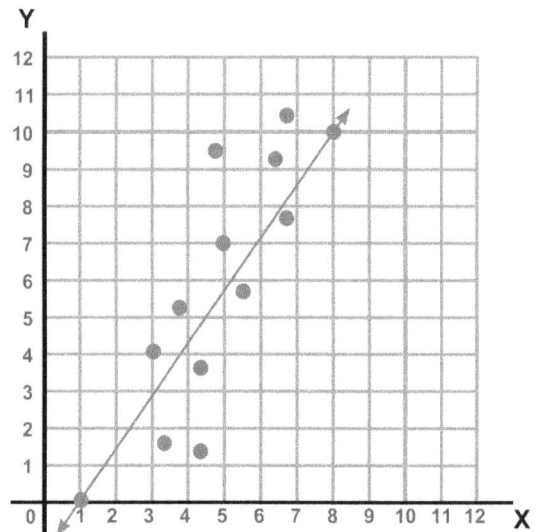

15 The data points on a scatter plot show a strong positive linear correlation. The line p is the line of best fit. Which graph represents this situation?

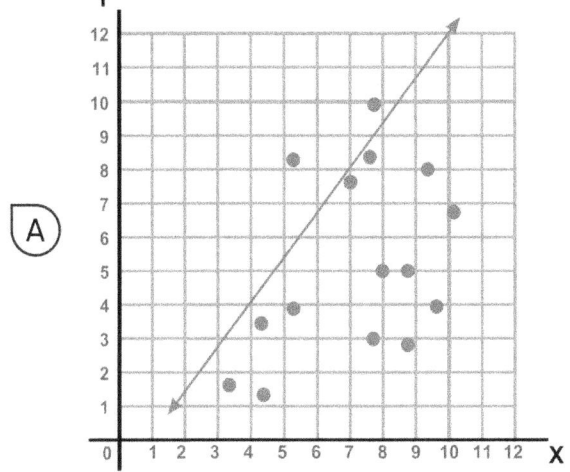

A

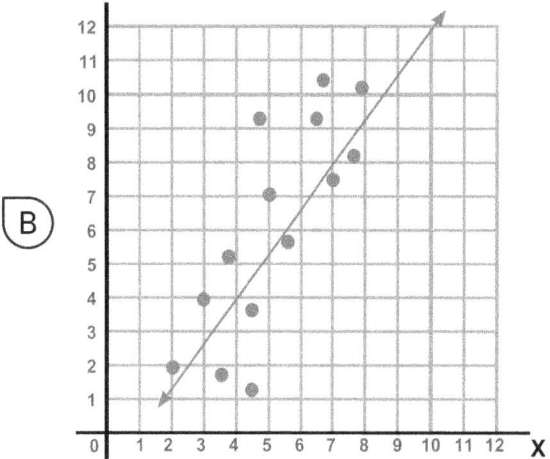

B

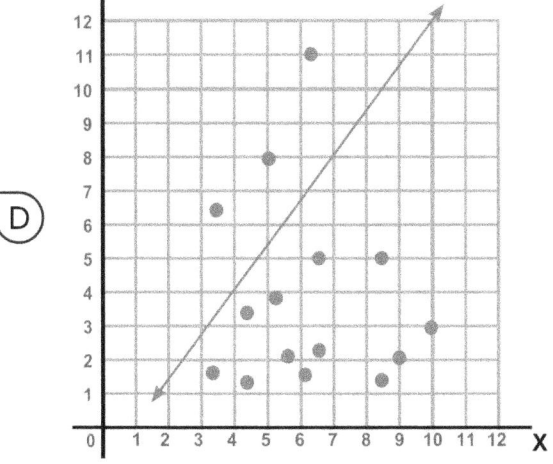

D

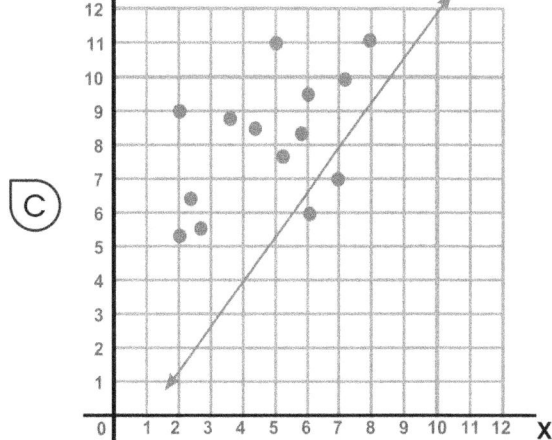

C

7.1 Construct and Interpret Scatterplots

16 The data points on a scatter plot show a weak positive linear correlation. Line p is the line of best fit. Which graph represents this situation?

(A)
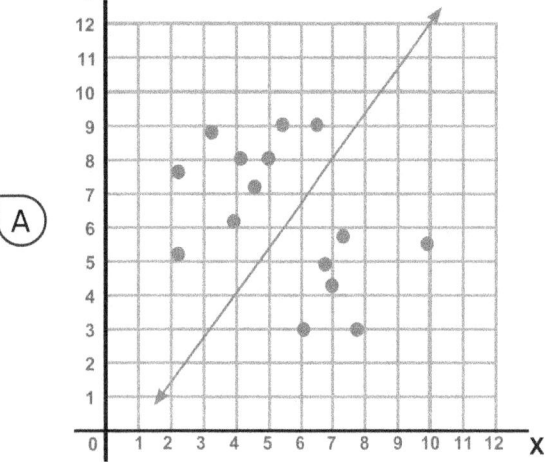

(B)
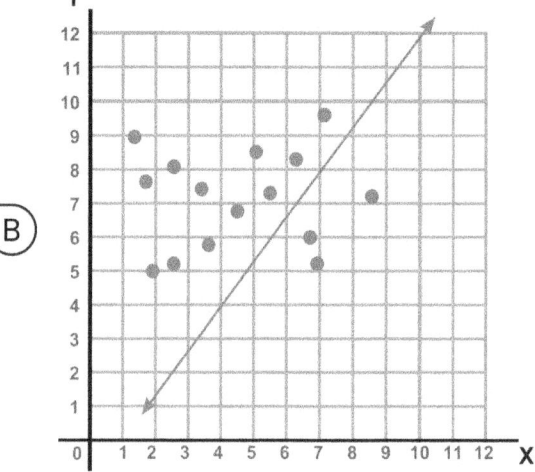

(D)
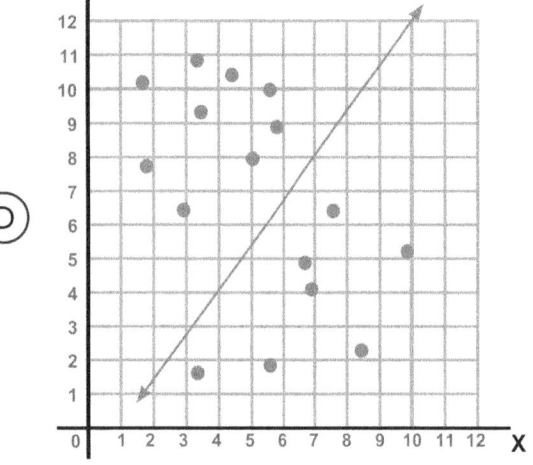

(C)
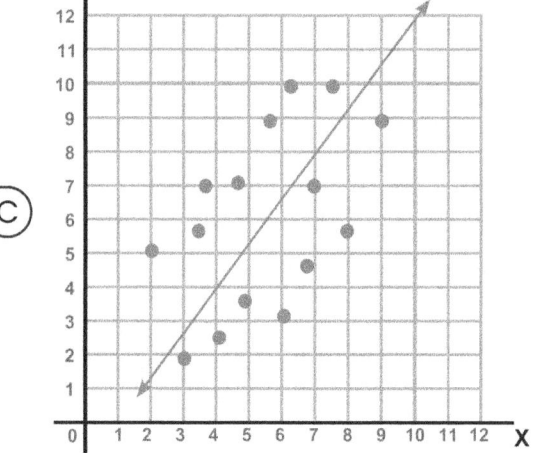

17 Which relationship could be modeled by the line of best fit shown on this graph?

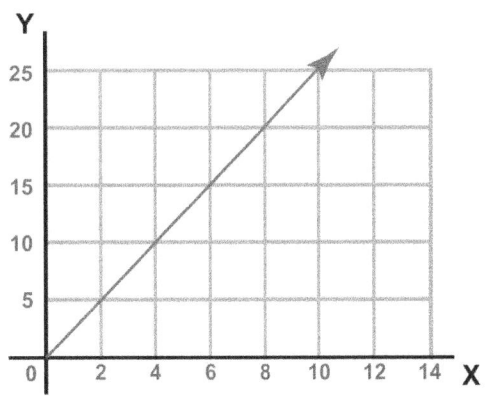

A The relationship between the distance traveled in miles y by a bus waiting at a stop sign for x seconds.

B The relationship between the height y of a burning candle over time x.

C The relationship between the cost of ice-cream y and the amount x of candy purchased.

D The relationship between the amount of weight y a person loses on a diet over x weeks.

18 Which trend does this scatter plot show?

A Positive

B Negative

C No correlation

D Discontinuous

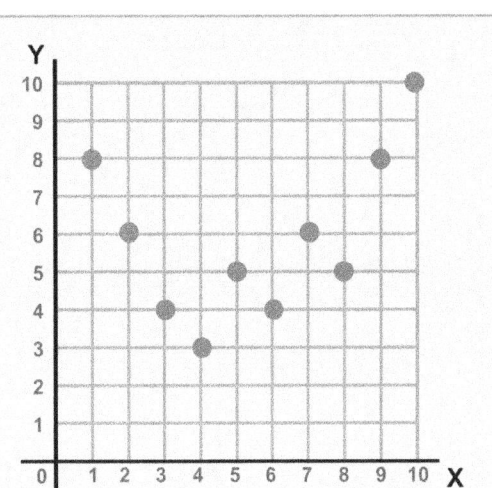

7.1 Construct and Interpret Scatterplots

19 David creates a scatterplot and determines these two possible lines of best fit.

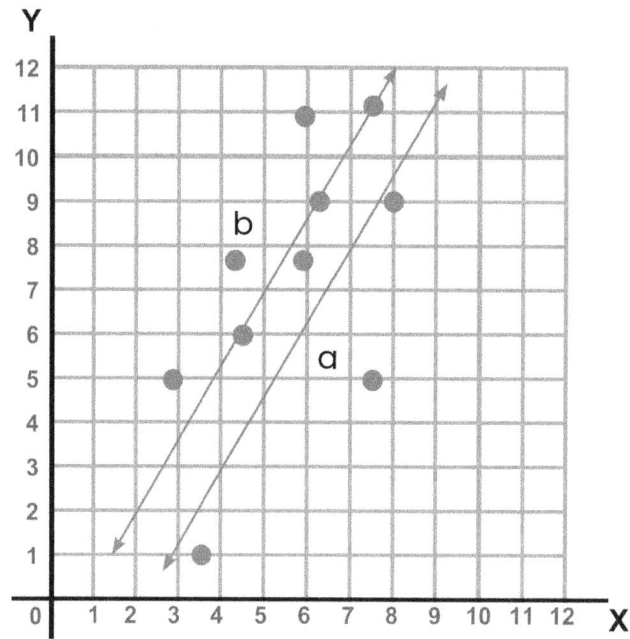

Which line of best fit is the most accurate? Explain your reasoning.

_____

20 Kirana creates a scatterplot and determines these two possible lines of best fit.

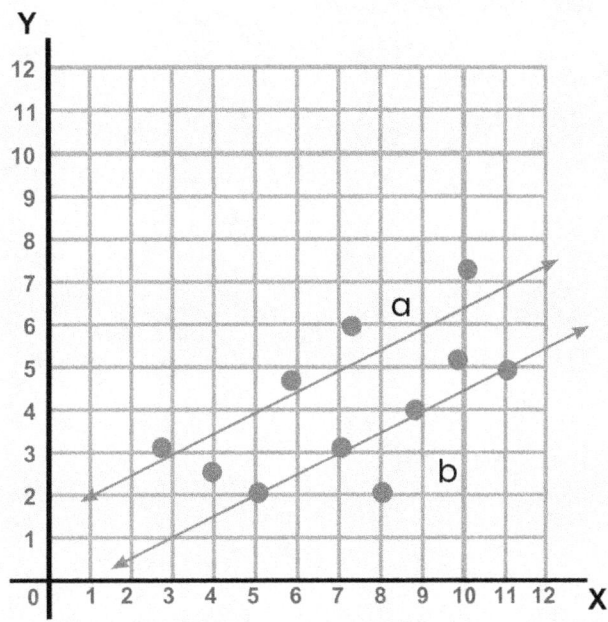

Which line of best fit is the most accurate? Explain your reasoning.

_____

Next Section: Interpret Slope and
y–Intercept of Line of Best Fit

INTERPRET SLOPE AND Y – INTERCEPT OF LINE OF BEST FIT

A line of best fit is a line on a scatterplot that shows the direction that plotted points follow.

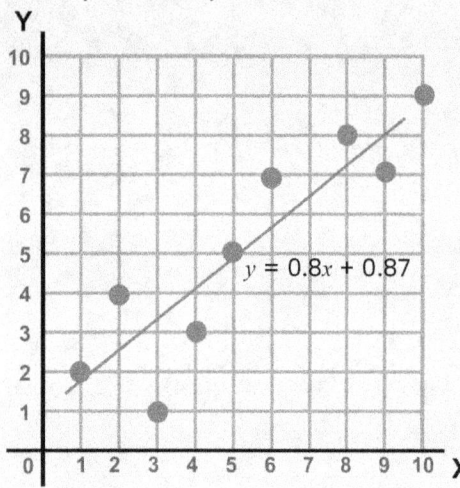

The equation of line of best fit is

$y = mx + b$

m – slope

b - y – intercept

Example:

According to the line of best fit in the scatterplot shown above, which of the following statements is true?

A) A line of best fit intercepts the x –axis at 0.8

B) A line of best fit intercepts the x-axis at 0.87

C) A line of best fit intercepts the y–axis at 0.8

D) A line of best fit intercepts the y–axis at 0.87

Solution: D

Interpret Slope and y-Intercept of
Line of Best Fit

7.2

1 The graph shows how the time required to ring up a customer at a cash register (in seconds) is related to the number of items the customer purchases. How long does it take to ring up an item? Round to the nearest whole number.

A) 1 second

B) 2 seconds

C) 3 seconds

D) 4 seconds

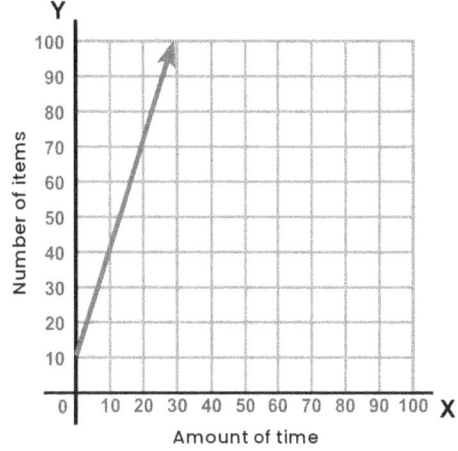

2 This graph shows how the amount of peanut butter Peter makes, in liters, is related to the number of days she spends making the peanut butter. What is the rate of change in the amount of peanut butter Peter makes per day? Round to the nearest whole number.

A) 1

B) 2

C) 3

D) 4

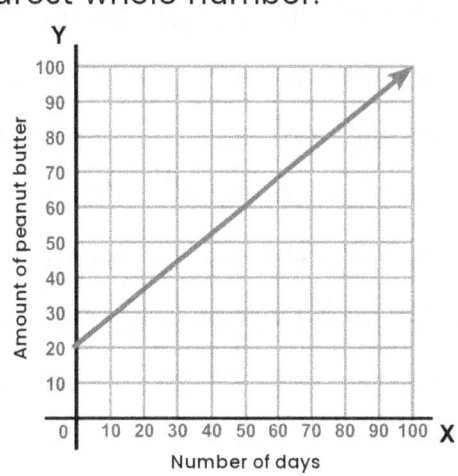

7.2 Interpret Slope and y-Intercept of
Line of Best Fit

3 This graph shows how the total cost, in dollars, of a members-only
speaking series is related to the number of events attended.
What is the rate of change? Round to the nearest whole number?

(A) 1 dollar per event

(B) 2 dollars per event

(C) 3 dollars per event

(D) 4 dollars per event

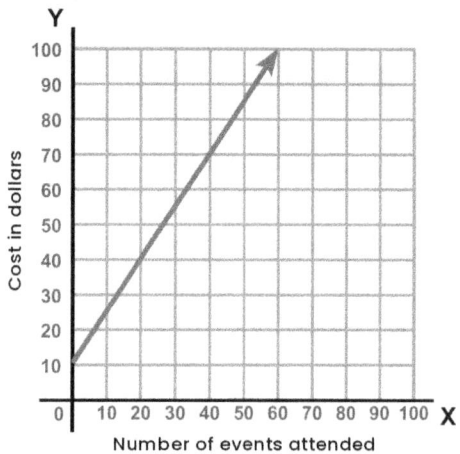

4 This graph shows how the total number of story books Noah has
in his collection is related to the amount of money, in dollars, he
spends on additional storybooks. What is the rate of change?
Round to the nearest whole number?

(A) 1 dollar per book

(B) 2 dollars per book

(C) 3 dollars per book

(D) 4 dollars per book

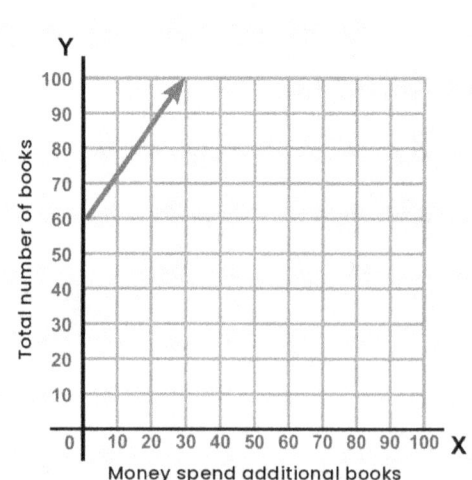

5 This graph shows how the total cost, in dollars, of a member visiting an art gallery is related to the number of visits.
What is the rate of change? Round to the nearest whole number?

(A) 1 dollar per visit

(B) 2 dollars per visit

(C) 3 dollars per visit

(D) 4 dollars per visit

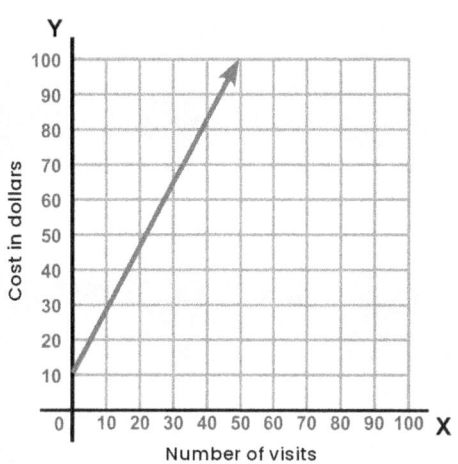

6 The graph shows how the total number of headbands Mercy owns is related to the amount of money, in dollars, she spends on additional headbands. What is the rate of change?
Round to the nearest whole number.

(A) 1 dollar per head band

(B) 2 dollars per head band

(C) 3 dollars per head band

(D) 4 dollars per head band

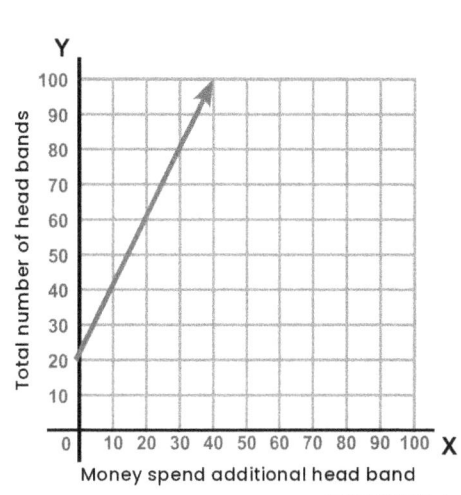

7.2 Interpret Slope and y-Intercept of Line of Best Fit

7 The equation below is used to fit a data set representing the value of a motorcycle y after x years.

$$y = 34,000 - 1,500x$$

What does the slope of the graph of this equation represent?

(A) Depreciation in the value of the motorcycle each year.

(B) Amount of interest paid on the motorcycle .

(C) Value of the motorcycle after 1 year.

(D) Original cost of the motorcycle.

8 The graph shows the relationship between the amount of hot coffee sold and the temperature on a given day.

(A) The average amount of money earned.

(B) The difference between the highest and lowest temperatures.

(C) The amount of money earned altogether.

(D) How the average amount of money earned changes based on the outside temperature.

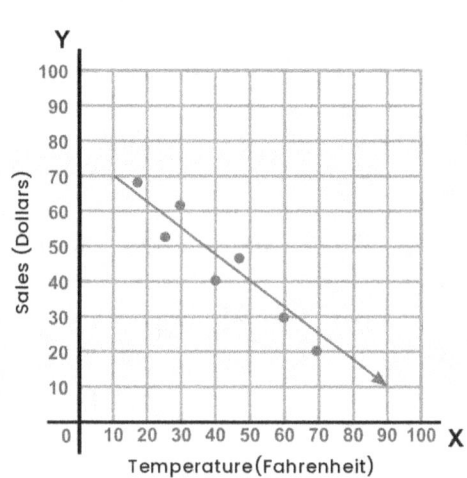

9 The equation below was used to fit a data set representing the total monthly cost y of a mobile plan, based on the number of minutes used m

$$y = 33 + 0.66m$$

What does the slope of the graph of this equation represent?

(A) Cost per minute

(B) Cost per plan

(C) Monthly fee

(D) Cost after speaking for 33 minutes

10 The mobile company determines the equation below represents the number of hours y of battery life remaining after x hours of use.

$$y = 130 - 5.55x$$

Based on this equation, what is the best prediction of the percent of power remaining after 15 hours?

_____

11 Berlin determines the equation below represents the number of hours y of battery life remaining in her phone, after x hours of use.

$$y = 65 - 8.25x$$

What does the y-Intercept of this equation?

_____

7.2 Interpret Slope and y-Intercept of
Line of Best Fit

12 The computers in the library are charging on the power station. The equation below is used to fit the data which represents the total percent y of battery power of the computers after x minutes.

$$y = 40 + 8x$$

What does the y-Intercept of the equation?

_____

13 **True or False:** Ryan bikes 20 kilometers during each trip to work. The equation shows the relationship between the number of trips to work (x) and the total distance biked (y) is $y = 20/x$.

    Ⓐ True   Ⓑ False

14 Emma learns to play an average of 12 new pieces each week in piano lessons. What equation shows the relationship between the weeks of lessons (x) and the total number of pieces learned (y)?

_____

15 Grace spends 10 minutes routing each incoming phone call. What equation shows the relationships between the phone calls routed (x) as well as the minutes (y) Grace is on the phone, routing calls?

_____

16 The graduation picnic costs $3.65 for each attendee. What equation represents the relationships between the number of attendees (x) and the cost (y)?

_____

17 Racheal reads 14 books each month as part of her book club. What equation shows the relationships between the months (x) and the total books Racheal reads (y)?

_____

18 Julia's birthday party costs $300 for each guest she invites. What equation shows the relationships between the number of guests (x) and the cost (y) of the birthday party?

_____

19 Lilly can grow 15 flowers with every seed packet. What equation shows the relationships between the number of seed packets (x) and the total number of flowers (y) Lilly can grow?

_____

7.2 Interpret Slope and y-Intercept of Line of Best Fit

20 Jose reads 5 books each month as part of his book club. What equation shows the relationships between the months (x) and the total books Jose reads (y).

_____

Next Section: Construct and Interpret Two-Way Tables

CONSTRUCT AND INTERPRET TWO-WAY TABLES

Lesson Introduction:

A two-way table is a statistical table that displays the observed number or frequency for two variables, with the rows representing one category and the columns representing the other.

Example: A table below shows a relationship between two categorical variables. Create a table of relative frequencies.

Category B

Category A	Column 1	Column 2	Total
Row 1	12	18	30
Row 2	10	20	30
Total	22	38	60

Answer:

Category B

Category A	Column 1	Column 2	Total
Row 1	0.12	0.30	0.50
Row 2	0.17	0.33	0.50
Total	0.37	0.13	1.00

SCHOOL BUS

255

7.3

Construct and Interpret Two-Way Tables

1

Mr. Austin wonders if boys and girls like different ice cream flavors. He collects data on three flavors: chocolate, strawberry, and vanilla. The results are as follows:

- Of the 25 students who prefer vanilla ice cream, 16 are boys.
- Of the 40 students who prefer strawberry ice cream, 18 are girls.
- Of the 50 students who prefer chocolate, 31 are girls.

Which statement correctly describes the results of Mr. Austin's survey?

(A) About 16% of the students surveyed prefer vanilla ice cream.

(B) About 18% of those surveyed were boys who prefer strawberry ice cream

(C) About 31% of the girls surveyed prefer chocolate ice cream.

(D) About 8% of those surveyed were girls who prefer vanilla ice cream.

2

Blake wants to know whether most baseball players are left-handed, right-handed, or able to use both hands to throw a pitch. He collects data on pitchers from 3 baseball teams: The Angels, Red Sox, and Rangers. The results are as follows:

- Of the 11 pitchers on the Angels, 6 are left-handed and 4 are right-handed.
- Of the 11 pitchers on the Red Sox, 7 are right-handed and 2 can use both hands.
- Of the 15 pitchers on the Rangers, 4 can use both hands, and 5 are left-handed.

Which statement correctly describes the results of Blake's survey?

(A) About 55% of the right-handed pitchers play for the Rangers.

(B) About 14% of the players surveyed are left-handed pitchers for the Red Sox.

(C) About 13% of the pitchers can play with both hands.

(D) About 18% of the players surveyed are right-handed pitchers for the Angels.

7.3 Construct and Interpret Two-Way Tables

3 Kayla wants to know whether most baseball players are left-handed, right-handed, or able to use both hands to hit the ball. She collects data on batters from 3 baseball teams: The Dingers, Devils, and Sharks. The results are as follows:

- Of the 22 players on the Dingers, 7 are right-handed and 15 can use both hands.
- Of the 22 players on the Devils, 11 are right-handed and 11 are left-handed.
- Of the 22 players on the Sharks, 12 are left-handed and 10 are right-handed.

Which statement correctly describes the results of Kayla's survey?

(A) About 42% of the players surveyed are right-handed batters.

(B) About 100% of the Devils players surveyed are left-handed batters.

(C) About 22% of the Sharks players are right-handed batters.

(D) About 22% of the Dingers players are left-handed or right-handed batters.

Construct and Interpret Two-Way
Tables

7.3

		Amount Earned			
		Less than $40,000	At least $40,000 and less than $60,000	At least $60,000 and less than $80,000	Greater than $80,000
Age	18-24	200	550	572	166
	25-34	355	644	678	676
	35-55	568	789	1000	888
	60 and older	400	360	1111	989

4 Morgan conducts a survey to determine the average income of the residents in her city. This table shows her results.

What is the approximate relative frequency, as a decimal rounded to the nearest hundredth, of the residents between the ages of 35 and 55 who earn at least $60,000 and less than $80,000?

_____

		Amount Earned			
		Less than $40,000	At least $40,000 and less than $60,000	At least $60,000 and less than $80,000	Greater than $80,000
Age	18-24	200	550	572	166
	25-34	355	644	678	676
	35-55	568	789	1000	888
	60 and older	400	360	1111	989

5 Jace conducts a survey to determine the average income of the residents in his city. This table shows his results.

What is the approximate relative frequency, as a decimal rounded to the nearest hundredth, of the residents of the city who are between the ages of 25 and 34 and earn at least $40,000 and less than $60,000?

_____

BIVARIATE DATA

Construct and Interpret Two-Way Tables

6 Leo surveys residents in his city for an academic report. This table shows the results of his survey.

	HS Graduate	Bachelor's Degree	Master's Degree
Took an SAT class	10,222	12,098	8,379
Did not take an SAT class	15,567	29,456	23,699

What is the relative frequency, as a two-digit decimal, of residents of the city who have a Master's degree and have taken an SAT course?

_____

7 Owen surveys residents in his city for an academic report. This table shows the frequencies he determined.

	HS Graduate	Bachelor's Degree	Master's Degree
Took an SAT class	12,467	10,205	9,876
Did not take an SAT class	20,092	14,656	9,986

What is the relative frequency, as a decimal rounded to the nearest 10 digits, of residents in the city who have a Master's degree and who did not take an SAT course?

_____

8 This relative frequency table reflects the number of people who prefer different pets.

		Men	Women
	Fishes	0.09	0.10
Pet	Birds	0.08	0.07
	Cats	0.12	0.32

What does the relative frequency of 0.12 represent?

_____

9 This relative frequency table reflects the number of people who prefer different colors.

		Men	Women
	Pink	0.10	0.30
Colors	Green	0.20	0.21
	Red	0.11	0.24

What does the relative frequency of $(0.30 + 0.21 + 0.24)$ represent?

_____

7.3 Construct and Interpret Two-Way Tables

10 This relative frequency table reflects the income of 400 people

		Men	Women
Income	Under $ 30,000	0.29	0.23
	$ 30,000 to $ 49,999	?	0.22
	$ 50,000 or greater	0.07	0.06

What is the relative frequency of the individuals who are men and earn between $ 30,000 and $ 49,999?

_____

11 The table below shows a relationship between gender and the favorite leisure activity of 40 people.

		Activity	
		Sports	TV
Gender	Male	0.23	0.24
	Female	?	0.25

12 The table below shows a relationship between cars model and color in the parking lot of 54 cars.

		Color	
		Black	White
Car Model	BMW	?	0.15
	Audi	0.25	0.33

---

13 A table below shows a relationship between age and support for visiting an aqua park with a total of 72 people.

	Opinion	
	Yes	No
Children	0.14	?
Adults	0.29	0.34

7.3 Construct and Interpret Two-Way Tables

14 The table below shows a relationship between 66 students' gender and their favorite subject.

		Activity	
		Math	English
Gender	Boys	0.34	0.22
	Girls	0.25	?

15 The table below shows a relationship between 59 students' nationality and scores on a math test.

		Activity	
		Math	English
Nationality	European	?	0.21
	Australian	0.34	0.27

16

Luke conducts a survey to determine how many people use social media. Using the data from this survey, create a frequency table in the space below:

- Of the 88 people surveyed between the ages of 20 and 25, 55 people use social media.
- Of the 98 people surveyed between the ages of 26 and 32, 7 do not use social media.
- Of the 100 people surveyed that are 33 and older, 10 do not use social media.

7.3 Construct and Interpret Two-Way Tables

17 Caleb conducts a survey to determine whether people prefer cherries, kiwis, or apples. Use the data from this survey to create a frequency table in the space below:

- Of the 66 people surveyed under the age of 18, 27 people prefer apples and 19 people prefer kiwis.
- Of the 70 people surveyed between the ages of 18 and 34, 25 prefer cherries and 30 prefer kiwis.
- Of the 82 people surveyed who are 35 and older, 28 prefer cherries, and 42 prefer apples.

18 Riley conducts a survey to determine whether people prefer smartphones, tablets, or laptops. Use the data from her survey to create a relative frequency table in the space below:

- Of those under the age of 15 surveyed, 15 people prefer smartphones, 10 prefer tablets and 8 prefer laptops.
- Of the people between the ages of 15 and 20 surveyed, 12 people prefer smartphones, 15 prefer tablets and 17 prefer laptops.
- Of the people over the age of 20, 15 people prefer smartphones, 22 prefer tablets and 28 prefer laptops.

BIVARIATE DATA

7.3   Construct and Interpret Two-Way Tables

19 Hailey conducts a survey of 100 friends to determine which power is preferred in superheroes. Use the data from the survey to create a relative frequency table in the space below. Round each relative frequency to the nearest two decimal places.

- 17 girls and 11 boys vote for invisibility.
- 4 girls and 15 boys vote for superhuman strength.
- 17 girls and 8 boys vote for telepathy.
- 13 girls and 15 boys vote for flying.

20 This frequency table shows the food preferences of a group of students.

	Pizza	Tacos	Hamburgers
Girls	10	11	5
Boys	8	12	9

What is the difference between the relative frequency of boys who like pizza and the relative frequency of girls who like pizza?

Next Section: Chapter Review

7.4 **Chapter Review**

1 Which correlation does this scatter plot show?

(A) Positive

(B) Negative

(C) No correlation

(D) Discontinuous

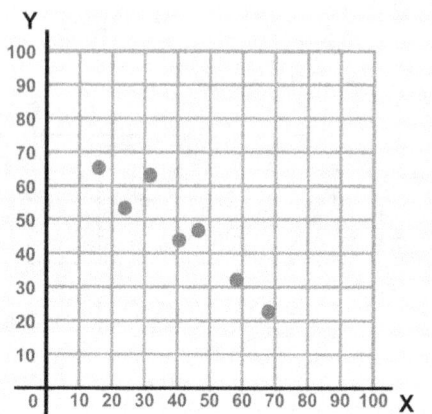

2 Which correlation does this scatter plot show?

(A) Positive

(B) Negative

(C) No correlation

(D) Discontinuous

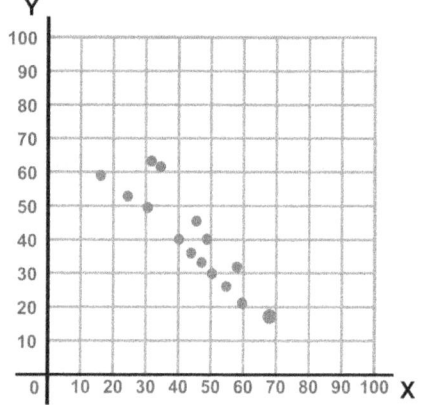

3 Which correlation does this scatter plot show?

(A) Positive

(B) Negative

(C) No correlation

(D) Discontinuous

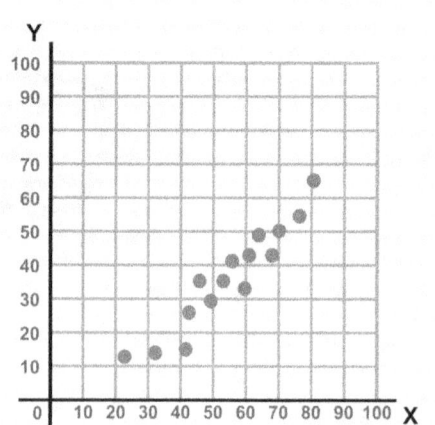

4 Which correlation does this scatter plot show?

- (A) Positive
- (B) Negative
- (C) No correlation
- (D) Discontinuous

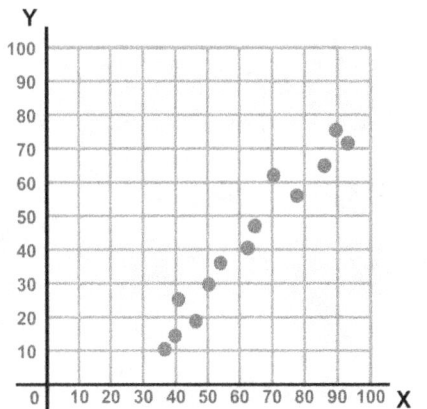

5 Which correlation does this scatter plot show?

- (A) Positive
- (B) Negative
- (C) No correlation
- (D) Discontinuous

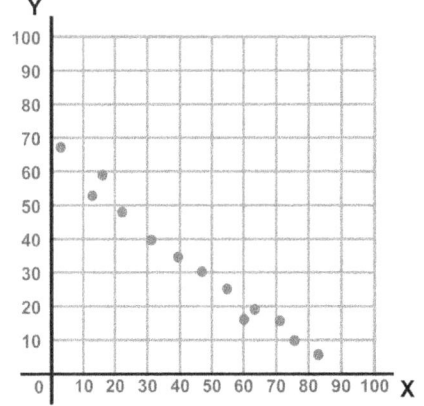

6 What is the equation of the trend line in the scatter plot?

- (A) $y = -\dfrac{100}{3} - \dfrac{10}{3}x$
- (B) $y = \dfrac{100}{3} + \dfrac{10}{3}x$
- (C) $y = \dfrac{100}{3} - \dfrac{10}{3}x$
- (D) $y = -\dfrac{100}{3} + \dfrac{10}{3}x$

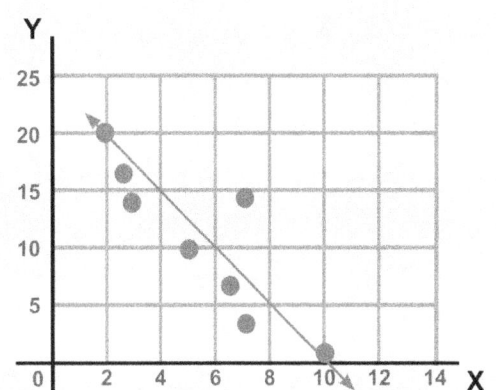

7.4   Chapter Review

---

7 What is the equation of the trend line in the scatter plot?

(A) $y = -2x + 15$

(B) $y = 2x + 15$

(C) $y = -2x - 15$

(D) $y = 2x - 15$

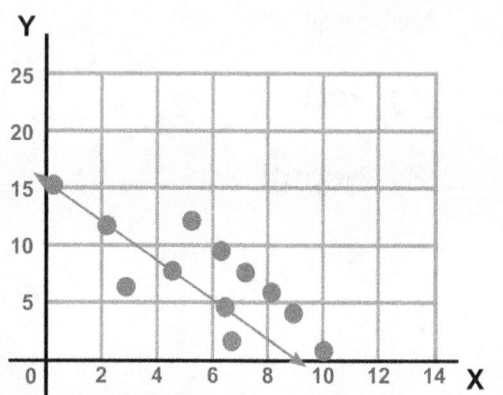

---

8 What is the equation of the trend line in the scatter plot?

(A) $y = -10 - \dfrac{5}{3}x$

(B) $y = 10 - \dfrac{5}{3}x$

(C) $y = 10 + \dfrac{5}{3}x$

(D) $y = -10 + \dfrac{5}{3}x$

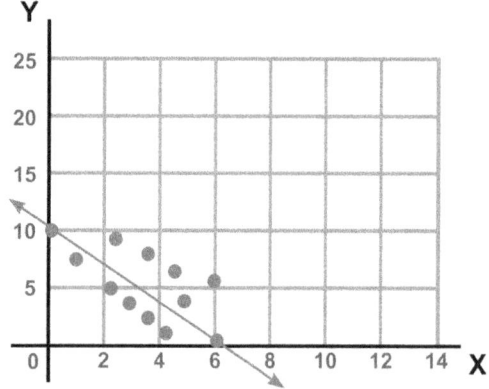

---

9 **True or False:**

There is a specific formula for defining outliers.

(A) True   (B) False

10

True or False: An outlier is a point in a data set that is connected to all other points in the data set.

(A) True   (B) False

11

True or False: A scatter plot shows no correlation if there is an obvious pattern.

(A) True   (B) False

12

True or False: A scatter plot shows a negative correlation if y tends to decrease as x increases.

(A) True   (B) False

13

True or False: A scatter plot shows a positive correlation if y tends to increase as x increases.

(A) True   (B) False

14

What is the relationship between two variables in a trend line data set?

(A) Positive   (B) Negative

(C) Best fit   (D) Outlier

7.4 Chapter Review

15 This graph shows how the distance Ayden's motorbikes depend on the number of trips he takes to work. What is the rate of change? Round to the nearest whole number.

A) 1 kilometers per trip

B) 2 kilometers per trip

C) 3 kilometers per trip

D) 4 kilometers per trip

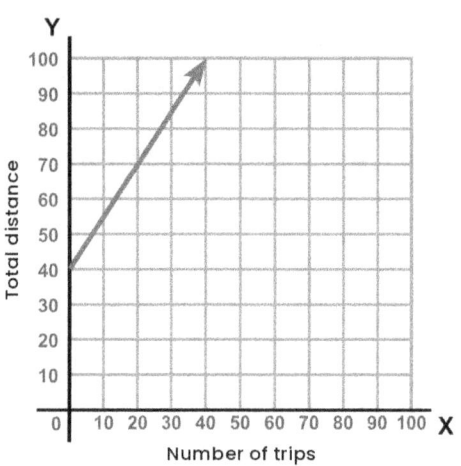

16 This graph shows how the total number of pages of notes in Kevin's class workbook depends on the number of hours he spends in class. What is the rate of change? Round to the nearest whole number.

A) 1 pages per class

B) 2 pages per class

C) 3 pages per class

D) 4 pages per class

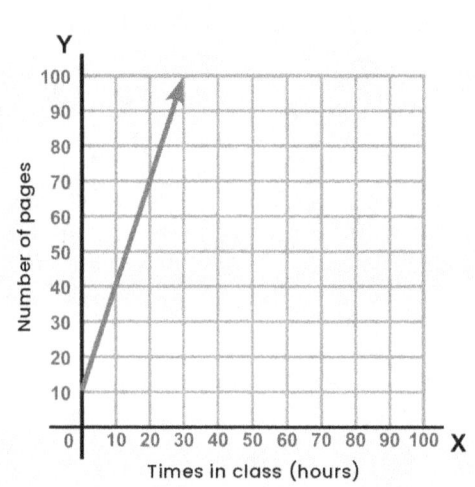

17 This graph shows how the total amount of paper Jaxon's office recycles depends on the number of weeks since they started the new recycling plan. What is the rate of change? Round to the nearest whole number.

A) 1 kg per week

B) 2 kg per week

C) 3 kg per week

D) 4 kg per week

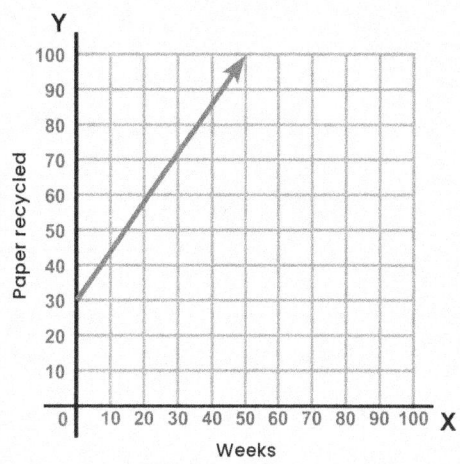

18 This table shows bivariate measurement data for the height of a plant, in cm, over a period of 11 weeks.

Time (weeks)	1	2	6	9	11
Height (cm)	9	12	15	23	28

Explain what the slope of the line of best fit could represent in this situation.

7.4   Chapter Review

19 The data in this table shows the results of a survey. What is the relative frequency of females who had a positive opinion about the topic? (Round to the nearest tenths place.)

Gender	Positive Opinion	Negative Opinion	Neutral Opinion
Female	65	45	9
Male	34	58	8

---

20 The table below shows the results of a survey. The participants indicated whether they have a college degree and their income. How many more participants do not have a college degree and have an income that is below $35,000 than those participants who do not have a college degree and make more than $35,000?

	Income Below $ 35,000	Income Above $ 35,000
Have a college Degree	12	44
Do not a college Degree	22	18

Next Chapter: Assessment 1 & 2 ›››

COMPREHENSIVE ASSESSMENT

3		4		5				7
	9				3		4	
5		2	7					1
		3			2			5
	8	1	5			4	7	
9				1				8
				4			6	
4					1	7		9
1	2		9	7			5	

1 Which of these numbers has the greatest value?

(A) -2   (B) -3   (C) -0.004   (D) $-\frac{2}{3}$

2 Which set of equations can be used to determine x, the fractional value of 2.062?

(A) $x = 2.062$ and $100x = 2{,}062.062$

(B) $x = 2.062$ and $1{,}000x = 2{,}062.062$

(C) $x = 2.062$ and $10x = 2.062062$

(D) $x = 2.062$ and $x = 2{,}06.2062$

3 What is the decimal value of this fraction?

$\frac{1}{2^2 \times 5^2}$ = _____.

4 Aaron constructs a large mirror in the living room of his new house. The mirror is a square, with an area of 41 square feet. Which type of number represents the length of one side of the mirror?

(A) Rational   (B) Integer   (C) Natural   (D) Irrational

5 Juliet's yard is a square with an area of 161 square centimeters. Exactly how long is each side of the yard?

_____

6 The length of one side of a square is $4\frac{1}{7}$ inches. Write an expression to show the calculation of the area of the square using decimals.

_____

7 Sherlyn states that $\frac{1}{5}$ is a rational number because it can be represented as 20%. Do you agree with Sherlyn? Explain your reasoning.

_____

8 Jim sees a drawing of a circle, with a diameter of 12 inches, and writes this expression to represent its area: $(4)(4)(5)$
Is Jim correct? Explain your reasoning.

_____

9 Jennifer draws a cone with a base area of 169π square centimeters and a height of 15 centimeters. What is the approximate area of the base of the cone, to the nearest whole square centimeter?

_____

10 Given the function, $h(x) = \sqrt{6-x}$, evaluate $h(7)$.

(A) 1   (B) 0   (C) Undefined   (D) 5

11 What is the value of y when x = 5? $y = -3x + 9$.

(A) 6   (B) -6   (C) -5   (D) 5

12 John has two car washes near his house. Car wash A charges $ 0.55 per minute. Car wash B charges $2.50 for three minutes and $2.50 for each additional minute. Which car wash should John choose if it takes him 10 minutes to wash his car?

(A) Car Wash A

(B) Car Wash B

(C) Car Wash A and Car Wash B are the same cost.

(D) There is not enough information to determine which is a better deal.

13 Which of the following characteristics of a graph can be determined from the vertical line test?

(A) The vertical line test determines whether the points create a line.

(B) The vertical line test determines whether the points create a nonlinear function.

(C) The vertical line test determines whether the points represent a function.

(D) The vertical line test determines how many points are on the y-axis.

14 Which equation represents a nonlinear function?

(A) $y = (x+2)^2$ (B) $y = x+2$ (C) $y = 2$ (D) $y = 2x$

15 A coffee club offers a membership y with an annual fee of $ 49.99 and charges $20 per coffee d. Which algebraic function represents this situation?

(A) $y = 49.99 + d$

(B) $y = 20d$

(C) $y = 14 + 49.99d$

(D) $y = 49.99 + 20d$

16 Which strategy could you use to graph this function?
$$5y + 8x = 15.$$

(A) Identify whether the function is linear or nonlinear.

(B) Rewrite the equation in standard form.

(C) Use the vertical line test.

(D) Rewrite the equation in slope-intercept form.

17 Sarah created a graph to represent the equation $y = 4x + 4$. Which option best describes the characteristics of this graph?

(A) The graph is increasing.

(B) The graph is decreasing.

(C) The slope is greater than the y-intercept.

(D) The slope is less than the y-intercept.

18 Which equation represents a linear and not a function?

(A) $y = 5x^2$ (B) $x = 2$ (C) $y = |x+4|$ (D) $y = x^4+6$

19 What is the rate of change of this function? $y = -8x + 15$.

(A) $y = -8$ (B) $x = 8$ (C) $y = 15$ (D) $y = -15$

20 The volume of a box can be found by using the formula V= lwh. The length of a box is x^3, the width of the box is 3x and the height of the box is 7x. Which option below is the correct expression for the volume of the box?

A) V = $10x^4$ B) V = $21x^4$ C) V = $21x^5$ D) V = $4x^5$

21 Simplify the expression $(3x^4y)(4x^2y^2)^2$.

A) $12x^6y^3$ B) $48x^8y^5$ C) $12x^8y^5$ D) $48x^8y^3$

22 The area of a circle is found with the formula $A=\pi r^2$, where r is the radius. Suppose the radius of a circle is y^6. Which of the following options is the correct expression for the area of the circle?

A) πy^6 B) πy^8 C) πy^{10} D) πy^{12}

23 Linda finds the cube root of a number x and then doubles the result to get 12. Which of the following is equal to x?

A) 125   B) 216   C) 343   D) 64

24 The area of a square is calculated using the formula $A=s^2$, where s is the length of a side of the square. Mike would like to create a square with an area of 196 square inches. What is the length of one side of the square?

(A) 15　　　(B) 16　　　(C) 13　　　(D) 14

25 A farm raises goats and pigs. There are a total of 357 goats and pigs on the farm. There are twice as many pigs as goats. How many goats are on the farm?

(A) 199　　　(B) 119　　　(C) 129　　　(D) 139

26 Earth's core temperature is 16,700,000 degrees Celsius at its core. How would you express this number in scientific notation?

(A) 1.67×10^7　　(B) 1.67×10^5　　(C) 1.67×10^9　　(D) 16.7×10^7

27 Which of the following options determines if the second-factor exponent is positive or negative?

(A) Exponents are always negative.

(B) Exponents are always positive.

(C) Very large numbers have positive exponents, and very small numbers have negative exponents.

(D) Very large numbers have negative exponents, and very large numbers have positive exponents.

28 The equation 8.85 + 0.65s = c gives the cost c in dollars that a website charges for downloading songs. The variable s stands for the number of songs downloaded. Find out how much it costs to download 26 songs.

_____

29 270° How much of a full rotation?

(A) Half

(B) Third

(C) Fourth

(D) None of the above

30 If the number of degrees an image is rotated is positive, which way would you rotate the image?

(A) Counterclockwise

(B) Along the y-axis

(C) Along the x-axis

(D) Clockwise

31 **True or False:** A reflection flips a figure across a line or point to create a mirror image.

(A) True

(B) False

32 The legs of a right triangle are 20 centimeters and 15 centimeters long. What is the length of the hypotenuse?

(A) 22^2

(B) 9^2

(C) 16^2

(D) 25^2

33 Irene's ladder is 12 feet long. If she places the bottom of the ladder 6 feet from the wall, how far from the ground surface does the ladder touch the wall?

---

34 The legs of a right triangle are 12 centimeters and 14 centimeters long. What is the length of the hypotenuse?

---

35 What is the approximate distance, to the nearest tenth of a unit, between the points (– 3, 6) and (7, – 4), without using a graph?

---

36 What is the approximate distance, to the nearest tenth of a unit, between the points (– 2, –4) and (8, –4), without using a graph?

---

37 **True or False:** The approximate volume of a cylinder with a height of 11 yards and a radius of 6 yards is 1,243.44 yd³.

A) True   B) False

38 **True or False:** The approximate volume of a cone with a radius of 6 in and a height of 14 in is 515 in³.

A) True   B) False

39 **True or False:** To choose the correct scatter correlation, we can check along the outlier.

A) True   B) False

40 Chris's birthday party costs $3 for every guest he invites. Write an equation that shows the relationship between the guests (x) and the cost (y)?

_____

41 **True or False:** One outlier can have a drastic effect on the correlation and on the least squares regression line.

A) True   B) False

42 Eda learns 30 new appetizer recipes each week of culinary school.
True or False: The equation that shows the relationship between the number of weeks (x) and the number of appetizer recipes (y) is x/30.

_____

43 Benny buys 120 postcards each day of vacation.
True or False: The equation that shows the relationship between the days of vacation (x) and the number of postcards bought (y) is y=120x.

_____

44 Based on the table below, how many people prefer apples?

	Prefer Apples	Prefer Oranges
Male	3	8
Female	5	10

_____

45 Based on the table below, how many people do not prefer carrots?

	Prefer Carrot	Prefer Cucumber
Male	8	11
Female	7	12

Next Chapter: Assessment – 2 ➤➤

COMPREHENSIVE ASSESSMENT

4		2	5				3	
	1					8			4
	5		7			1	2	
9			1				6	8
	2	7		3		4		
	6		4		2			3
		9		5				2
6	8				7		5	
	4		9	1		3		

1 According to the table below, how many pencils are red?

Color	Pen	Pencil
Yellow	1	3
Red	5	8
Green	3	4

---

2 According to the table below, how many students, who did not listen to music as they studied, made a 90 or above on the assessment?

	Made a 90 or above on assesment	Made below a 90 on assesment
Student listened to music as they studied	9	43
Student did not listen to music as the studied	48	7

---

3 According to the table below, how many people prefer Milkshakes?

Age	Prefer Milkshake	Prefer Juice
Under 18	29	44
18 to 30	13	25
Over 30	36	20

4 Which of the following square roots is a rational number?

(A) $\sqrt{15}$ (B) $\sqrt{17}$ (C) $\sqrt{49}$ (D) $\sqrt{39}$

---

5 Find the value of y in the ordered pair $(-1, y)$ given the equation.
$y = \frac{1}{3}x - 3$

(A) $\frac{1}{3}$ (B) $-\frac{1}{3}$ (C) $-3\frac{1}{3}$ (D) -3

---

6 Which situation below best represents the equation:
$f(m) = 16 + 8m$?

(A) The membership of a gym costs $16 per month plus an $8 join fee.

(B) The membership of a gym costs $8 per month plus a $16 join fee.

(C) The membership of a gym costs $24 per month.

(D) The membership of a gym costs $16 per month for adults and $8 per month for minors.

7 Students are presented with the following algebraic statement: $y = -6x - 6$. Which student draws the correct conclusion?

(A) John says the graph is increasing because its slope is negative.

(B) Kaitlyn says the graph is decreasing because its slope is negative.

(C) Akbar says the graph is decreasing because its y-intercept is negative.

(D) Edward says the graph is increasing because its slope is positive.

8 What is the value of this expression? $5^2 \times 5^3$.

(A) 3125   (B) 625   (C) 3.125   (D) 6.900

9 The cubed root of a number n is one less than 5. What is the value of the number n?

(A) 4   (B) 25   (C) 64   (D) 125

10 Find the value of $(\sqrt[3]{-64})^2$.

(A) 4   (B) 2   (C) 25   (D) 16

11 Which number is 1000 times larger than $8×10^7$?

- (A) $8×10^8$
- (B) $8×10^9$
- (C) $8×10^{10}$
- (D) $8×10^7$

12 Which equation has a slope greater than the function represented in the table below?

x	1	2	3
y	3	6	9

_____

13 Solve for g.

$5g + 3 = 6g - 2$.

- (A) $g = 2$
- (B) $g = 4$
- (C) $g = 5$
- (D) $g = 6$

14 If the lengths of the legs of a right triangle are 15 centimeters and 30 centimeters, what is the length of the hypotenuse?

- (A) $\sqrt{1125}$
- (B) $\sqrt{1155}$
- (C) $\sqrt{1145}$
- (D) $\sqrt{1165}$

15 If the lengths of the legs of a right triangle are 6 centimeters and 9 centimeters, what is the length of the hypotenuse?

- (A) $\sqrt{112}$
- (B) $\sqrt{117}$
- (C) $\sqrt{114}$
- (D) $\sqrt{116}$

16 Eda is playing hide-and-seek with Susan and Charles. Charles is hiding 13 meters south of Eda, and Susan is hiding east of Charles. If Eda is 22 meters from Susan, how far apart are Charles and Susan?

_____

17 Shirley takes a rectangular piece of fabric and makes a diagonal cut from one corner to the opposite corner. The cut she makes is 6 inches long with a width of 5 inches. What is the fabric length?

_____

18 Without using a graph, determine the distance between the points (3,7) and (5,12). Round your answer to the nearest tenth.

_____

19 Without using a graph, determine the distance between the points (9,-6) and (10,-12). Round your answer to the nearest tenth.

_____

20 **True or False:** A cylinder with a diameter of 10 mm and a height of 14 mm has an approximate volume of 1254 mm³.

(A) True   (B) False

21 According to the data in this table, how many students use black pens?

	Male	Female
Use Black Pen	4	6
Use Blue Pen	5	7

22 What fraction is equivalent to 0.75?

(A) $\frac{6}{9}$ (B) $\frac{6}{8}$ (C) $\frac{75}{100}$ (D) $\frac{6}{10}$

23 Which expression has a value between 12 and 13?

(A) π (B) 4π (C) 5π (D) 6π

24 Find the value of x in the given ordered pair, (x, 6) y=x−4.

(A) 10   (B) 40   (C) 1   (D) 3

25 Which of the ordered pairs satisfies the function in the table?

x	4	5	6
y	64	125	216

(A) (3,9) (B) (1,1) (C) (2,8) (D) (7,323)

26 Which of the following statements is true about vertical lines?

(A) Vertical lines have undefined slopes.

(B) Vertical lines can be used to test whether a line is a function.

(C) Vertical lines are perpendicular to horizontal lines.

(D) All these statements above are true.

27 The area of a circle is found with the formula $A = \pi r^2$, where r is the radius. If the radius of a circle is a^{-4}. Which of the following is the area of the circle?

(A) πa^8 (B) $\dfrac{\pi}{a^8}$ (C) πa^{16} (D) $\dfrac{\pi}{a^{16}}$

28 Find the value of $\sqrt[3]{512}$.

(A) 9 (B) 8 (C) 7 (D) 6

29 Which option below represents all real solutions to the equation $\frac{1}{9}x^2 = 16$?

(A) 16   (B) ±12   (C) 12   (D) −12

30 Which expression represents a number 10 times smaller than nine hundred million?

(A) $\frac{9 \times 10^8}{10^1}$ (B) $\frac{9 \times 10^{10}}{10^2}$ (C) $\frac{9 \times 10^9}{10^1}$ (D) $\frac{9 \times 10^8}{10^0}$

31 What expression, as a product in scientific notation, represents the number six-hundredths times 50.

_____

32 Which value is missing from this table?

x	4	8	12
y	3.4	?	10.2

(A) 6.8   (B) 7.8   (C) 6   (D) 9

33 Solve for x.

$(6.982 \times 10^{-7}) - (2.567 \times 10^{-7}) = x$

(A) 4.415×10^{-7}

(B) 4.415×10^{-8}

(C) 3.415×10^{-7}

(D) 3.415×10^{-8}

34 What is the value of x if $2(x-3) = 3(x + 2)$?

(A) -12

(B) 12

(C) 0

(D) 6

35 Which equation has no solution?

(A) $2x + 5 = 3x - 2$

(B) $4x + 5 = 5x - 2$

(C) $10x + 6 = 12x + 7$

(D) $4x + 5 = 4x + 2$

36 At an exhibition hall, two sandwiches and two juices cost $6. Four sandwiches and one juice cost $ 8.50. How much does a sandwich cost?

(A) 0.875 cents

(B) $8.75

(C) 0.895 cents

(D) 0.975 cents

37 A transformation is performed on Triangle XYZ to create Triangle X'Y'Z'. Point X is located at (4,0). The transformation will create a similar image and enlarge the side lengths of the triangle to 5 times its original size. One vertex is at the origin and does not move. What are the coordinates of X?

_____

38 A transformation is performed on Triangle XYZ to form Triangle X'Y'Z'. Point X is located at $\left(\frac{3}{4},\frac{5}{4}\right)$. The transformation will create a similar image and enlarge the side lengths of the triangle to 4 times the original size. One vertex is at the origin and does not move. What are the coordinates of X'?

_____

39 If the lengths of the legs of a right triangle are 14 centimeters and 18 centimeters, what is the length of the hypotenuse?

(A) $\sqrt{820}$ (B) $\sqrt{520}$ (C) $\sqrt{720}$ (D) $\sqrt{920}$

40 If the lengths of the legs of a right triangle are 12 centimeters and 16 centimeters, what is the length of the hypotenuse?

(A) $\sqrt{440}$ (B) 20   (C) 40   (D) 30

41 The floor of a rectangular storage unit is 5 meters long and 7 meters wide. What is the distance between two opposite corners of the floor?

_____

42 Two window washers, Tesla and Linda, lean a ladder against the side of a building so Tesla can wash a window while Linda holds the ladder. The top of the ladder reaches the window, 20 feet off the ground. The base of the ladder is 6 feet away from the building. How long is the ladder? Round your answer to the nearest tenth of a foot.

_____

43 What is the distance between the points $(3, 3)$ and $(8, 10)$, without using a graph? Round your answer to the nearest tenth.

(A) 9.6   (B) 10   (C) 8.6   (D) 7.5

44 **True or False:** A cone with a diameter of 6 ft and a height of 12 ft has a volume of about 110 ft³.

(A) True   (B) False

45 Without using a graph, determine the distance between the following points: (- 3,5) and (-3, -3) ?

(A) 1.5   (B) 1.4   (C) 2   (D) 3

Next Chapter: Answers ❯❯

ANSWERS AND EXPLANATIONS

TABLE OF CONTENTS

TABLE OF CONTENTS

1. RATIOS AND RATES

1.1 RATIONAL AND IRRATIONAL NUMBERS

1. Answer: A
Explanation: $\frac{4}{5}$ is a rational number. $\sqrt{5}$ is an irrational number.

2. Answer: B
Explanation: $\frac{\pi}{0}$ is not a rational because 0 is the denominator. $\sqrt{3}$ is an irrational number.

3. Answer: D
Explanation: The fraction $\frac{3\sqrt{6}}{5}$ contains an irrational part $\sqrt{6}$. Thus, it is an Irrational number.

4. Answer: B
Explanation: Divide the numerator by the denominator to convert the fraction to a decimal. $17 \div 20 = 0.85$.

5. Answer: A
Explanation: Divide the numerator by the denominator to convert the fraction to a decimal.

6. Answer: B
Explanation: The sum of a rational and an irrational number is always an irrational number

7. Answer: A
Explanation: $A = hw\sqrt{100} = h \times 2\sqrt{2}h$

$= \frac{\sqrt{200}}{2\sqrt{2}} = \frac{\sqrt{\frac{200}{2}}}{2} = \frac{\sqrt{100}}{2} = \frac{10}{2} = 5$ units.

8. Answer: C
Explanation: A repeating decimal is a fraction with one 9 in the denominator for each digit that repeats. The given decimal has 3 digits that repeat. Then simplify the resulting fraction.

9. Answer: B
Explanation: A repeating decimal is a fraction with one 9 in the denominator for each digit that repeats. The given decimal has 2 digits that repeat. Then simplify the resulting fraction.

10. Answer: A
Explanation: A repeating decimal is a fraction with one 9 in the denominator for each digit that repeats. The given decimal has 2 digits that repeat. Then simplify the resulting fraction.

11. Answer: D
Explanation: The exact value of cannot be written as a fraction, so it is Irrational.

12. Answer: A
Explanation: Divide the numerator by the denominator to convert the fraction to a decimal.

13. Answer: A
Explanation: Divide the numerator by the denominator to convert the fraction to a decimal. Dividing by 9 always gives a repeating decimal.

14. Answer: B
Explanation:
$A = \pi r^2$ $r = \sqrt{3}$, which is irrational.

15. Answer: B
Explanation:
$P = 2(h+w)$ $w = \frac{7\pi}{6} - \frac{\pi}{2} = \frac{4\pi}{6} = \frac{2\pi}{3}$, π is irrational.

16. Answer: A
Explanation: m and n must be rational. Therefore, m is a rational number.

17. Answer: B
Explanation: The quotient of a rational and an irrational number is an irrational number. So is m an irrational number.

18. Answer: A
Explanation: The product of two rational numbers is a rational number. So m is a rational number.

19. Answer: A
Explanation: m and n must be rational. Therefore, m is a rational number.

20. Answer: C
Explanation: A repeating decimal is a fraction with one 9 in the denominator for each digit that repeats. The given decimal has 2 digits that repeat. Then simplify the resulting fraction.

1.2 EXPRESSIONS USING PROPERTIES OF EXPONENTS

1. Answer: B
Explanation: According to the exponent rule for multiplication with the same base, we add the powers.

2. Answer: A
Explanation: $\left(4^3\right)^2 = 4^{3\times2} = 4^6$.

3. Answer: D
Explanation: $m^2 \times n^2 = (mn)^2$.

4. Answer: C
Explanation: $10^{-4} = \frac{1}{10^4}$.

5. Answer: A
Explanation: $\left(m^{-2}\right)^4 = m^{-2\times4} = m^{-8} = \frac{1}{m^8}$.

6. Answer: B
Explanation: Numbers to the power of zero are equal to one.

7. Answer: A
Explanation: $A = lw = a^5 \times a^3 = a^8$ mm^2.

8. Answer: B
Explanation: $A = a^2 = \left(4^5\right)^2 = 4^{10}$ mm^2.

9. Answer: D
Explanation: $A = \pi r^2 = \pi\, a^{4\times2} = a^8\pi$ mm^2.

10. Answer: C
Explanation: $V = a^3 = 7^{4\times3} = 7^{12}$ mm^2.

11. Answer: A
Explanation: $A = lw = a^6 a^2 = a^{6+2} = a^8$.

12. Answer: $b^0+b^1+b^3$
Explanation:
A man has b sons = man+b son = $b^0 + b^1$ and each of his sons have 3 sons = b^3.

13. Answer: $a^{16}\pi$ mm^2
Explanation: $A = \pi r^2 = \pi\, a^{8\times2} = a^{16}\pi$ mm^2.

14. Answer: a^4 m
Explanation:
$A = lw = \frac{A}{l} = \frac{a^7}{a^3} = a^{7-3} = a^4$ m.

15. Answer: 6^6 cm^2
Explanation: $\left(6^3\right)^2 = 6^{3\times2} = 6^6$ cm^2.

16. Answer: A
Explanation: $V = r^2 = a^{7\times2} = a^{14}$ seats.

17. Answer: C
Explanation: $A = rs = \frac{A}{s} = \frac{8^4}{8} = 8^{4-1} = 8^3$ rows.

18. Answer: D
Explanation: $V = a^3 = 4^{3\times3} = 4^9$ cm^3.

19. Answer: 6^{15} cm^3
Explanation: $V = a^3 = 6^{5\times3} = 6^{15}$ cm^3.

20. Answer: $\dfrac{1}{a^6+16a^2}$

Explanation: $\dfrac{a^4\left(a^2\right)^{-3}}{\left(a^4\right) + 4^2} = \dfrac{a^4\, a^{-6}}{\left(a^4\right) + 16} = \dfrac{a^{-2}}{a^4 +16}$

$\dfrac{1}{(a^4+16)a^2} = \dfrac{1}{a^6+16a^2}$.

1.3 NEGATIVE BASES AND EQUIVALENT EXPRESSIONS INVOLVING EXPONENTS

1. Answer: B
Explanation: $(-a)^3 \times (-a)^7 = -a^{3+7} = -a^{10} = a^{10}$.

2. Answer: A
Explanation: When multiplying the same bases with exponents, the rule is adding the exponents. Filling 5^7 into the blank gives $5^2 \times 5^7 = 5^9$, since $2 + 7 = 9$, the answer is 5^7.

3. Answer: D
Explanation: When multiplying the same bases with exponents, the rule is adding the exponents. The area is length times width, so add 5 and 6. Do not multiply the bases.

4. Answer: C
Explanation: Substituting any integer for x will yield a positive number. Recall that 0 is neither positive nor negative.

5. Answer: B
Explanation: To simplify this expression, consider 3^2 which is equal to 9. Then consider 4^2, which is equal to 16.
Finally, multiply $9 \times 16 = 144$.

6. Answer: A
Explanation: When you substitute the value in for x you get, $(-2)^4 = -2 \cdot -2 \cdot -2 \cdot -2 = 16$.

7. Answer: B
Explanation: $(-3)^5 = -3^5$ and $3^{-5} = \frac{1}{3^5}$
$(-3)^5 \neq 3^{-5}$.

8. Answer: $\frac{100}{b^4}$ cm

Explanation: $|(-b)^{-4}| = |\frac{1}{(-b)^4}| = \frac{1}{-b^4}$ m

$= \frac{1}{b^4} \times 100$ cm $= \frac{100}{b^4}$ cm.

9. Answer: A
Explanation: $|(-b)^{-2}| = |\frac{1}{(-b)^2}| = |\frac{1}{b^2}| = b^{-2}$.

10. Answer: B
Explanation: $\frac{5^5}{4^5} = (\frac{5}{4})^5 = 1.25^5 > 1$.
$5^5 > 4^5$.

11. Answer: C
Explanation: $V = x^3 = (|(-a)^4|)^3 = a^{4 \times 3} = a^{12}$ cm^3.

12. Answer: B
Explanation:

$$\frac{2^2}{2^3((-4)^{-2})^3} = \frac{2^2}{2^3(\frac{1}{(-4)^2})^3} = \frac{2^2}{2^3(\frac{1}{4^2})^3} = \frac{2^2}{2^3(\frac{1}{2^4})^3} = \frac{2^2}{2^3(2^{-4})^3}$$

$$= \frac{2^2}{2^3 \, 2^{-12}} = \frac{2^2}{2^{-9}} = 2^{2+9} = 2^{11}.$$

13. Answer: $(\frac{5}{2})^2$cm
Explanation:
$(-4)^{-2}$ m $= \frac{1}{(-4)^2}$ m $= \frac{1}{4^2}$ m $= \frac{1}{4^2} \times 100$cm $=$

$\frac{10^2}{4^2}$ cm $= (\frac{10}{4})^2$ cm $= (\frac{5}{2})^2$ cm.

14. Answer: B
Explanation: $(2^3)^2 = 2^{3 \times 2} = 2^6$,
$2^3 \times 2^2 = 2^{3+2} = 2^5$.
$(2^3)^2 \neq 2^3 \times 2^2$.

15. Answer: a^9 cm
Explanation: $A = hw \rightarrow h = \frac{A}{w} = \frac{|(-a)^{11}|}{(-a^2)}$

$= \frac{a^{11}}{a^2} = a^{11-2} = a^9$cm.

16. Answer: A
Explanation: $(\frac{5}{3})^6 = \frac{5^6}{3^6}$
$5^6 3^{-6} = \frac{5^6}{3^6}$
$(\frac{5}{3})^6 = 5^6 3^{-6}$.

17. Answer: B
Explanation: $6^{-4} = \frac{1}{6^4} = \frac{1}{1296}$

$4^{-6} = \frac{1}{4^6} = \frac{1}{4096}$
$6^{-4} \neq 4^{-6}$.

18. Answer: $\frac{100}{2^6}$ **cm**
Explanation: $(-2)^{-6}$ m $= \frac{1}{(-2)^6}$ m $= \frac{1}{2^6}$ m $= \frac{100}{2^6}$ cm

19. Answer: A
Explanation: $4^{-20} = (2^2)^{-20} = 2^{2 \times -20} = 2^{-40}$
$\rightarrow 4^{-20} = 2^{-40}$.

20. Answer: Equal
Explanation: $|(-2)^{-6}| = |\frac{1}{(-2)^6}| = \frac{1}{2^6} = 2^{-6}$
$\rightarrow |(-2)^{-6}| = 2^{-6}$.

1.4 SQUARE ROOTS AND CUBE ROOTS

1. Answer: C
Explanation: The number 42 in $\sqrt{42}$ is not a perfect square, therefore, it is irrational.

2. Answer: A
Explanation: The largest value is 8.8 because $\sqrt{64} = 8$ and $\sqrt{36} = 6$.

3. Answer: A
Explanation: A rational number can be written as a fraction. $\sqrt{81} = 9$, Therefore, it is a rational number. Only square roots that contain a perfect square are rational numbers.

4. Answer: D
Explanation: To solve the equation, take the square root of both sides. This would give x = 7. However, when taking the square root to solve an equation, consider a negative value that makes the equation true. This gives x = - 7. Therefore, the solution of the equation is x = ±7.

5. Answer: A
Explanation: First, Substitute 25 into the area formula for A. This gives $25 = x^2$. To solve, take the square root of both sides of the equation, which gives x = ±5. Since the context of the problem is a side length of a square, reject the negative solution.

6. Answer: $\frac{2\sqrt[3]{5}}{5}$ **m**
Explanation:
$V = x^3 \rightarrow x^3 = 0.320 = \frac{320}{1000}$.
$\rightarrow x = \sqrt[3]{\frac{320}{1000}} = \frac{\sqrt[3]{4^3 \times 5}}{\sqrt[3]{10^3}} = \frac{4\sqrt[3]{5}}{10} = \frac{2\sqrt[3]{5}}{5}$.

7. Answer: 0.8
Explanation: $\sqrt{0.64} = \sqrt{(0.8) \times 0.8} = \sqrt{0.8^2} = 0.8$.

8. Answer: –1
Explanation: $\sqrt[3]{-1} = -\sqrt[3]{1} = -\sqrt[3]{1 \times 1 \times 1} = -\sqrt[3]{1^3} = -1$.

9. Answer: $\frac{1}{3}$
Explanation: $\sqrt{\frac{16}{144}} = \sqrt{\frac{4^2}{12^2}} = \frac{4}{12} = \frac{1}{3}$.

10. Answer: $9\sqrt[3]{9}$
Explanation: $\sqrt[3]{6561} = \sqrt[3]{9 \times 9 \times 9 \times 9} = \sqrt[3]{9^3 \times 9} = 9\sqrt[3]{9}$.

11. Answer: B
Explanation: $V = x^3 \rightarrow x^3 = 64$.
$x = \sqrt[3]{64} = \sqrt[3]{4^3} = 4m$.

12. Answer: A
Explanation:
Area of a square $= (\text{side length})^2$
Let x be the width of the mobile phone.
Then, $x^2 = 196$
$x = \sqrt{196} = \sqrt{14 \times 14} = 14$ cm.
So, the width of the mobile phone is 14 cm.

13. Answer: C
Explanation: $V = x^3 \rightarrow x^3 = 0.049$
$x = \sqrt[3]{0.049} = \sqrt[3]{\frac{49}{1000}} = \frac{\sqrt[3]{49}}{10}$ m.

14. Answer: D
Explanation:
Area of a square $= (\text{side length})^2$
Let x be the side length of the paper.
Then, $x^2 = 3600$.
$x = \sqrt{3600} = \sqrt{60 \times 60} = \sqrt{60^2} = 60$ cm.
So, the side length of the paper is 60 cm.

15. Answer: 20 cm
Explanation: $V = x^3 \rightarrow x^3 = 8000$

$x = \sqrt[3]{8000} = \sqrt[3]{1000 \times 8} = \sqrt[3]{10^3 \times 2^3} = 10 \times 2 = 20$.

16. Answer: 2.3

Explanation:

Area of a square = (side length)^2

Let x be the width of the desk.

Then, $x^2 = 5.29$

$x = \sqrt{2.3 \times 2.3} = \sqrt{2.3^2} = 2.3$ m.

So, the width of the desk is 2.3 m.

17. Answer: $4\sqrt[3]{6}$ m

Explanation: $V = x^3 \rightarrow x^3 = 384$.

$x = \sqrt[3]{64 \times 6} = \sqrt[3]{4^3 \times 6} = 4\sqrt[3]{6}$ m.

18. Answer: 1960

Explanation: $(\sqrt{250} + \sqrt{810})^2 = (\sqrt{25 \times 10} + \sqrt{81 \times 10})^2 = (5\sqrt{10} + 9\sqrt{10})^2$

$= (14\sqrt{10})^2 = 14^2 \times 10 = 196 \times 10 = 1960$.

19. Answer: A

Explanation:

Area of a square = (side length)^2

Let x be the width of the painting.

Then, $x^2 = 0.36$

$x = \sqrt{0.36} = \sqrt{0.6 \times 0.6} = 0.6$m

So, the width of the painting is 0.6 m

20. Answer: $\frac{4}{5}$ m

Explanation: $V = x^3 \rightarrow x^3 = 0.512$

$x = \sqrt[3]{\left(\frac{512}{1000}\right)} = \sqrt[3]{\frac{8^3}{10^3}} = \frac{8}{10} = \frac{4}{5}$ m.

1.5 SCIENTIFIC NOTATION

1. Answer: A

Explanation: To write a number in scientific notation, the first factor is greater than or equal to 1 and less than 10. The second factor is a power of ten. In this problem, 4.23 is the first factor. The decimal must move eight places to the right to give the original number, making the second factor of 10^8.

2. Answer: B

Explanation: To write a number in scientific notation, the first factor is greater than or equal to 1 and less than 10. The second factor is a power of ten. In this example, 7.65 is the first factor. The decimal must move seven places to the left i.e., the original number, making the second factor 10^{-7}.

3. Answer: C

Explanation: When she rewrote the number in scientific notation, she should have written it as 5.309×10^{10}. All significant digits must be included in the first factor.

4. Answer: B

Explanation: The number is 5 times larger than 90,000. Recognize that number in scientific notation.

5. Answer: A

Explanation: The number is very small so the second-factor exponent should be negative. Alternatively, when converting a standard number to scientific notation, if the decimal point moves to the right to create the first factor, the exponent is the negative of the number of places the decimal point is moved.

6. Answer: 3.5×10^{-5}

Explanation:

$5.0 \times 10^{-5} - 1.5 \times 10^{-5} = 10^{-5}(5.0 - 1.5) = 3.5 \times 10^{-5}$.

7. Answer: C

Explanation: $5.4 \times 10^{-5} = 0.000054$

$\rightarrow 0.000054 = 5.4 \times 10^{-5}$.

8. Answer: B

Explanation: $3.2 \times 10^{-6} = 0.0000032$

$\rightarrow 3.2 \times 10^{-6} < 0.000032$.

9. Answer: B

Explanation: When converting a standard number to scientific notation, if the decimal point moves to the right to create the first factor, the exponent is the negative of the number of places the decimal point is moved. In this problem, the decimal was moved 6 places to the left, and no significant digit in the first factor is changed.

10. Answer: D
Explanation: The original problem already contains the correct first factor for the scientific notation. The expression $0.1 \times 0.1 \times 0.1$ is equivalent to 10^{-3}.

11. Answer: D
Explanation: The original problem already contains the correct first factor for the scientific notation. The expression $10 \times 10 \times 10 \times 10$ is equivalent to 10^4.

12. Answer: 2.0
Explanation: $\dfrac{c}{b} = \dfrac{8.0 \times 10^{-4}}{4.0 \times 10^{-4}} = 2.0$.

13. Answer: D
Explanation: Move the decimal 11 places to the left.

14. Answer: 2.2×10^{-5}
Explanation: $6.6 \times 10^{-3} \div 3.0 \times 10^2 = \dfrac{6.6 \times 10^{-3}}{3.0 \times 10^2}$ $= 2.2 \times 10^{-5}$.

15. Answer: A
Explanation: Place the decimal after the first non-zero digit then count the number of places between the original and new location.

16. Answer: B
Explanation: $(6.4 \times 10^{-4}) \times (2.3 \times 10^{-3}) = (6.4 \times 2.3) \times (10^{-4} \times 10^{-3}) = 14.72 \times 10^{-7} = 1.472 \times 10^{-6}$.

17. Answer: B
Explanation: Move the decimal 3 places to the right.

18. Answer: 4.7×10^{-1}
Explanation: $7.5 \times 10^{-1} - 2.8 \times 10^{-1} = (7.5 - 2.8)10^{-1} = 4.7 \times 10^{-1}$.

19. Answer: C
Explanation: Place the decimal after the first non-zero digit then count the number of places between the original and new location.

20. Answer: 8
Explanation:

$$(4.0 \times 10^9) \div (5.0 \times 10^8) = \frac{(4.0 \times 10^9)}{(5.0 \times 10^8)}$$

$$= 0.8 \times 10^1 = 8 \times 10^0.$$

1.6 CHAPTER REVIEW

1. Answer: B
Explanation: The cube root of 216 is 6 because $6 \cdot 6 \cdot 6 = 216$.

2. Answer: C
Explanation: The radical $\sqrt{49}$ irrational because 49 is not a perfect cube

3. Answer: D
Explanation: First, substitute 729 into the formula for V. This gives $729 = s^3$. To find s, take the cube root of both sides. This gives $\sqrt[3]{729} = s = 9$.

4. Answer: C
Explanation: In scientific notation, the first-factor base contains the significant digits of the standard notation number as a number greater than or equal to 1 and less than 10, and the second-factor base is 10 to the power equal to the number of places the decimal point is moved to the left.

5. Answer: 6.22×10^6
Explanation: Multiply 6.22×10^5 by 10, which adds 1 to the exponent making the second factor 10^6.

6. Answer: A
Explanation: The product rule for exponents states that when multiplying two numbers with exponents and the same base, add their exponents, but do not multiply the bases.

7. Answer: C
Explanation: The quotient rule for exponents states that when dividing two numbers with the same base, subtract the exponent in the denominator from the exponent in the numerator.

8. Answer: C
Explanation: The square root of 16 is 4 and $2\frac{6}{4} = 12.$ → $2\frac{6}{4} > \sqrt{16}$.

9. Answer: B
Explanation: The square root of 38 is approximately 6.164.

10. Answer: B
Explanation: Compare 24 and 36. Although there is no need to find the square roots, the square root of 24 is approximately 4.899 and the square root of 36 is 6.

11. Answer: A
Explanation: Evaluate $\sqrt{68}$. The result is approximately 8.25.

12. Answer: D
Explanation: The square root of 30 is approximately 5.477 and the square root of 32 is approximately 5.657, which makes 6.71 the largest number

13. Answer: C
Explanation: The square root of 59 is approximately 7.745, which makes it larger than 7.62.

14. Answer: A
Explanation:
Step 1: $x = \overline{0.246} \to 1000x = 246.\overline{246}$
Step 2: Subtract $x = \overline{0.246}$ from $1000x = 246.\overline{246}$
Step 3: $999x = 246$
Step 4: $x = \frac{246}{999}$
Step 5: Simplify the fraction which gives $\frac{82}{333}$.

15. Answer: B
Explanation:
Step 1: $x = \overline{0.27} \to 100x = 27.\overline{27}$
Step2: Subtract $x = \overline{0.27}$ from $100x = 27.\overline{27}$
Step 3: $99x = 27$
Step 4: $x = \frac{27}{99}$
Step 5: Simplify the fraction which gives $\frac{3}{11}$.

16. Answer: D
Explanation: The square root of 3 is an irrational number and cannot be expressed as a fraction.

17. Answer: D
Explanation: The expression to $2\sqrt{7}+7$ contains an irrational number $(\sqrt{7})$ and cannot be expressed as a fraction.

18. Answer: A
Explanation: $A = lw \to l = \frac{A}{w} = \frac{75}{\sqrt{25}} = \frac{75}{5} = 15$.

19. Answer: 5.9611×10²⁴
Explanation:
$5.9736 \times 10^{24} - 1.25 \times 10^{22} = 5.9736 \times 10^{24} - 0.0125 \times 10^{24} = (5.9736 - 0.0125) \times 10^{24} = 5.9611 \times 10^{24}$.

20. Answer: B
Explanation:
$\sqrt[3]{512} - \sqrt[3]{-343} = \sqrt[3]{8^3} - \sqrt[3]{(-7)^3} = 8 - 7 = 8 + 7 = 15$.

2. FUNCTIONS

2.1 EVALUATE FUNCTION AND LINEAR FUNCTION

1. Answer: A
Explanation: A function has exactly one output for each input.

2. Answer: D
Explanation: Two identical inputs have different outputs.

3. Answer: D
Explanation: Two identical inputs have different outputs. Thus, the graph fails the vertical line test.

4. Answer: A
Explanation: A function has one output for each input. A slanted line automatically represents a function because the graph passes the vertical line test.

5. Answer: A
Explanation: There are no restrictions on the inputs of x which come from the domain.

6. Answer: B
Explanation: The inside of a square root must be greater than or equal to 0. Thus, the values that can be input for x must make the expression $4x - 5 \geq 0$.

7. Answer: C
Explanation: The given expression is a rational expression. Dividing by 0 is undefined. If x=1, the denominator is zero and the function expression is undefined.

8. Answer: B
Explanation: The given expression is a rational expression. Dividing by 0 is undefined. If $x=\frac{2}{3}$, the denominator is zero and the function expression is undefined.

9. Answer: B
Explanation: The domain includes the x-values, or inputs, of the graph. The inputs are between these two values, inclusive.

10. Answer: B
Explanation: The input value -2 maps to multiply output values of y.

11. Answer: D
Explanation: Let a represent the missing value of y. Since the difference between any two consecutive values of y must be the same, we setup equation to find the missing value a. $8 - 6 = 6 - b \Rightarrow b = 4$. Therefore, we fill 4 in the missing value of y.

12. Answer: A
Explanation: Vertical line Test: A vertical line intersects the graph at exactly one point of the graph for all input values of x.

13. Answer: B
Explanation: Vertical line Test: A vertical line intersects the graph at more than one point of the graph.

14. Answer: 6, 36, 66, 96
Explanation: The problem statement is represented as a linear function $y = 15x + 6$ where x represents the working hours and y the total earnings.

We substitute each value of x into the linear equation to find the corresponding y values.
For x = 0, $y = 15(0) + 6 = 6$
For x = 2, $y = 15(2) + 6 = 36$
For x = 4, $y = 15(4) + 6 = 66$
For x = 6, $y = 15(6) + 6 = 96$.

15. Answer: 20, 40, 60,80
Explanation: The problem statement is represented as a linear function as y = 4x where x represents the length of the square and y represents the perimeter of the square. We substitute each value of x into the equation to get the corresponding y value. Let's find for one of the x value.
For x = 5, y = 4(5) = 20. In a similar way we calculate the corresponding y values for the other x values and complete the table.

16. Answer:
Domain: $x \in [0,5]$ and Range: $y \in [300,7800]$
Explanation: From the table, we see the domain of the function is $x \in [0,5]$ and the range is $y \in [300,7800]$.

17. Answer:
Domain: $x \in [0,4]$ and Range: $y \in [0,5]$
Explanation: Clearly, from the table, we can see that the domain of the function is 0 to 4 and the range of the function is 0 to 5.

18. Answer:
Domain: $x \in [0,6]$ and Range: $y \in [2,32]$
Explanation: Finding Domain: Since the tank is 32 feet high, we substitute 32 for y in the given equation to find the corresponding value of x.
$$32 = 5x + 2 \Rightarrow x = 6.$$
The maximum height that the water can rise is to the height of tank at 6 hours.
The minimum value of x is 0 hours.
Therefore, domain is $x \in [0,6]$
Finding Range:
Substitute x=0 in the equation to find the corresponding y value.
$$y = 5(0) + 2 = 2.$$
Substitute x = 6 in the equation to find the corresponding y value.
$$y = 56 + 2 = 32.$$
Therefore, range is $y \in [2,32]$.

19. Answer: 40,70,100,130
Explanation: The problem statement is represented as a linear function as y = 30x + 10 where x represents the working hours and y is the total earnings.
We substitute each value of x into the linear equation to find the corresponding y values.
For x = 1, y = 30 (1) + 10 = 40
For x = 2, y = 30 (2) + 10 = 70
For x = 3, y = 30 (3) + 10 = 100
For x = 4, y = 30 (4) + 10 = 130.

20. Answer:
Domain: $x \in [0,20]$ and Range: $y \in [0,60]$
Explanation: Finding domain: After giving away all marbles to the children the number of marbles left in the box will be 0. We setup this situation in the equation by substituting 0 for y to determine the value of x.
$$0 = 60 - 3x \Rightarrow x = 20$$
So, the maximum children can be 20.
Therefore, the domain is $x \in [0,20]$.
Finding range:
Substitute x = 0 in the equation to find the corresponding y-value.
$$y = 60 - 3 (0) \Rightarrow y = 60$$
Substitute x = 20 in the equation to find the corresponding y-value.
$$y = 60 - 3 (20) \Rightarrow y = 0$$
Therefore, The range is $y \in [0,60]$.

2.2 COMPARE THE LINEAR FUNCTION

1. Answer: B
Explanation: The rate of change is calculated by dividing the amount of change of y by the amount of change of x:
$$m = \frac{y_2 - y_1}{x_2 - x_1} = \frac{-1 + 2}{-2 + 4} = \frac{1}{2}.$$

2. Answer: D
Explanation: The rate of change is calculated by dividing the amount of change of y by the amount of change of x:
$$m = \frac{y_2 - y_1}{x_2 - x_1} = \frac{4-2}{2-1} = \frac{2}{1} = 2.$$

3. Answer: A
Explanation: A line passes through the points $(0,4)$ and $(4,0)$, The rate of change is calculated by dividing the amount of change of y by the amount of change of x:
m$= \frac{y_2-y_1}{x_2-x_1} = \frac{0-4}{4-0} = \frac{-4}{4} = -1$.

4. Answer: C
Explanation: A line passes through the points $(-2,-2)$ and $(4,0)$. The rate of change is calculated by dividing the amount of change of y by the amount of change of x:
m$= \frac{y_2-y_1}{x_2-x_1} = \frac{0+2}{4+2} = \frac{2}{6} = \frac{1}{3}$.

5. Answer: C
Explanation: Find the rate of change i.e., the number in front of x.
So, the height of the bird increases each minute by 30 feet.

6. Answer: B
Explanation: Find the slope. A line passes through the points 0,20 and 10, 40, The rate of change is calculated by dividing the amount of change of y by the amount of change of x:
m$= \frac{y_2-y_1}{x_2-x_1} = \frac{40-20}{10-0} = \frac{20}{10} = 2$.

7. Answer: C
Explanation: The number in front of x i.e., –10 is the rate of change.

8. Answer: 16
Explanation: Rate of change, m=2, The rate of change is calculated by dividing the amount of change of y by the amount of change of x:
m$= \frac{y_2-y_1}{x_2-x_1} = \frac{24-y_1}{2+2} = \frac{24-y_1}{4}$
So,
$2 = \frac{24-ay_1}{4}$
Multiply both sides by 4,
$8 = 24 - y_1$
$\rightarrow y_1 = 16$.

9. Answer: A
Explanation: Find the rate of change i.e. the number in front of x. So there are 25 students in each van.

10. Answer: B
Explanation: Noah charges $15 per day and Peter charges $10 per day.

11. Answer: A
Explanation: John will charge $10 and James will charge $15.

12. Answer: D
Explanation: The rate of change is calculated by dividing the amount of change of y by the amount of change of x:
m$= \frac{y_2-y_1}{x_2-x_1} = \frac{20-10}{4-2} = \frac{10}{2} = 5$.

13. Answer: A
Explanation: The rate of change for Function A is $\frac{1}{3}$ and the rate of change for Function B is 5.

14. Answer: A
Explanation: The movie club would cost $240 (40 + 10 × 20) per year. Buying movies individually would cost $280 (14×20).

15. Answer: A
Explanation: Equation: $2x - 5y + 3 = 0$
$\rightarrow -5y = -2x - 3$
$\rightarrow y = \frac{2}{5}x + \frac{3}{5}$
$m = \frac{2}{5}$
Table:

x	5	8	11
y	-1	0	1

$m = \frac{y_2-y_1}{x_2-x_1} = \frac{0+1}{8-5} = \frac{1}{3}$.

16. Answer: A
Explanation: Graph:
A line passes through the points-3,0 and 0,3
$m = \frac{y_2-y_1}{x_2-x_1} = \frac{3}{0+3} = 1$.

Equation:
$2x + 4y = 8$
$\rightarrow 4y = -2x - 8$
$\rightarrow y = -\frac{1}{2}x - 2$

$\rightarrow m = -\frac{1}{2}$.

17. Answer: 90 bacteria are in each minute
Explanation: Find the rate of change i.e., the number in front of x.
So there are 90 bacteria in each minute.

18. Answer: D
Explanation: Find the rate of change i.e., the number in front of x.
So, the height of the bird increases each minute by 60 feet.

19. Answer: B
Explanation: Equation:
$\frac{x}{2}+\frac{y}{3}=1$
$\rightarrow 3x + 2y = 6$
$\rightarrow 2y = -3x + 6$
$\rightarrow y = -\frac{3}{2}x+3$
$\rightarrow m=-\frac{3}{2}$

Table:

x	3	8	13
y	-8	-5	-2

$m = \frac{Y_2-Y_1}{X_2-X_1} = \frac{8-3}{-5+8} = \frac{5}{3}.$

20. Answer: B
Explanation: The graph shows that it does not snow during the cold snap, then snow accumulating and finally a rapid drop, and since the snow melted until it is gone. B best represents the graph.

2.3 IDENTIFY AND REWRITE EQUATIONS IN SLOPE-INTERCEPT FORM

---

1. Answer: C
Explanation:
$4x - 5y = 3 \rightarrow -5y = -4x + 3 \rightarrow y = \frac{4}{5}x-\frac{3}{5}.$

2. Answer: A
Explanation:
$-6x - 2y + 3 = 0 \rightarrow -2y = 6x - 3 \rightarrow y = -3x +\frac{3}{2}.$

3. Answer: D
Explanation:
$5y - 11x - 22 = 0 \rightarrow 5y = 11x + 22 \rightarrow y = \frac{11}{5}x+\frac{22}{5}.$

4. Answer: B
Explanation: Slope $\rightarrow m = \frac{5-7}{2-4} = \frac{-2}{-2}=1$
$y = mx + b$
Substituting the point $A(4,7)$
$b = y - mx = 7 - 1 \times 4 = 3$
So, $y = x + 3$ is the equation in slope–intercept form given two points.

5. Answer: A
Explanation: Slope $\rightarrow m = \frac{2-10}{-1-3} = \frac{-8}{-4}=2$
$y = mx + b$
Substituting the point $A(3,6)$
$b = y - mx = 10 - 2 \times 3 = 4$
So, $y = 2x + 4$ is the equation in slope–intercept form given two points.

6. Answer: D
Explanation: Slope $\rightarrow m = \frac{6-3}{4-2} = \frac{3}{2}$
$y = mx + b$
Substituting the point $A(2,3)$
$b = y - mx = 3 -\frac{3}{2} \times 2 = 3 - 3 = 0$
So, $y = \frac{3}{2}x$ is the equation in slope-intercept form given two points.

7. Answer: A
Explanation: A line passes through the points $(0,2)$ and $(2,3)$
Slope $\rightarrow m = \frac{3-2}{2-0} = \frac{1}{2}$
$y = mx + b$
Substituting the point $A(0,2)$
$b = y - mx = 2-\frac{1}{2} \times 0 = 2 - 0 = 2$
So, $y =\frac{1}{2}x + 2$ is the equation in slope-intercept form given two points.

8. Answer: C
Explanation: A line passes through the points $(0,-1)$ and $(4,0)$
Slope $\rightarrow m = \frac{0+1}{4-0} = \frac{1}{4}$
$y = mx + b$
Substituting the point $A(0,-1)$
$b = y - mx = -1 - \frac{1}{2} \times 0 = -1$
So, $y = \frac{1}{4}x - 1$ is the equation in slope-intercept form given two points.

9. Answer: D
Explanation: A line passes through the points $(0,5)$ and $(2,2)$
Slope $\rightarrow m = \frac{2-5}{2-0} = \frac{-3}{2}$
$y = mx + b$
Substituting the point $A(0,5)$
$b = y - mx = 5 - \frac{-3}{2} \times 0 = 5 - 0 = 5$
So, $y = \frac{-3}{2}x + 5$ is the equation in slope-intercept form given two points.

10. Answer: B
Explanation: The line intersects the y-axis at the point $(0,3)$. So, y-intercept is 3.

11. Answer: C
Explanation: The line intersects the y-axis at the point $(0,5)$. So, y-intercept is 5.

12. Answer: D
Explanation: The line intersects the y-axis at the point $(0,-7)$. So, y-intercept is -7.

13. Answer: A
Explanation: Interpret the Slope and y-intercept from the problem statement. The initial level of water is 8 inches, which means y-intercept 'b' is 8.

Water increases 2 inches per hour, which means slope 'm' is 2.
$y = mx + b$ is the slope-intercept form equation.

Substituting m = 2 & b = 8 ,
$y = 2x + 8$ is the equation that represents the level of water.

14. Answer: C
Explanation: Interpret the Slope and y-intercept from the problem statement. Neha has $500 in the bank account, means y-intercept 'b' is 100. Neha saves $100 each week, means the slope 'm' is 100
$y = mx + b$ is the slope-intercept form equation.
Substituting m = 100 & b = 500,
$y = 100x + 500$ is the equation that represents the balance.

15. Answer: B
Explanation: Interpret the Slope and y-intercept from the problem statement. The height of the balloon is 40 yards, which means y-intercept 'b' is 40.
It increases 4 yards per minute, which means the slope 'm' is 4.
$y = mx + b$ is the slope-intercept form equation.
Substituting m = 4 & b = 40,
$y = 4x + 40$ is the equation that represents the height of the balloon.

16. Answer: A
Explanation: Interpret the Slope and y-intercept from the problem statement. Ava weighs 90 kg means y-intercept 'b' is 90. She gains in weight 4 kg each month, means slope 'm' is 2.
$y = mx + b$ is the slope-intercept form equation.
Substituting m = 4 & b = 90 ,
$y = 4x + 90$ is the equation that represents Ava's weight.

17. Answer: D
Explanation: Interpret the Slope and y-intercept from the problem statement.
The level of water is 16 inches, which means y-intercept 'b' is 16.
It decreases 2 inches per hour, which means the slope 'm' is -2.
y = mx + b is the slope-intercept form equation.
Substituting m = -2 & b = 16,
y = -2x + 16 is the equation that represents the level of water.

18. Answer: B
Explanation: Interpret the Slope and y-intercept from the problem statement.
Jack has 300 bottles of Soda means y-intercept 'b' is 300.
He sells bottles in six-packs, which means the slope 'm' is -6
y = mx + b is the slope-intercept form equation.
Substituting m = -6 & b = 300,
y = -6x + 300 is the equation that represents the total number of bottles.

19. Answer: $y = -\frac{3}{2} + 6$
Explanation:
$\frac{x}{2} + \frac{y}{3} = 2 \rightarrow \frac{3x + 2y}{6} = 2 \rightarrow 3x + 2y = 12 \rightarrow 2y =$
$-3x + 12 \rightarrow y = -\frac{3}{2} + 6$

20. Answer: $y = -\frac{5}{2}x + 1$
Explanation: A line passes through the points (-2,6) and (2,-4)
Slope → $m = \frac{-4-6}{2+2} = \frac{-10}{4} = -\frac{5}{2}$
y = mx + b
Substituting the point A(-2,6)
$b = y - mx = 6 + \frac{5}{2}x - 2 = 6 - 5 = 1$
So, $y = -\frac{5}{2}x + 1$ is the equation in slope-intercept form given two points.

2.4 ANALYZING GRAPH

1. Answer: B
Explanation: The line goes down from left to right, i.e., the slope of the line is negative.

2. Answer: A
Explanation: The line goes up from left to right, i.e., the slope of the line is positive.

3. Answer: B
Explanation: A curve is a non-linear graph.

4. Answer: A
Explanation: A straight line is a linear graph.

5. Answer: C
Explanation: The domain of the function is all values of x including and greater than -3.

6. Answer: D
Explanation: The domain of the function is all values of x that are less than or equal to -1.

7. Answer: A
Explanation: The range of the function is all values of y.

8. Answer: C
Explanation: The range of the function is all values of y greater than or equal to-4.

9. Answer:
Domain: 0 < x < 20 and Range: 16 < y < 96
Explanation: The given situation represented in linear function as y = 16 + 4x represents time in minutes, y represents cakes baked.
Domain: 0 < x < 20
Finding range: Substituting the domain-endpoints into the linear equation
y = 16 + 4 (0) = 16
y = 16 + 4 (20) = 96
Range: 16 < y < 96.

10. Answer:
Domain: 0 ≤ x ≤ 20 and Range: 0 ≤ y ≤ 40
Explanation: The given situation represented in linear function as y = 40 − 2x, x represents a number of days, y represents a number of books.
Range: 0 ≤ y ≤ 40
y = 40 − 2x
2x = 40 − y
$x = 20 - \frac{y}{2}$
Substituting range-end points,
$x = 20 - \frac{0}{2} = 20$
$x = 20 - \frac{40}{2} = 0$
Domain: 0 ≤ x ≤ 20.

11. Answer: B
Explanation: $\frac{6-3}{2-0} = \frac{3}{2} \neq \frac{12-6}{4-2} = \frac{6}{2} = 3$.
A nonlinear function does not have a constant slope

12. Answer: A
Explanation: Slope of the function is constant as shown below. Hence linear.
$\frac{14-7}{4-3} = 7 = 7 = \frac{21-14}{5-4}$.

13. Answer: B
Explanation: x increases and y decreases ⇒ decreasing function

14. Answer: A
Explanation: x increases and y increases ⇒ increasing function

15. Answer: y ∈ {6,15,24}
Explanation: A triangle has 3 sides.

x	2	5	8
y	6	15	24

16. Answer: A
Explanation: m=5>0 ⇒ Increasing

17. Answer: B
Explanation: m=−4<0 ⇒ Decreasing

18. Answer: D
Explanation: The only function given that is a line is choice D. It is the only function that can be written in one of the linear forms.

19. Answer: A
Explanation: Any function that includes an exponent other than 1 is nonlinear. The graph of the given function is a curve, and therefore, it is a nonlinear function.

20. Answer: B
Explanation: When you graph a graph in y = mx + b form, it forms a line.

2.5 CHAPTER REVIEW

1. Answer: A
Explanation: The outputs (y-values) are between these two values, inclusive.

2. Answer: C
Explanation: Substitute −1 for x to calculate the correct output.

3. Answer: D
Explanation: Substitute −4 for x to calculate the correct output.

4. Answer: C
Explanation: The x-value of this function is the number of pounds and the y-value is the cost. Multiply each number of pounds by 2.

5. Answer: B
Explanation: Check the values of x and y in the table against the graph, the values in the table in choice B match the points on the graph.

6. Answer: A
Explanation: While the bike is not moving, the line representing distance remains constant. Since the line is horizontal, the bike is not moving.

7. Answer:A
Explanation: When given a function in slope-intercept form, the coefficient of the x-variable is the slope or rate of change of the linear function.

8. Answer: D
Explanation: Function A has a positive slope which means it is increasing and function B has a negative slope which means it is decreasing.

9. Answer: B
Explanation: The y-intercept is the b value in the slope-intercept equation ($y = mx + b$). In this situation, the y-intercept is 4.

10. Answer: B
Explanation: Mia was incorrect because when you graph this function, its shape is like a V, and it passes the vertical line test

11. Answer: D
Explanation: Choice D is a linear function in the slope-intercept form.

12. Answer: B
Explanation: The larger the slope, the steeper the graph of the line will be.

13. Answer: C
Explanation: When x=0, y = -16 for this function.

14. Answer: C
Explanation: Choice C is a cubic function that is not linear.

15. Answer: B
Explanation: The function can be defined as $f(x) = x^2$. When graphed, the function is not a line. It's a curve.

16. Answer: Create a table with enough points to see the pattern of the graph.
Explanation: Depending on the points you choose; you may need to use more than three points for this function to clearly see the pattern created by the graph. The absolute value graph looks like a V.

17. Answer: No, this line is a horizontal line and is neither increasing nor decreasing
Explanation: The graph is that of a horizontal line and therefore neither increases or decreases.

18. Answer: A
Explanation: This function is a linear decreasing function because the values of y decrease from left to right.

19. Answer: D
Explanation: Use the points in the table. There is no set number of points needed to graph a function. Create more points if needed.

20. Answer: C
Explanation: A linear function is a line when graphed. Additionally, any function that includes only exponents of 1 is linear.

3.EQUATIONS AND INEQUALITIES

3.1 PROPORTIONAL RELATIONSHIPS

1. Answer: D
Explanation: In the form, y=mx, m is the slope.

2. Answer: B
Explanation: Lines in direct variation form always intersect the x-axis at (0,0) or the origin.

3. Answer: D
Explanation: In a direct variation relationship, all of the terms are proper ways to refer to m.

4. Answer: C
Explanation: Lines in this form are referred to as direct variations. As different x values are substituted into the equation, the m values change but the m remains the same. It is called the "constant" of the variation.

5. Answer: B
Explanation: Lines in direct variation form always intersect the y-axis at $(0,0)$ or the origin. If the intersection is elsewhere, then the relation is not a direct variation.

6. Answer: 1.25
Explanation: $k = \frac{y}{x} = \frac{2.5}{2}$.

7. Answer: A
Explanation:
A line passes through the point $(2,4)$.
$k = \frac{y}{x} = \frac{4}{2} = 2$.

8. Answer: C
Explanation: When the line follows the form $y = mx$, the slope is the m-value, also called the constant of the variation. In the equation $y = \frac{1}{6}x$ and $k = \frac{1}{6}$.

9. Answer: D
Explanation: When the line follows the form $y = mx$, the k-value is the slope. In the equation $y = 9x$, $k = 9$.

10. Answer: B
Explanation: Each y-value is 20 times its corresponding x-value.

11. Answer: A
Explanation: Each y-value is $\frac{1}{2}$ times its corresponding x-value. Alternatively, when x increases by 1, y increases by $\frac{1}{2}$.

12. Answer: 0.3
Explanation:

$k = \frac{y}{x} = \frac{0.6}{2} = 0.3$.

13. Answer: C
Explanation: By picking two points on the line, the constant of proportionality, or the slope, can be calculated as $\frac{3}{4}$.

14. Answer: D
Explanation: By picking two points on the line, the constant of proportionality, or the slope, can be calculated as $\frac{5}{2}$.

15. Answer: D
Explanation: Each set of ordered pairs represents 2 points on the line which can be used to create 2 similar triangles. To calculate the slope accurately, those points should always contain integer values for both x and y.

16. Answer: B
Explanation: Each set of ordered pairs represents 2 points on the line which can be used to create 2 similar triangles. To calculate the slope accurately, those points should always contain integer values for both x and y.

17. Answer: C
Explanation: The line passes through the origin, meaning it will take the form of $y = mx$. The slope of the line is $\frac{1}{4}$ and the y-intercept is $(0,0)$.

18. Answer: B
Explanation: The line passes through the origin, meaning it will take the form of $y = mx$. The slope of the line is $\frac{4}{5}$ and the y-intercept is $(0,0)$.

19. Answer: $y = \frac{7}{5}x$
Explanation: The line passes through the origin, meaning it will take the form of $y = mx$. From the origin, the rise is 7 and the run is 5. The slope of the line is $\frac{7}{5}$.

20. Answer: $y = \frac{2}{7}x$

Explanation: The line passes through the origin, meaning it will take the form of y=mx. From the origin, the rise is 2 and the run is 7. The slope of the line is $\frac{2}{7}$.

> ## 3.2 FINDING SLOPE AND GRAPH OF A SLOPE

1. Answer: C

Explanation: slope $= \frac{y}{x} = \frac{9}{4}$.

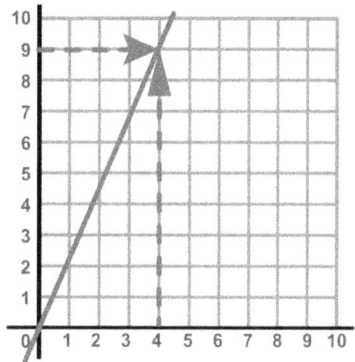

2. Answer: B

Explanation: slope $= \frac{y}{x} = \frac{-4}{3}$.

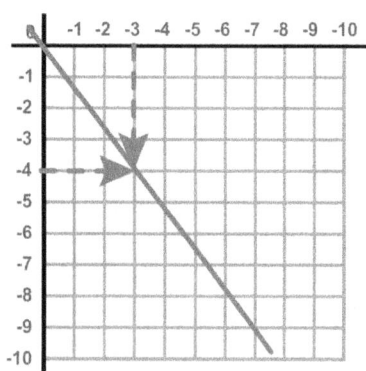

3. Answer:

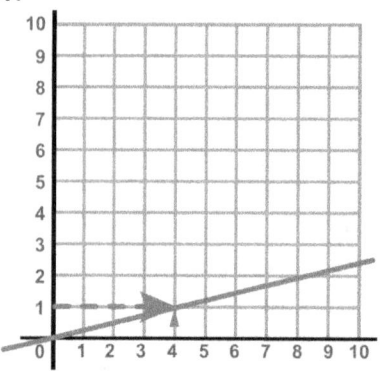

Explanation: Slope is $\frac{1}{4}$ means the rise of 1 unit and a run of 4 units.

4. Answer:

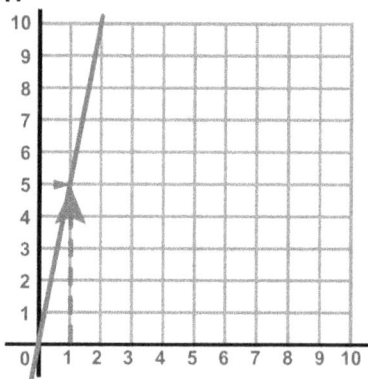

Explanation: Slope is 5 means rise of 5 unit and a run of 1 units.

5. Answer:

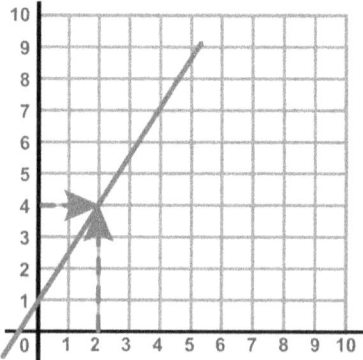

Explanation: The y-intercept of the line is 1 and the slope is $\frac{3}{2}$.
Slope is $\frac{3}{2}$ means rise of 3 units and a run of 2 units. So, mark a point at y = 1 and move up 3 units and right 1 units and mark the next point.

6. Answer:

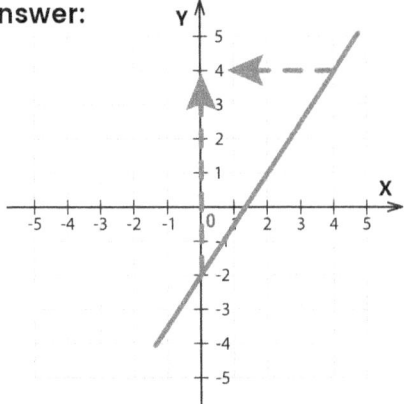

Explanation: Equation of the line: $y = \frac{5}{4}x - 2$
The y-intercept of the line is -2 and the slope is $\frac{5}{4}$. Slope is $\frac{5}{4}$ means rise of 5 units and a run of 4 units. So, mark a point at $y = -2$, and move up 5 units and right 4 units and mark the next point.

7. Answer: A
Explanation:
slope $= \frac{y_2-y_1}{x_2-x_1} = \frac{5-6}{3-5} = \frac{-1}{-2} = \frac{1}{2}$.

8. Answer: D
Explanation:
slope $= \frac{y_2-y_1}{x_2-x_1} = \frac{-6+3}{4-7} = \frac{-3}{-3} = 1$.

9. Answer: B
Explanation: $y = mx + b$
$y = 5 - 7x = -7x + 5$
$m = -7$
slope $= m = -7$.

10. Answer: C

Explanation: $y = mx + b$
$y = \frac{3x - 5}{6}$
$y = \frac{3}{6}x - \frac{5}{6}$
$y = \frac{1}{2}x - \frac{5}{6}$
$m = \frac{1}{2}$
slope $= m = \frac{1}{2}$.

11. Answer: B
Explanation: Find the slope of two points
$A(4,200)$, $B(8,280)$
Slope $= \frac{280-200}{8-4} = \frac{80}{4} = 20$.

12. Answer: A
Explanation:
Find the slope of $-4x + \frac{1}{2}y - 10 = 0$.
Adding 4x and 10 to both sides, we get
$\frac{1}{2}y = 4x + 10$
Multiplying both sides by 2
$y = 8x + 20$; Slope = 8
There are 8 chairs around a table.

13. Answer: D
Explanation: Find the slope of two points
$A(2,80)$, $B(5,155)$
Slope $= \frac{155-80}{5-2} = \frac{75}{3} = 25$.
Babysitter earns $ 25 per hour.

14. Answer: B
Explanation: Find the slope of two points
$A(2,17), B(7,47)$
Slope $= \frac{47-17}{7-2} = \frac{30}{5} = 6$.
There are 6 flowers in a bouquet.

15. Answer: The cost of a single ticket is $12.
Explanation: Find the slope of
$-4x + \frac{1}{3}y - 10 = 0$
Adding 4x and 10 to both sides, we get
$\frac{1}{3}y = 4x + 10$
Multiplying both sides by 3
$y = 12x + 30$
slope = 12
The cost of a single ticket is $12.

16. Answer: The taxi driver charges $8 per mile.
Explanation: Find the slope of $8x - y + 5 = 0$.
Subtracting 8x and 5 from both sides, we get
$-y = -8x - 5$
Multiplying both sides by -1
$y = 8x + 5$
slope = 8
The taxi driver charges $8 per mile.

17. Answer:

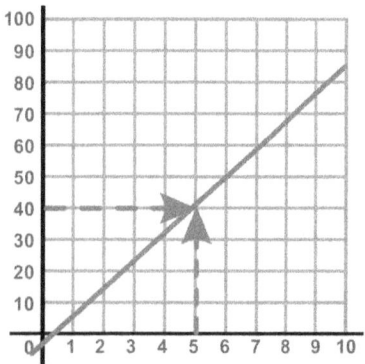

Explanation:
Slope is $\frac{40}{5}$ means rise of 40 units and a run of 5 units.
$m = \frac{\text{change of } y}{\text{change of } x} = \frac{40}{5}$.

18. Answer:

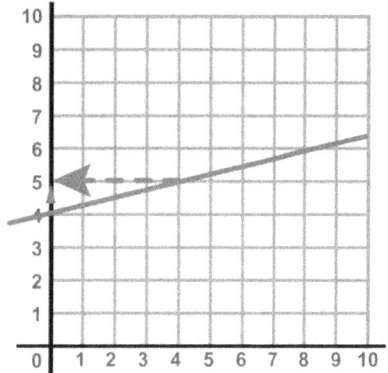

Explanation:
Equation of the line: $y = 0.25x + 4 = \frac{1}{4}x + 4$
The y-intercept of the line is 4 and the slope is $\frac{1}{4}$. Slope is $\frac{1}{4}$ means the rise of 1 unit and a run of 4 units. So, mark a point at $y = 4$, and move up 1 unit and right 4 units and mark the next point.

19. Answer: $-\frac{4}{3}$
Explanation: $\frac{x}{3} + \frac{y}{4} = -1$
Multiplying both sides by 12, we get
$4x + 3y = -12$
Subtracting 4x from both sides,
$3y = -4x - 12$
Dividing both sides by 4
$y = -\frac{4}{3}x - 4$
slope = $m = -\frac{4}{3}$.

20. Answer: $-\frac{1}{8}$
Explanation: $\frac{x}{4} + 2y = -5$
Subtracting $\frac{1}{4}x$ from both sides, we get
$2y = -\frac{1}{4}x - 5$
Dividing both sides by 2
$y = -\frac{1}{8}x - \frac{5}{2}$.
Slope $m = -\frac{1}{8}$.

3.3 SOLVE TWO-STEP AND MULTI-STEP EQUATIONS

1. Answer: B
Explanation: To solve $k + 8 = 18$, subtract 8 from both sides resulting in $k = 10$.

2. Answer: B
Explanation: When working in inverse order of operations, add and subtract before multiplying and dividing.

3. Answer: B
Explanation: To solve for n, first subtract 8 from both sides. Then divide each side by 3. The result is $n = -6$.

4. Answer: A
Explanation: The first step to solve an equation, is to simplify by combining like terms

5. Answer: D
Explanation: $\frac{7x+2}{2} = 9$

Multiplying 2 on both sides → 7x + 2 = 18

Subtract 2 on both sides → 7x = 16

Divide 7 on both sides → x = $\frac{16}{7}$.

6. Answer: B
Explanation: First, distribute 8 to the terms in the parentheses on the left side of the equation. the new equation is
20u + 8u - 48 = 32 . Next, combine like terms on the left side to get the following equation:
28u - 48 = 32. Now, add 48 to both sides. Lastly, divide both sides by 28 giving m = $\frac{80}{28} = \frac{40}{14} = \frac{20}{7}$.

7. Answer: C
Explanation: 4x - 2 = 10
Adding 2 to both sides: 4x = 10 + 2
4x = 12
Dividing both sides by 4
x = 3.

8. Answer: D
Explanation:
Add the like terms. 2x - 2 = 2x + 2
This equation is false for any value of x. Therefore, it has no solution.

9. Answer: Five pizzas are ordered
Explanation: 9x + 3 = 48
Subtracting 3 from both sides 9x = 48 - 3
9x = 45
Dividing both sides by 9
→ x=5.

10. Answer: D
Explanation: 8x + 3x - 6 = 5 + 11x - 11
We move all the variables to LHS and numbers to RHS and their signs are reversed
8x + 3x - 11x = 5 - 11 + 6
Adding the like terms
0x = 0
This equation is true for any value of x. Therefore, it has infinitely many solutions.

11. Answer: A
Explanation:

-8 - 4(x-1) = 4x + 12 → -8 - 4x + 4 = 4x + 12
We move all the variables to LHS and numbers to RHS and their signs are reversed
-4x - 4x = 12 + 8 - 4

Adding the like terms -8x = 16 → x = -2,This equation has exactly one solution.

12. Answer: C
Explanation: -5x + 8 - 3x = 3 - 8x - 11
We move all the variables to LHS and numbers to RHS and their signs are reversed
-5x - 3x + 8x = 3 - 11 - 8
Adding the like terms 0x = -16
This equation is false for any value of x . Therefore, it has no solution.

13. Answer: Eleven pencils are ordered
Explanation: x + 4 = 15
Subtract 4 from both sides: x = 15 - 4
x = 11.

14. Answer: D
Explanation: cx + 8 - 4x = 6 - 8x
We move all the variables to LHS and numbers to RHS and their signs are reversed
cx - 4x + 8x = 6 - 8
Factoring out x from all terms in LHS
x(c - 4 + 8) = -2
Since the given equation has no solutions
c - 4 + 8 = 0
c = 4 - 8
c = -4.

15. Answer: Six packs of chewing gums are ordered
Explanation: 6x + 5 = 41
Subtracting 5 from both sides
6x = 41 - 5
6x = 36
Dividing both sides by 6
x = 6.

16. Answer: Four hours elapsed
Explanation: $52 - 11x = 8$
Subtract 52 from both sides: $-11x = 8 - 52$
$-11x = -44$
Dividing both sides by -11
$x = 4$.

17. Answer: $x = 14/11$
Explanation: $6x - 4(3 - 5x) - 2 = 8 + 2(2x + 3)$
$6x - 12 + 20x - 2 = 8 + 4x + 6$
We move all the variables to LHS and numbers to RHS and their signs are reversed
$6x + 20x - 4x = 8 + 6 + 12 + 2$
Adding the like terms $22x = 28$
Dividing both sides by 22
$x = \frac{28}{22} = \frac{14}{11}$.

18. Answer: $x = 16$
Explanation: $(3 - 2x) - 4(x + 1) = -4x - 3(x-5)$
$3 - 2x - 4x - 4 = -4x - 3x + 15$
We move all the variables to LHS and numbers to RHS and their signs are reversed.
$-2x - 4x + 4x + 3x = 15 - 3 + 4$
Add the like terms: $x = 16$.

19. Answer: Fourteen donuts are ordered
Explanation: $2x + 4 = 32$
Divide 2 on both sides
$x + 2 = 16$
Subtract 2 on both sides: $x = 14$.

20. Answer: Nine hours elapsed
Explanation: $65 - 7x = 2$
Subtract 65 from both sides: $-7x = 2 - 65$
$-7x = -63$
Divide both sides by -7:
$x = 9$.

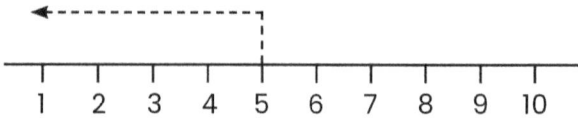

1. Answer:

Explanation: $15 \geq 3x$
$5 \geq x$ or $x \leq 5$.

2. Answer: B
Explanation: $8 + 6x > 4x - 8$
$6x - 4x > -8 - 8$
$-2x > -16$
Dividing both sides by -2 changes the sign of the inequality $x < 8$.

3. Answer: Sara can order at most 7 cakes
Explanation: $7x + 2 \leq 51$
Subtract 2 on both sides $\rightarrow 7x \leq 49$
Divide 7 on Both sides $\rightarrow x \leq 7$.

4. Answer: C
Explanation: $x + 5 \geq 9$,
Subtract 5 on both sides $\rightarrow x \geq 9 - 5 = 4$
$\rightarrow x \geq 4$.

5. Answer: A
Explanation: $3x + 2 \leq 32$.
Subtract 2 on both sides $\rightarrow 3x \leq 30$
Divide 3 on Both sides $\rightarrow x \leq 10$.

6. Answer: A
Explanation: $26 - 4x > 2$
Subtract 26 on both sides $\rightarrow -4x > 2 - 26 = -24$
Dividing both sides by -4 changes the sign of the inequality $x < 6$.

7. Answer: D
Explanation: $49 - 5x < 9$
Subtract 49 on both sides $\rightarrow -5x < 9 - 49 = -40$
Dividing both sides by -5 changes the sign of the inequality $x > 8$.

8. Answer:

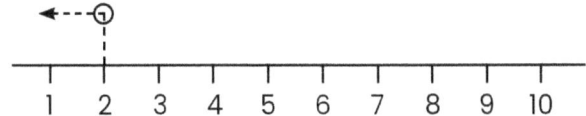

Explanation: 6 – 3x > 3x – 8 + x

Solve for x

–3x – 3x – x > –8 – 6

–7x > –14

Dividing both sides by –7 changes the sign of the inequality. x < 2 .

9. Answer:

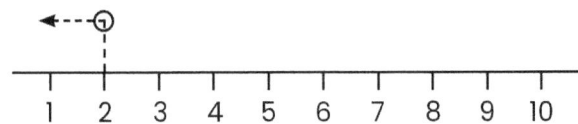

Explanation: 6 – 3x > 4x – 12 + 2x

Solve for x.

–3x – 4x – 2x > –12 – 6

–9x > –18

Dividing both sides by –9 changes the sign of the inequality. x < 2.

10. Answer:

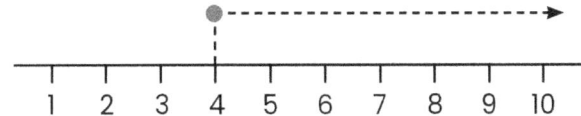

Explanation: 7x – 3 – 8x + 1 ≥ 8 – 3x + 6 – 2x

7x – 8x + 3x + 2x ≥ 8 + 6 + 3 – 1

4x ≥ 16

x ≥ 4.

11. Answer:

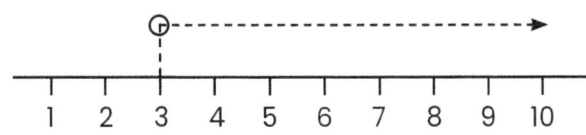

Explanation: 5 < 6x – 13

Solve for x

5 + 13 < 6x

18 < 6x

3 < x or x > 3.

12. Answer: Less than 7

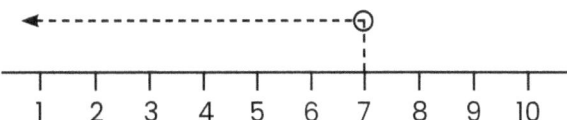

Explanation: 61 – 8x > 5

Subtract 61 on both sides → –8x > 5 – 61 = –56

Dividing both sides by –8 changes the sign of the inequality. x<7.

13. Answer: Nancy ordered at least 4 packs of Soda.

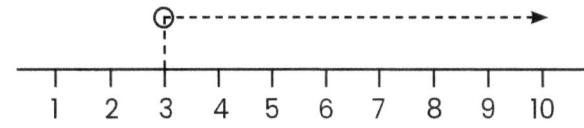

Explanation: 9x + 6 > 42

Subtract 6 on both sides → 9x > 42 – 6 = 36

Dividing both sides by 9 changes the sign of the inequality x > 4.

14. Answer: Nancy ordered at least 6 breads.

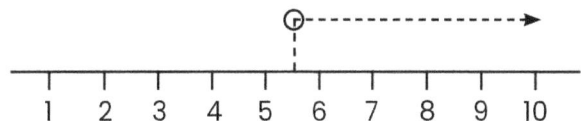

Explanation: 3x + 1 > 18

3x > 17

x > 5.7 Nancy ordered at least 6 breads.

15. Answer: Less than or equal to 5

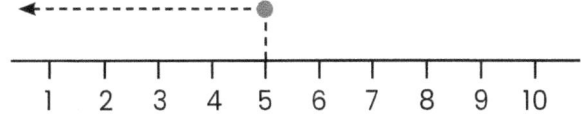

Explanation: 7 – x ≥ 2

→ –x ≥ 2 – 7

→ –x ≥ – 5

→ x ≤ 5 .

16. Answer: A
Explanation: $-4 + 3x > 4x - 8$
$3x - 4x > -8 + 4$
$-x > -4$
Dividing both sides by -1 changes the sign of the inequality $x < 4$.

17. Answer: B
Explanation: $2x + 14 > 7x - 6$
$2x - 7x > -14 - 6$
$-5x > -20$
Dividing both sides by -5 changes the sign of inequality $x < 4$.

18. Answer: C
Explanation: $3x - 9 < -4x + 5$
$3x + 4x < 5 + 9$
$7x < 14$
$x < 2$.

19. Answer: B
Explanation: $20 - 7x \geq 5 - 2x$
$-7x + 2x \geq 5 - 20$
$-5x \geq -15$
Dividing both sides by -5 changes the sign of inequality $x \leq 3$.

20. Answer: C
Explanation: $1 - 8x > -7$
$-8x > -8$
Dividing both sides by -8 changes the sign of the inequality $x < 1$.

3.5 SOLVE A SYSTEM OF EQUATIONS

1. Answer: B
Explanation: A system of equations can have one solution if the lines intersect, no solution if the lines are parallel, or infinite solutions if the lines are one and the same, but the system cannot have two solutions.

2. Answer: C
Explanation: The solution to a system of equations is usually represented by an ordered pair.

3. Answer: C
Explanation: When graphing two equations, the point at which the graphs intersect is the solution to both equations. The values satisfy both equations.

4. Answer: D
Explanation: The system has no solution because, when graphed, parallel lines do not intersect because there is no solution that makes both equations true.

5. Answer: D
Explanation: When solving by substitution, first isolate one variable in one equation. Then, substitute the expression in that equation into the other equation for that variable to get an equation with one variable. Solve to find the solution.

6. Answer: A
Explanation: Since the two lines intersect the number of solutions is: 1

7. Answer: A
Explanation: Since the two lines parallel the number of solutions is: 0

8. Answer: D
Explanation: Since the two lines Coincide the number of solutions is: ∞.

9. Answer: B
Explanation: Since the line p is parallel to the line n it forms a system of equations with no solution to line n.

10. Answer: A
Explanation: Since the two lines intersect at a point the point of intersection is the moment where the profits are equal.

11. Answer: B
Explanation: Since the two lines are parallel there is not a moment when the cars are at the same distance from the city.

12. Answer: B
Explanation: Since the two lines coincide the heights of kites are the same everywhere So, there is not a moment when their heights are different.

13. Answer: C
Explanation: If x is the number of nights, then both Ava and Merlin's total pages can be represented by y as it is dependent on x. For Ava, the total pages are $y = 4x + 24$ and for Merlin, the total pages are $y = 5x + 9$.

14. Answer: A
Explanation: The solution to the system of equations is the point of intersection for these two equations: $(-2,2)$.

15. Answer: C
Explanation: The solution to the system of equations is the point of intersection for these two equations: $(4,-3)$.

16. Answer: D
Explanation: The solution to the system of equations is the point of intersection for these two equations: $(-2,-1)$.

17. Answer: x = 20, y = 4
Explanation: Let x & y represent the two numbers. According to the problem statement, the first and second equations are
$x + y = 24$
$x - y = 16$
Eliminate y. Add both equations.
$2x = 40 \Rightarrow x = 20$
Solve for y
$20 + y = 24 \quad y = 4$
$x = 20, y = 4$.

18. Answer: x = 2, y = 5
Explanation: Let x represent the base and y represent one of the lateral sides of the isosceles triangle. Then the perimeter is $x+2y$ and the difference of lateral side and base is $y-x$. Therefore, according to the problem statement, the first and second equations are $x + 2y = 12$
$y - x = 3$
Eliminate x: Add both equations,
$3y = 15 \Rightarrow y = 5$
Solve for x
$5 - x = 3 \Rightarrow x = 2$
$x = 2, y = 5$.

19. Answer: x = 36, y = 18
Explanation: $x = 2y$
$x - y = 18$
Substitute for $x = 2y$ in the second equation.
$2y - y = 18$
Solve for y
$y = 18$
Solve for x
$x = 2 \times 18 = 36$
$x = 36, y = 18$.

20. Answer: x = 44, y = 22
Explanation: Let x & y represent the two numbers. According to problem statement, the first and second equations are
$x + y = 3(x-y) \Rightarrow x = 2y \Rightarrow x - 2y = 0$
$x - y = 22$
Eliminate x.
Multiply the second equation by -1
$x - 2y = 0$
$-x + y = -22$
Adding both equations,
$-y = -22 \Rightarrow y = 22$
Solve for x
$x - 2(22) = 0 \Rightarrow x = 44$
$x = 44, y = 22$.

ANSWERS AND EXPLANATIONS

1. Answer: C
Explanation:
The rise over run in this graph is $\frac{20}{4}$ or 5.

2. Answer: B
Explanation: The relation in the table can be represented by the equation $y = 6x$. The only choice with a higher slope than 6 is B

3. Answer: A
Explanation: The line passes through $(0, -8)$, which means in the form $y = mx + b$, the slope of the line is -1 and the y-intercept is -8.

4. Answer: D
Explanation: To remove the fractions, multiply each term by 4, the least common denominator of the fractions.
The result is $1 + 2y = 12$.

5. Answer: D
Explanation: To remove the decimals, multiply each term by 10, which results in $56 = 23y - 68$.

6. Answer: B
Explanation: Evan's amount is represented by the expression $2w + 8$. Emma's amount is represented by the expression $w + 12$. Set the expressions equal to each other and solve for w.

7. Answer: at least 52 jobs to break even
Explanation: Using the variable u to represent each job, solve the equation: $10u + 1.50u = 600$. Solving for u, gives 52.17, so they must do at least 52 jobs to break even.

8. Answer: B
Explanation: Substitute the values of x and y in the first equation.
$2 + 2 = 4$
$4 = 4$
Substitute the values of x and y in the second equation.
$2 - 2 = -4$
$0 = -4$
The ordered pair $(2,2)$ does not satisfy the second equation. Therefore, the ordered pair is not a solution of the system of equations.

9. Answer: A
Explanation: According to the problem statement, the system of equations are shown below.
$x + y = 8$
$x - y = 4$
Check:
$x = 6, y = 2$
$6 + 2 = 8$
$6 - 2 = 4$
The ordered pair $(6,2)$ satisfies both equations. Therefore, it is a solution.

10. Answer: B
Explanation: According to the problem statement, the system of equations is shown below.
$x + y = 24$
$x - y = 14$
$x = 18, y = 6$
Check:
$18 + 6 = 24$
$18 - 6 \neq 14$
The ordered pair $(18,6)$ doesn't satisfy both equations. Therefore, it is not a solution.

11. Answer: B
Explanation: When extended both the graphs meet at a point.
So, there is 1 solution for the system of equations.

12. Answer:

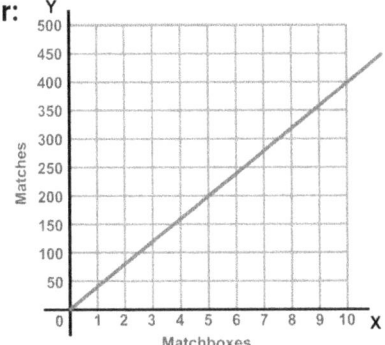

Explanation: $y = 50x = \frac{50}{1} x = \frac{250}{5} x$.

13. Answer: 8 scissors are ordered
Explanation: $8x + 3 = 67$
Subtracting 3 from both sides,
$8x = 67 - 3$
$8x = 64$
Dividing both sides by 8,
$x=8$
So, 8 scissors are ordered.

14. Answer: A
Explanation: The answer is $\frac{x}{2} - \frac{y}{4} = 1$.
Multiply both sides by 4,
$2x - y = 4$
Subtracting 2x from both sides,
$-y = -2x + 4$
Dividing both sides by -1,
$y = 2x - 4$

15. Answer: 7
Explanation: $3x + 8 = 29$
Subtracting 8 from both sides,
$3x = 29 - 8$
$3x = 21$
Dividing both sides by 3, $\rightarrow x = 7$.

16. Answer: C
Explanation: $4x - 9x = 4 - 5x + 13$
We move all variables to LHS and numbers to RHS and their signs are reversed.
$-5x + 5x = 4 + 13$
Adding the like terms, $0x = 17$
This equation is false for any value of x, therefore it has no solutions.

17. Answer: x = 19 & y = 13
Explanation: $2(x+y) = 64$
$x - y = 6$
Dividing both sides of first equation by 2,
$x + y = 32$
$x - y = 6$
Adding above two equations,
$2x = 38$
$x = 19$
Therefore,
$x - y = 6$
$19 - y = 6$
$y = 13$.

18. Answer: A
Explanation: Both the graphs meet at a point. So, both salaries are equal at a point.

19. Answer: A
Explanation: Plan A can be represented by the equation A = 30m + 35and Plan B can be represented by B = 19m + 50.

20. Answer: $\frac{12}{3} = \frac{4}{1}$
Explanation: The line passes through the origin, meaning it will take the form of $y = mx$. From the origin, the rise is 12 and the run is 3.The slope of the line is $\frac{12}{3} = \frac{4}{1}$.

4. TRANSFORMATIONS

4.1 ROTATIONS AND DILATIONS

1. Answer: A
Explanation: Point A' is the image of the point A under a rotation in the clockwise direction.

2. Answer: B
Explanation: Point A' is the image of the point A under a rotation about the point D in the count counterclockwise direction.

3. Answer: A
Explanation: Point A' is the image of the point A under a rotation about the point E in the clockwise direction.

4. Answer: B
Explanation: Point A' is the image of the point A under rotation in a Counterclockwise direction about the point C.

5. Answer: D
Explanation: Quadrilateral A'B'C'D is the image of quadrilateral ABCD when rotated about the point D. So, point D is the center of rotation.

6. Answer: C
Explanation: Quadrilateral A'B'CD' is the image of the quadrilateral ABCD when rotated about point C. So, point C is the center of rotation.

7. Answer: B
Explanation: Line segment A'B' is obtained by rotating line segment AB about the point C. So, the transformation is a rotation.

8. Answer: A
Explanation: A line segment A'B' is a reduction of the line segment AB about the point D. So, the transformation is a dilation

9. Answer: B
Explanation: Here, △ A'B'C' is an enlargement of △ ABC about the center of dilation D. Dilation takes place in the opposite direction of the center of dilation D.
So, the scale factor of a dilation is negative.

10. Answer: A
Explanation: Here, △ A'B'C' is the image of △ ABC about the center of dilation D. Note that the image points are in the same direction as the center of dilation D.
So, the scale factor of a dilation is positive.

11. Answer: A
Explanation: From East Parker turns 90°clockwise towards the South.

12. Answer: D
Explanation: The angle around a point is 360° So, the angle of rotation is 360°.

13. Answer: C
Explanation: $\frac{3}{4}$ of a full turn $= \frac{3}{4} \times 360° = 270°$
So, the angle of rotation is 270°.

14. Answer: D
Explanation: When the arm of the clock moves from 12 to 4, it is 20 minutes.
20 minutes $= \frac{1}{3}(60 \text{ min}) = \frac{1}{3}(1 \text{ full rotation}) = \frac{1}{3}(360°) = 120°$.
So, the angle of rotation is 120°.

15. Answer: Sun
Explanation: Mercury, Venus, and Earth orbits around the Sun.
So, the Sun is the center of rotation.

16. Answer: A
Explanation: $\frac{1}{5}$ of a full turn $= \frac{1}{5}(360°) = 72°$
So, the angle of rotation is 72°.

17. Answer: 400,000
Explanation: 1 km = 100,000 cm
4 km = 400,000 cm
So, 1 centimeter on a map represents an actual distance of 4 km (=400,000 cm)
Scale factor = $\frac{400,000}{}$ =400,000 .

18. Answer: B
Explanation: 1 ft = 12 inches
3 ft = 3×12 inches = 36 inches
1 inch of the width of the model of a swimming pool represents an actual width of 3 ft (=36 inches) Scale factor = $\frac{36}{1}$ = 36.

19. Answer: 22
Explanation: 1 m = 100 cm
5.5 m = 5.5×100 cm = 550 cm
25 centimeters represents 5.5 meters (=550 cm) Scale factor = $\frac{550}{25}$ = 22.

20. Answer: 18 feet
Explanation: 1 yard = 3 feet
6 yards = 6×3 feet = 18 feet
1 foot of the length of the model of a courtyard represents an actual length of 3 yards(=18 feet)Scale factor = $\frac{18}{1}$ = 18.

> **4.2 REFLECTIONS AND TRANSLATIONS**

1. Answer: B
Explanation: In a given diagram, every point in the translation is moved the same distance and in the same direction.

2. Answer: A
Explanation: In a given diagram, every pair of the corresponding points in the reflection is the same distance from the mirror line.

3. Answer:A
Explanation: In a given diagram, every pair of the corresponding points in the reflection is the same distance from the mirror line.

4. Answer: B
Explanation: In a given diagram, every point in the translation is moved the same distance and in the same direction.

5. Answer:A
Explanation: In a given diagram, every pair of the corresponding points in the reflection is the same distance from the mirror line.

6. Answer: B
Explanation: In a given diagram, every point in the translation is moved the same distance and in the same direction.

7. Answer: B
Explanation: In a given diagram, every point in the translation is moved the same distance and in the same direction.

8. Answer:A
Explanation: In a given diagram, every pair of the corresponding points in the reflection is the same distance from the mirror line.

9.Answer: B
Explanation: The given statement doesn't represent Translation.

10. Answer: A
Explanation: The given statement represents Translation.

11.Answer: A
Explanation: The given statement represents Translation.

12.Answer: B
Explanation: The given statement doesn't represent Translation.

13.Answer: B
Explanation: The elevator moved the same distance and in the same direction.

14.Answer: A
Explanation: Noah is looking at the surface of the water pot, which is the same distance from the mirror line.

15.Answer: B
Explanation: The ball dropped from the hand moved the same distance and in the same direction.

16.Answer: A
Explanation:

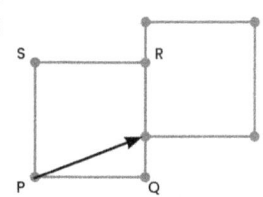

17.Answer: A
Explanation:

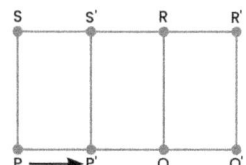

18.Answer: D
Explanation:

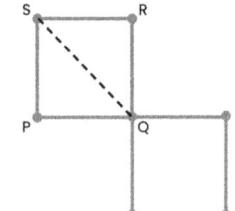

19.Answer: 10
Explanation:

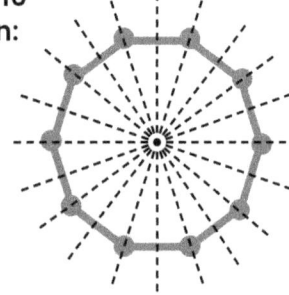

20.Answer: 8
Explanation:

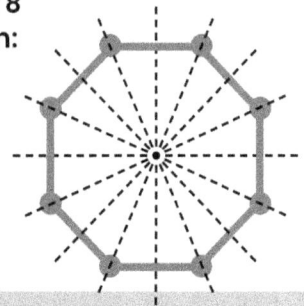

4.3 SIMILAR FIGURES AND CONGRUENT FIGURES

1.Answer: B
Explanation:

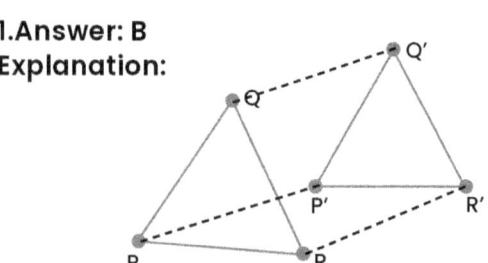

The transformation that exhibits congruence between the two triangles is translation.

2.Answer: C
Explanation:

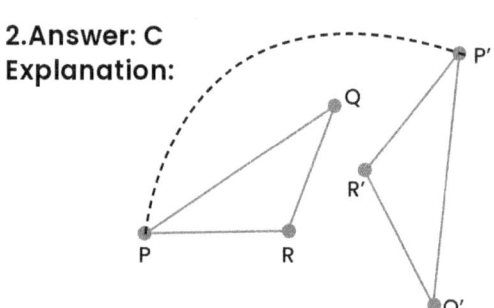

The transformation that exhibits congruence between the two triangles is rotation.

3.Answer: A
Explanation: The transformation that exhibits congruence between the two hexagons is reflection.

4.Answer: D
Explanation:

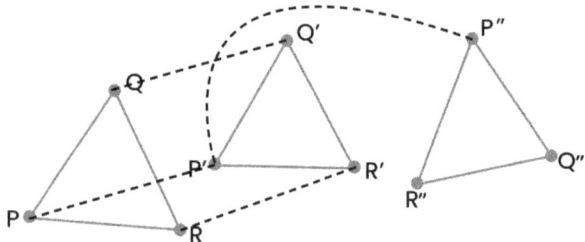

The transformation exhibited here is the translation and then rotation.

5.Answer: A
Explanation:

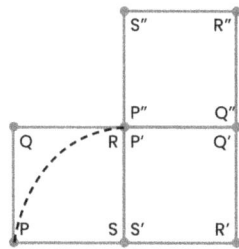

Congruence between PQRS and P'Q'R'S' is by rotation.
Congruence between P'Q'R'S' and P''Q''R''S'' is by reflection.
Congruence between PQRS and P''Q''R''S'' is by rotation and reflection.

6.Answer: A
Explanation: Vector of translation moves point A 3 units right and 2 units up
$A(-3,-1) → A'(-3+3,-1+2) → A'(0,1)$

7.Answer: C
Explanation: Vector of translation moves point A 3 units left and 4 units up
$A(3,-2) → A'(3-3,-2+4) → A'(0,2)$

8. Answer: B
Explanation: Vector of translation moves point A 4 units right and 1 unit up.
$A(-3,2) → A'(-3+4,2+1) → A'(1,3)$

9. Answer: D
Explanation: Interchange the coordinates. A' is in the III quadrant, so both coordinates are negative. $A(3,-1) → AT(-1,3) → A'(-1,-3)$

10. Answer: A
Explanation: Interchange the coordinates. A' is in the I quadrant, so both coordinates are positive. $A(-3,3) → AT(3,-3) → A'(3,3)$

11.Answer: B
Explanation: Reflection around the x-axis changes the sign of the y-coordinate.
$A(-1,3) → A'(-1,-3)$.

12.Answer: C
Explanation: Reflection around the y-axis changes the sign of the x-coordinate.
$A(1,3) → A'(-1,3)$.

13.Answer: A
Explanation: $A(-2,-1) → x_1 = -2, y_1 = -1$
$B(1,-4) → x_2 = 1, y_2 = -4$
$x_2 - x_1 = 1-(-2) = 3 > 0 →$ translation 3 units right
$y_2-y_1 = -4-(-1) = -3 < 0$ translation 3 units down. Vector $\vec{AB}$ translates the marble 3 units right and 3 units down
$(4,2) → (4+3, 2-3) → (7,-1)$.

14.Answer: D
Explanation: The boat is in the I quadrant. Interchange the coordinates. After rotation the point is in the II quadrant, so the x-coordinate is negative and the y-coordinate is positive.
$(-5,-2) → (-2,-5) → (-2,5)$

15.Answer: B
Explanation: The point is in the II quadrant. Interchange the coordinates. After rotation the point is in the I quadrant, so both coordinates are positive.
$(-4,1) → (4,-1) → (4,1)$.

16.Answer: C
Explanation: $A(-2,-4) → x_1 = -2, y_1 =-4$
$B(-4,3) → x_2 = -4, y_2=3$
$x_2 - x_1 = -4 - (-2) = -2 < 0 →$ translation 3 units left
$y_2 - y_1 = 3 - (-4) = 7 > 0$ translation 7 units up
Vector $\vec{AB}$ translates the globe 2 units left and 7 units up
$(6,2) → (6-2, 2+7) → (4,9)$.

17.Answer: B
Explanation: The asteroid is in the IV quadrant. Interchange the coordinates. After rotation the asteroid is in the I quadrant, so both coordinates are positive
$(4,-1) → (-1,4) → (1,4)$.

18.Answer: D
Explanation: Reflection around the x-axis changes the sign of the y-coordinate $(-6,3) \rightarrow (-6,-3)$.

19.Answer: C
Explanation:

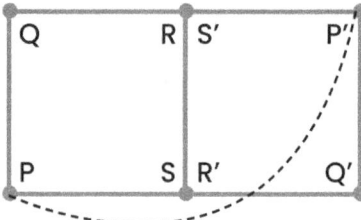

The transformation that exhibits the congruence between the two rectangles is rotation.

20.Answer: B
Explanation:

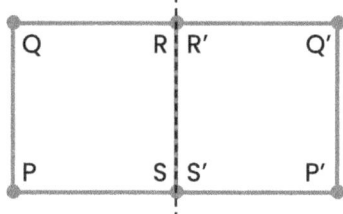

The transformation that exhibits the congruence between the two rectangles is Reflection.

4.4 CHAPTER REVIEW

1.Answer: C
Explanation: Figure A is translated along the x-axis in a positive direction, then translated along the y-axis in a negative direction, and then rotated clockwise.

2.Answer: B
Explanation: Note that Figure Q is a "flip" of Figure P. Thus, Figure P is reflected across the horizontal line, y = 6 to create Figure Q.

3.Answer: A
Explanation: Note from the graph that Triangle B is 6 units higher and 5 units to the right of Triangle A.

4.Answer: B
Explanation: The x-coordinates are the same, but the y-coordinates become opposites. Each angle should correspond as well: Angle P with Angle A, Angle B with Angle Q, Angle C with Angle R, and Angle D with Angle S.

5.Answer: (-2,-2), (-2,-5) and (-6-2)
Explanation: Rotating the shape 180 degrees about the origin transforms each vertex from (x, y) to $(-x, -y)$. Translating the shape 1 unit down will decrease the y-coordinate by 1.

6.Answer: (5,-1), (4,-4), (1,-4) and (2,-1)
Explanation: A reflection across the y-axis transforms each vertex from (x, y) to $(-x, y)$. The reflection across the x-axis translates each translated vertex from $(-x, y)$ to $(-x, -y)$.

7.Answer: A
Explanation: A translation slides a figure to a different location. Moving 3 units to the right, the x-coordinate increases by 3. The y-coordinate remains the same.

8.Answer: B
Explanation: A translation slides a figure to a different location. Moving 6 units to the right, the x-coordinate increases by 6. The y-coordinate remains the same.

9.Answer:D
Explanation: A translation slides a figure to a different location. Moving the point up 1 unit, adds 1 to the y-coordinate. The x-coordinate remains the same.

10.Answer: C
Explanation: A translation slides a figure to a different location. Moving 1 unit to the right, the x-coordinate increases by 1. The y-coordinate remains the same.

11. Answer: (-10,-5), (-8,-1) and (-6,-5)
Explanation: In the dilation, every coordinate of the original triangle is multiplied by the scale factor (2). Then, translating the shape up 1 units increase the y-coordinates by 1.

12. Answer: (-8,-32), (-32,-8) and (-48,-32)
Explanation: In the dilation, every coordinate of the original triangle is multiplied by the scale factor (4). Then, reflecting across the y-axis changes the sign of the x-coordinate.

13. Answer: (1, 1), (2, 1), (2, 0), (1, 0)
Explanation: In the dilation, every coordinate of the original quadrilateral has been multiplied by the scale factor $\frac{1}{3}$.

14. Answer: (-6,6), (-4,6), (-2,-4) and (-8,-4)
Explanation: In the dilation, every coordinate of the original triangle is multiplied by the scale factor (2).

15. Answer: D
Explanation: Figure P is rotated counter clockwise.

16. Answer: B
Explanation: A translation slides the figure to a different location; in this case up 2 units. The coordinates of Point S' coordinates are (3, 2).

17. Answer: B
Explanation: $\frac{3}{20}$ of a full turn $= \frac{3}{20} \times 360 = 54°$

18. Answer: (0,0), (1,3) and (5,0)
Explanation: Translation 4 units right and 1 unit up.

19. Answer: (-5,0), (-3,3) and (-1,2)
Explanation: Translation 4 units left and 1 unit up

20. Answer: (0,0), (-3,2) and (2,-5)
Explanation: Translation 2 units left and 4 unit down.

5. ANGLES & SIDES

5.1 MISSING ANGLES IN TRIANGLES AND EXTERIOR ANGLE THEOREM

1. Answer:
Explanation: $\beta = 3\alpha$

$\gamma = 3\beta = 9\alpha$

$\alpha + \beta + \gamma = 180°$

$\alpha + 3\alpha + 9\alpha = 180°$

$13\alpha = 180°$

$\alpha = \frac{180°}{13}$

$\beta = 3\alpha = 3 \times \frac{180°}{13} = \frac{540°}{13}$

$\gamma = 9\alpha = 9 \times \frac{180°}{13} = \frac{1620°}{13}$.

2. Answer: B
Explanation: $\beta = \alpha + 20°$

$\gamma = \beta + 20° = \alpha + 20° + 20° = \alpha + 40°$

$\alpha + \beta + \gamma = 180°$

$\alpha + \alpha + 20° + \alpha + 40° = 180°$

$3\alpha + 60° = 180°$

$3\alpha = 120°$

$\alpha = 40°$

$\beta = \alpha + 20° = 40° + 20° = 60°$

$\gamma = \alpha + 40° = 40° + 40° = 80°$.

3. Answer: A
Explanation: $\beta = \alpha - 20°$

$\gamma = \beta - 20° = \alpha - 20° - 20° = \alpha - 40°$

$\alpha + \beta + \gamma = 180°$

$\alpha + \alpha - 20° + \alpha - 40° = 180°$

$3\alpha - 60° = 180°$

$3\alpha = 240°$

$\alpha = 80°$

$\beta = \alpha - 20° = 80° - 20° = 60°$

$\gamma = \alpha - 20° = 80° - 40° = 40°$.

4. Answer: A
Explanation: $\alpha = \beta + \gamma$

$90° = \beta + \gamma \Rightarrow$ A right triangle a triangle is 180°

5. Answer: A-b, B-c, C-a
Explanation: The sum of the interior angles of a triangle is 180°.

6. Answer: A-c, B-a, C-b
Explanation: The sum of the interior angles of a triangle is 180°.

7. Answer: A-c, B-a, C-b
Explanation: The sum of the interior angles of a triangle is 180°.

8. Answer: A
Explanation: $\theta = 148° = 92° + 56°$.

9. Answer: C
Explanation: $\theta = 156° = 93° + 63°$.

10. Answer: B
Explanation: $\theta = 162° = 77° + 85°$.

11. Answer: D
Explanation: $\beta = \frac{\alpha + \gamma}{2} \Rightarrow \alpha + \gamma = 2\beta$
$\alpha + \beta + \gamma = 180°$
$\beta + 2\beta = 180°$
$3\beta = 180°$
$\beta = 60°$
$\alpha = 90°$
$\gamma = 180° - (\alpha + \beta) = 180° - (90° + 60°) = 180° - 150° = 30°$

12. Answer: B
Explanation: $\beta = \frac{\alpha + \gamma}{2} \Rightarrow \alpha + \gamma = 2\beta$
$\alpha + \beta + \gamma = 180°$
$\beta + 2\beta = 180°$
$3\beta = 180°$
$\beta = 60°$
$\alpha = 40°$
$\gamma = 180° - (\alpha + \beta) = 180° - (40° + 60°) = 180° - 100° = 80°$.

13. Answer: C
Explanation: $\beta = \alpha + \gamma$
$\alpha + \beta + \gamma = 180°$
$\beta + \beta = 180°$
$2\beta = 180°$
$\beta = 90°$
$\alpha = 55°$
$\gamma = 180° - (\alpha + \beta) = 180° - (55° + 90°) = 180° - 145° = 35°$.

14. Answer: A
Explanation: $\beta = \frac{\alpha + \gamma}{3} \Rightarrow \alpha + \gamma = 3\beta$
$\alpha + \gamma = 3\beta$
$\alpha + \beta + \gamma = 180°$
$\beta + 3\beta = 180°$
$4\beta = 180°$
$\beta = 45°$
$\alpha = 85°$
$\gamma = 180° - (\alpha + \beta) = 180 - (85° + 45°) = 180° - 130° = 50°$.

15. Answer: D
Explanation: $\beta = \frac{\alpha + \gamma}{4} \Rightarrow \alpha + \gamma = 4\beta$
$\alpha + \beta + \gamma = 180°$
$\beta + 4\beta = 180°$
$5\beta = 180°$
$\beta = 36°$
$\alpha = 110°$
$\gamma = 180° - (\alpha + \beta) = 180° - (110° + 36°) = 180° - 146° = 34°$.

16. Answer: A
Explanation: $\alpha_1 = \beta + \gamma$
$\alpha_1 = 3\beta$
$3\beta = \beta + \gamma$
$2\beta = \gamma$
The greatest interior angle is α or γ
$\gamma = 90° \Rightarrow \beta = 45° \Rightarrow \alpha = 45°$
$\alpha = 90° \Rightarrow \alpha_1 = 90° \Rightarrow \beta = \frac{90°}{3} = 30° \Rightarrow \gamma = 30°$

17. Answer: D
Explanation: $\alpha_1 = \beta + \gamma$
$\alpha_1 = 4\beta$
$4\beta = \beta + \gamma$
$3\beta = \gamma$
The smallest interior angle is α or β
$\beta = 40° \Rightarrow \gamma = 120° \Rightarrow \alpha = 60°$
$\alpha = 40° \Rightarrow \alpha_1 = 140° \Rightarrow \beta = \frac{140°}{4} = 35 \Rightarrow \gamma = 105°$.

18. Answer: C

Explanation: $\frac{x^\circ}{3} + x^\circ + 10^\circ + 2x^\circ - 10^\circ = 180^\circ$

$(\frac{x^\circ}{3} + x^\circ + 2x^\circ = 180^\circ) \times 3$

$x^\circ + 3x^\circ + 6x^\circ = 540^\circ$

$10x^\circ = 540^\circ$

$x^\circ = 54^\circ$.

19. Answer: C

Explanation: $x^\circ + 3x^\circ + 20^\circ + 2x^\circ - 20^\circ = 180^\circ$

$x^\circ + 3x^\circ + 2x^\circ = 180^\circ$

$6x^\circ = 180^\circ$

$x^\circ = 30^\circ$.

20. Answer: A

Explanation:

$x^\circ + 40^\circ + x^\circ - 20^\circ + x^\circ - 20^\circ = 360^\circ$

$x^\circ + x^\circ + x^\circ = 360^\circ$

$3x^\circ = 360^\circ$

$x^\circ = 120^\circ$.

5.2 ANGLES FORMED BY A TRANSVERSAL

---

1. Answer: C

Explanation: Transversals cut parallel lines and form angles in the diagram. From the given diagram, angles add up to
$180 \Rightarrow \alpha + \beta = 180^\circ$

2. Answer: C

Explanation: Transversals cut parallel lines and form angles in the diagram. From the given diagram, angles add up to
$180 \Rightarrow \alpha + \beta = 180^\circ$

3. Answer: B

Explanation: In the given diagram, the pair of angles α and β that are formed on the outer side of the parallel lines are on the opposite side of the transversal.

4. Answer: D

Explanation: Corresponding angles are equal
$\Rightarrow \alpha = \beta$

5. Answer: A

Explanation: From the given diagram, the angles α and β are formed inside the two parallel lines are equal to their alternate pairs.

6. Answer: A

Explanation: Corresponding angles are equal (62).

7. Answer: C

Explanation: Consecutive interior angles add up to 180°.
$\Rightarrow 180^\circ - 38^\circ = 142^\circ$.

8. Answer:

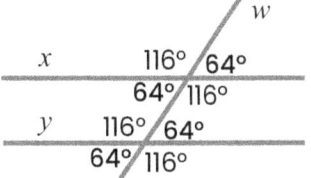

Explanation: In the given figures, transversal w cuts parallel lines x and y.

9. Answer: A

Explanation: Alternate exterior angles are equal – lines are parallel.

10. Answer: B

Explanation: Corresponding angles are not equal – lines are not parallel.

11. Answer: A

Explanation: Consecutive interior angles add up to 180° – lines are parallel.

12. Answer: 82°

Explanation: Alternate exterior angles are equal.

13. Answer: 128°

Explanation: Corresponding angles are equal.

14. Answer: 118°
Explanation: Interior angle = 62°
Supplementary exterior angle =
180° − 62° = 118°
Alternate exterior angles are equal.
Alternate exterior angle = 118°.

15. Answer: A
Explanation: $\alpha + \beta = 180°$
$\alpha - \beta = 64°$
$2\alpha = 244°$
$\alpha = 122°$
$\beta = 180° - \alpha = 180° - 122° = 58°$.

16. Answer: D
Explanation: $\alpha + \beta = 180°$
$\alpha - \beta = 42°$
$2\alpha = 222°$
$\alpha = 111°$
$\beta = 180° - \alpha = 180° - 111° = 69°$.

17. Answer: B
Explanation: Consecutive interior angles do not add up to 180°− lines that are not parallel.

18. Answer: A
Explanation: Consecutive interior angles add up to 180° − lines that are parallel.

19. Answer: 95°
Explanation: $\alpha - 20° + \alpha + 10° = 180°$
$2\alpha - 10° = 180°$
$2\alpha = 190°$
$\alpha = 95°$.

20. Answer: 22°
Explanation: $2\alpha + 20° = 64°$
$2\alpha = 44°$;
$\alpha = 22°$.

5.3 PYTHAGOREAN THEOREM

1. Answer: A
Explanation: Using the converse of the Pythagorean theorem, the triangle is a right triangle because $a^2+b^2 = 6^2+8^2 = 36+64 = 100 = 10^2 = c^2$.

2. Answer: B
Explanation: Using the converse of the Pythagorean theorem, the triangle is a right triangle because $a^2+b^2 = 2^2+3^2 = 4+9 = 13 < 4^2 = c^2$.

3. Answer: C
Explanation: Using the converse of the Pythagorean theorem, the triangle is a right triangle because $a^2+b^2 = 3^2+4^2 = 9+16 = 25^2 = c^2$.

4. Answer: B
Explanation: Using the converse of the Pythagorean theorem, the triangle is a right triangle because $a^2+b^2 = 2^2+5^2 = 4+25 = 29 < 6^2 = c^2$.

5. Answer: A
Explanation: Using the converse of the Pythagorean theorem, the triangle is a right triangle because $a^2+b^2 = 4^2+6^2 = 16+36 = 52 > 6.5^2 = c^2$.

6. Answer: D
Explanation: Use the equation $a^2+b^2 = c^2$ to find the hypotenuse: $5^2+6^2 = \sqrt{61}^2$

7. Answer: B
Explanation: Use the equation $a^2+b^2 = c^2$ to find the hypotenuse: $9^2+10^2 = \sqrt{181}^2$

8. Answer: A
Explanation: Use the equation $a^2+b^2 = c^2$ to find the hypotenuse: $11^2+12^2=\sqrt{265}^2$

9. Answer: B
Explanation: Use the equation $a^2+b^2 = c^2$ to find the hypotenuse: $8^2+10^2 = \sqrt{164}^2$

10. Answer: B
Explanation: Using the converse of the Pythagorean theorem, the triangle isn't a right triangle because
$a^2+b^2 \neq c^2 \Rightarrow 10^2+11^2 \neq 15^2$.

11. Answer: A
Explanation: Using the converse of the Pythagorean theorem, the triangle is a right triangle because
$a^2+b^2 = c^2 \Rightarrow 8^2+15^2 = 17^2$.

12. Answer: B
Explanation: Using the converse of the Pythagorean theorem, the triangle isn't a right triangle because
$a^2+b^2 \neq c^2 \Rightarrow 7^2+9^2 = 11^2$.

13. Answer: C
Explanation: To find the length of one of the legs, use the modified Pythagorean theorem equation $c^2-b^2 = a^2$; $10^2-6^2 = 8^2$.

14. Answer: D
Explanation: To find the length of one of the legs, use the modified Pythagorean theorem equation $c^2-b^2 = a^2$;$15^2 - 12^2 = 9^2$.

15. Answer: B
Explanation: To find the length of one of the legs, use the modified Pythagorean theorem equation $c^2-b^2 = a^2$; $20^2 - 16^2 = 12^2$.

16. Answer: 29 km
Explanation: To find the hypotenuse, use the Pythagorean theorem equation
$a^2+b^2 = c^2$; $20^2+21^2 = 29^2$.

17.Answer: 13 mi
Explanation: To find the hypotenuse, use the Pythagorean theorem equation
$a^2+b^2 = c^2$; $5^2+12^2 = 13^2$.

18.Answer: $\sqrt{113}^2$
Explanation: To find the hypotenuse, use the Pythagorean theorem equation
$a^2+b^2 = c^2$; $7^2+8^2 = \sqrt{113}^2$.

19. Answer: C
Explanation: Given two points on a coordinate system, imagine a right triangle and calculate the distance using the Pythagorean Theorem.

20. Answer: A
Explanation: Given two points on a coordinate system, imagine a right triangle and calculate the distance using the Pythagorean Theorem.

5.4 CHAPTER REVIEW

1. Answer: B
Explanation: By the triangle sum theorem, the measures of the three angles add up to 180 degrees. The sum of the measures of the interior angles of a triangle is 180 degrees

2. Answer: D
Explanation: The Triangle Sum Theorem states that the interior angles of a triangle have a sum of 180 degrees. The diagram shows how 3 angles are combined to add up to 180 degrees.

3. Answer: A
Explanation: The triangle MNO and NPQ are similar triangles that share two congruent angles formed by the parallel horizontal lines. This makes the two triangles similar triangles using the AA Similarity rule.

4. Answer: 116 degrees
Explanation: Angle N is a vertical angle to Angle M. Angle A is supplementary to the 64 degree angle and has a measure of 116 degrees.

5. Answer: : Angle o = 92 degrees
Angle w = 88 degrees
Explanation: Angle o and Angle w are alternate interior angles, so they have the same measure. Angle o is the same side interior angle as Angle, w so they are supplementary, which means their measures have a sum of 180 degrees.

6. Answer: A
Explanation: Use the equation $a^2+b^2 = c^2$ to find the hypotenuse: $8^2+11^2 = \sqrt{185}^2$

7.Answer: B
Explanation: Use the equation $a^2+b^2 = c^2$ to find the hypotenuse: $7^2+24^2 = \sqrt{25}^2$

8. Answer: 36
Explanation: Use the Pythagorean theorem equation $a^2+b^2 = c^2$ to find the hypotenuse: $9^2+12^2 = \sqrt{152}$. Then, add the hypotenuse and the legs together, which is
$9 + 12 + 15 = 36$.

9. Answer: 24
Explanation: Use the Pythagorean theorem equation $a^2+b^2 = c^2$ to find the hypotenuse: $6^2+8^2 = \sqrt{10}^2$. Then, add the hypotenuse and the legs together, which is
$6 + 8 + 10 = 24$.

10. Answer: D
Explanation: Given two points on a coordinate system, imagine a right triangle and calculate the distance using the Pythagorean Theorem.

11. Answer: B
Explanation: Given two points on a coordinate system, imagine a right triangle and calculate the distance using the Pythagorean Theorem.

12. Answer: D
Explanation: Given two points on a coordinate system, imagine a right triangle and calculate the distance using the Pythagorean Theorem.

13. Answer: A
Explanation: Given two points on a coordinate system, imagine a right triangle and calculate the distance using the Pythagorean Theorem.

14. Answer: $\sqrt{101}$
Explanation: The distance formula is an algebraic expression used to determine the distance between two points with the coordinates $(x1, y1)$ and $(x2, y2)$.
$d = \sqrt{1^2+10^2} = \sqrt{101}$

15. Answer: 12
Explanation: The distance formula is an algebraic expression used to determine the distance between two points with the coordinates $(x1, y1)$ and $(x2, y2)$.
$d = \sqrt{0^2+12^2} = 12$

16. Answer: A
Explanation: $4^2+(x+2)^2 = (x+4)^2$
$16 + x^2 + 4x + 4 = x^2 + 8x + 16$
$4x = 4$
$x = 1$.

17. Answer: B
Explanation: $c = 20$

$c = 2a$
$a = \frac{c}{2} = \frac{20}{2} = 10$
$b = \frac{a+c}{2} = \frac{10+20}{2} = 15$
$a^2+b^2 = 10^2+15^2 = 100+225 = 325 < 20^2 = c^2$.

18.Answer: A
Explanation: Yes, these towns form an obtuse triangle on the map
$a^2 + b^2 < c^2$ – obtuse triangle
$4^2 + 7^2 = 16+49 = 65 < 9^2 = 81$.

19.Answer: D
Explanation: An exterior angle of a triangle cannot be less than its corresponding interior opposite angle.

20.Answer: 64°
Explanation: $\alpha+\beta+\gamma=180°$
$44° + 72° + \gamma =180°$
$116° + \gamma = 180°$
$\gamma = 180° - 116° = 64°$.

6. VOLUME OF 3D

6.1 VOLUME OF CYLINDERS

1. Answer: B
Explanation: The formula for the volume of a cylinder is r^2h.This formula translates to the area of the base times the height.

2. Answer:C
Explanation: Enter the given values into the formula for the volume of a cylinder: πr^2h
$V = r^2\pi h = 2^2\pi 6 = 4\times 6\pi = 24\pi$.

3. Answer: A
Explanation: Enter the given values into the formula for the volume of a cylinder: πr^2h
$V = r^2\pi h = 7^2 9 = 49\times 9\pi = 441\pi$.

4. Answer: D
Explanation: To find the height, use the modified for the volume of a cylinder: πr^2h
$h=\frac{V}{r^2\pi} = \frac{64\pi}{16\pi} =4$.

5. Answer: D
Explanation: To find the height, use the modified for the volume of a cylinder: πr^2h
$h =\frac{V}{r^2\pi}= \frac{150\pi}{16\pi}=6$.

6. Answer: 8
Explanation: To find the radius, use the modified for the volume of a cylinder: πr^2h
$r = \sqrt{\frac{V}{h\pi}} = \sqrt{\frac{384\pi}{6\pi}} = \sqrt{64} = 8$.

7. Answer: 6
Explanation: To find the radius, use the modified for the volume of a cylinder: πr^2h
$r = \sqrt{\frac{V}{h\pi}} = \sqrt{\frac{80\pi}{5\pi}} = \sqrt{36} = 6$.

8. Answer: A
Explanation: Sample response: r = 2, h = 3
$V = \pi r^2h = 12$
If r = 2, h = (3+3) i.e., if double the height
$V = \pi r^2h = 24\pi$
The volume increased by two times.

9. Answer: C
Explanation: Sample response: r = 2, h = 4
$V = \pi r^2h = 16$
If h = 4, r = 2×2 = 4 i.e., if double the height
$V = \pi r^2h = 64\pi$
The volume of a cylinder increases four times.

10. Answer: A
Explanation: Enter the given values into the formula for the volume of a cylinder: πr^2h
$V = r^2\pi h = 1^2\pi 5 = 5\pi \approx 15.7$.

11. Answer: C
Explanation: h = 4
$C = 8\pi$
$C = 2r\pi$
$r = \frac{C}{2\pi} = 4$
$V = r^2\pi h = 4^2\pi \times 4 = 64\pi \approx 201.07$.

12. Answer: D
Explanation: h=6
$B = 36\pi$
$B = r^2\pi$
$r = B = 36\pi = 36 = 6$
$V =r^2\pi h = 62\pi \times 6 = 216\pi \approx 678.6$.

13. Answer: B
Explanation: h=2
d = 14
d = 2r
$r = \frac{d}{2} = \frac{14}{2} =7$
$V =r^2\pi h = 72\pi \times 2 = 98\pi \approx 307.9$.

14. Answer: D
Explanation: h = 6
d = 20
d = 2r
$r = \frac{d}{2} = 10$
$V = r^2\pi h = 10^2\pi \times 6 = 600\pi \approx 1{,}885.$

15. Answer: C
Explanation: h=1
d = 8
d = 2r
$r = \frac{d}{2} = 4$
$V = r^2\pi h = 4^2\pi \times 1 = 16\pi \approx 50.3 \text{ in}^3.$

16. Answer: B
Explanation: Enter the given values into the formula for the volume of a cylinder: $\pi r^2 h$.

17. Answer: C
Explanation: Enter the given values into the formula for the volume of a cylinder: $\pi r^2 h$.

18. Answer: A
Explanation: Enter the given values into the formula for the volume of a cylinder: $\pi r^2 h$.

19. Answer: 251 m³
Explanation: Enter the given values into the formula for the volume of a cylinder: $\pi r^2 h$.

20. Answer: A
Explanation: The formula for the volume of a cylinder: $\pi r^2 h$.

6.2 VOLUME OF CONE

1. Answer: D
Explanation: The formula for the volume of a cone is $\frac{1}{3}\pi r^2 h$. This formula translates to one-third times the area of the base times the height.

2. Answer: A
Explanation: Enter the given values into the formula for the volume of a cone: $\frac{1}{3}\pi r^2 h$
$V = \frac{1}{3}\pi r^2 h = \frac{1}{3}3^2\pi6 = 6\times3\pi = 18\pi.$

3. Answer: C
Explanation: Enter the given values into the formula for the volume of a cone: $\frac{1}{3}\pi r^2 h$
$V = \frac{1}{3}\pi r^2 h = \frac{1}{3}9^2\pi5 = 135\pi.$

4. Answer: A
Explanation: To find the height, use the modified for the volume of a cone: $\frac{1}{3}\pi r^2 h$
$h = \frac{3V}{r^2\pi} = \frac{3\times18\pi}{9\pi} = 6.$

5. Answer: B
Explanation: To find the height, use the modified for the volume of a cone: $\frac{1}{3}\pi r^2 h$
$h = \frac{3V}{r^2\pi} = \frac{3\times20\pi}{4\pi} = 15.$

6. Answer: 9
Explanation: To find the radius, use the modified for the volume of a cone: $\frac{1}{3}\pi r^2 h$
$r = \sqrt{\frac{3V}{h\pi}} = \sqrt{\frac{3\times108\pi}{4\pi}} = \sqrt{81} = 9.$

7. Answer: 6
Explanation: To find the radius, use the modified for the volume of a cone: $\frac{1}{3}\pi r^2 h$
$r = \sqrt{\frac{3V}{h\pi}} = \sqrt{\frac{3\times96\pi}{8\pi}} = \sqrt{36} = 6.$

8. Answer: A
Explanation: Sample response: r = 2, h = 3
$V = \frac{1}{3}\pi r^2 h = 4\pi$
If r = 2, h = (3+3) i.e.., if double the height
$V = \frac{1}{3}\pi r^2 h = 8\pi$
The volume increased by two times.

9. Answer: C
Explanation: Sample response: r=2, h=3
$V = \frac{1}{3}\pi r^2 h = 4\pi$
If h = 3, r = 2×2 = 4 i.e.., if double the radius
$V = \frac{1}{3}\pi r^2 h = 16\pi$
The volume of a cone increased four times.

10. Answer: B
Explanation: Given: s=5, r=3
$s^2 = r^2 + h^2$
$h^2 = s^2 - r^2 = 25 - 9 = 16$
$h = 4$
$V = \frac{1}{3}\pi r^2 h = \frac{1}{3} 3^2 \pi 4 = 3 \times 4\pi = 12\pi.$

11. Answer: D
Explanation: Given: s=10, h=8
$s^2 = r^2 + h^2$
$r^2 = s^2 - h^2 = 100 - 64 = 36$
$r = 6$
$V = \frac{1}{3}\pi r^2 h = \frac{1}{3} 6^2 \pi 8 = 12 \times 8\pi = 96\pi$

12. Answer: C
Explanation: Given: s = 13
$B = 144\pi$
$B = r^2\pi$
$r = \sqrt{\frac{B}{\pi}} = \sqrt{\frac{144\pi}{\pi}} = \sqrt{144} = 12$
We have
$s^2 = r^2 + h^2$
$h^2 = s^2 - r^2 = 169 - 144 = 25$
$h = 5$
$V = \frac{1}{3}\pi r^2 h = \frac{1}{3} 12^2 \pi 5 = 240\pi.$

13. Answer: A
Explanation: Given: $\alpha = 60°$, s = 16
$r = \frac{s}{2} = \frac{16}{2} = 8$
We have
$s^2 = r^2 + h^2$
$h^2 = s^2 - r^2 = 256 - 64 = 192$
$h = 8\sqrt{3}$
$V = \frac{1}{3}\pi r^2 h = \frac{1}{3} 8^2 \pi \times 8\sqrt{3} = \frac{512\sqrt{3}}{3}\pi.$

14. Answer: D
Explanation: Given: $\alpha = 30°$, s = 12
$h = \frac{s}{2} = \frac{12}{2} = 6$
We have
$s^2 = r^2 + h^2$
$r^2 = s^2 - h^2 = 144 - 36 = 108$
$h = 6\sqrt{3}$
$V = \frac{1}{3}\pi r^2 h = \frac{1}{3}(6\sqrt{3})^2 \pi \times 6 = 216\pi.$

15. Answer: B
Explanation: Given: $\alpha = 45°$, s = 4
$h = r$
We have
$s^2 = r^2 + h^2 = r^2 + r^2 = 2r^2$
$r^2 = \frac{s^2}{2} = \frac{16}{2} = 8$
$h = 2\sqrt{2}$
$V = \frac{1}{3}\pi r^2 h = \frac{1}{3}(2\sqrt{2})^3 \pi = \frac{8\sqrt{2}}{3}\pi.$

16. Answer: A
Explanation: Enter the given values into the formula for the volume of a cone: $\frac{1}{3}\pi r^2 h$

17. Answer: D
Explanation: Enter the given values into the formula for the volume of a cone: $\frac{1}{3}\pi r^2 h$

18. Answer: 641 cm³
Explanation: Enter the given values into the formula for the volume of a cone: $\frac{1}{3}\pi r^2 h$

19. Answer: 452 cm³
Explanation: Enter the given values into the formula for the volume of a cone: $\frac{1}{3}\pi r^2 h$
(Given: d = 12 → r = 6).

20. Answer: 63 in³
Explanation: Enter the given values into the formula for the volume of a cone: $\frac{1}{3}\pi r^2 h$
(Given: d = 4 → r = 2).

6.3 VOLUME OF SPHERE

1. Answer: B
Explanation: The formula for the volume of a sphere is $\frac{4}{3}\pi r^3$.

2. Answer: C
Explanation: Enter the given values into the formula for the volume of a sphere: $\frac{4}{3}\pi r^3$
$V = \frac{4}{3}\pi r^3 = \frac{4}{3} 4^3 \pi = \frac{256}{3}\pi.$

3. Answer: C
Explanation: Enter the given values into the formula for the volume of a sphere: $\frac{4}{3}\pi r^3$
$V = \frac{4}{3}r^3 = \frac{4}{3}6^3\pi = 288\ \pi$.

4. Answer: B
Explanation: To find the radius, use the modified formula for the volume of a sphere: $\frac{4}{3}\pi r^3$
$r = \sqrt[3]{\frac{3V}{4\pi}} = \sqrt[3]{\frac{3\times36\pi}{4\pi}} = 3$.

5. Answer: A
Explanation: To find the radius, use the modified formula for the volume of a sphere: $\frac{4}{3}\pi r^3$
$r = \sqrt[3]{\frac{3V}{4\pi}} = \sqrt[3]{\frac{3\times4500\pi}{4\pi}} = 15$.

6. Answer: 18,432π
Explanation: Enter the given values into the formula for the volume of a sphere: $\frac{4}{3}\pi r^3$
$V = \frac{4}{3}\pi r^3 = \frac{4}{3}24^3\pi = 18,432\pi$.

7. Answer: 7,776π
Explanation: Enter the given values into the formula for the volume of a sphere: $\frac{4}{3}\pi r^3$
$V = \frac{4}{3}\pi r^3 = \frac{4}{3}18^3\pi = 7,776\pi$.

8. Answer: D
Explanation: Sample response: r = 3.
$V = \frac{4}{3}\pi r^3 = 36\pi$
If r = 3+3 = 6 i.e.., if double the radius
$V = \frac{4}{3}\pi r^3 = 288\pi$
The volume increased by eight times.

9. Answer: D
Explanation: Sample response: r = 6.
$V = \frac{4}{3}\pi r^3 = 288\pi$
If r = 62 = 3 i.e.., if halve its radius
$V = \frac{4}{3}\pi r^3 = 36\pi$
The volume decreased by eight times.

10. Answer: C
Explanation: d = 24
d = 2r
$r = \frac{d}{2} = \frac{24}{2} = 12$
$V = \frac{4}{3}\pi r^3 = \frac{4}{3}\pi 12^3 = 7,234.6\ cm^3$.

11. Answer: B
Explanation: Given C = 18.02
$C = 2r\pi$
$r = \frac{C}{2\pi} = \frac{18.02}{2\times3.14} = 2.9$
$V = \frac{4}{3}\pi r^3 = \frac{4}{3}\pi\ 2.9^3 = 102.1\ in^3$.

12. Answer: A
Explanation: Given: a = 8
$2r = a \rightarrow r = \frac{a}{2} = 4$
Enter the given values into the formula for the volume of a sphere: $\frac{4}{3}\pi r^3$
$V = \frac{256}{3}\pi$.

13. Answer: D
Explanation: Given a = $4\sqrt{3}$
$d = a\sqrt{3} = 4\sqrt{3}\sqrt{3} = 12$
$d = 2r \rightarrow r = \frac{d}{2} = \frac{12}{2} = 6$
Enter the given values into the formula for the volume of a sphere: $\frac{4}{3}\pi r^3$
$V = 288\pi$.

14. Answer: B
Explanation: Given: h = d = 6
$d = 2r \rightarrow r = \frac{d}{2} = \frac{6}{2} = 3$
Enter the given values into the formula for the volume of a sphere: $\frac{4}{3}\pi r^3$
$V = 36\pi$.

15. Answer: B
Explanation: Given C = 14π
$C = 2r\pi$
$r = \frac{C}{2\pi} = \frac{14\pi}{2\pi} = 7$
Enter the given values into the formula for the volume of a sphere: $\frac{4}{3}\pi r^3$
$V = \frac{1372}{3}\pi$

16. Answer: C
Explanation: Enter the given values into the formula for the volume of a sphere: $\frac{4}{3}\pi r^3$

17. Answer: 33493.3
Explanation: Enter the given values into the formula for the volume of a sphere: $\frac{4}{3}\pi r^3$

18. Answer: 14.1
Explanation: Calculate the volume using $\frac{4}{3} \times \pi \times 1.5^3$

19. Answer: A
Explanation: The formula for the volume of a sphere is $\frac{4}{3}\pi r^3$

20. Answer: A
Explanation: The formula for the volume of a sphere is $\frac{4}{3}\pi r^3$

6.4 CHAPTER REVIEW

1. Answer: D
Explanation: Enter the given values into the formula for the volume of a cylinder:
$V = \pi r^2 h = \pi \times 2^2 \times 4 = 16\pi.$

2. Answer: B
Explanation: Enter the given values into the formula for the volume of a cone: $\frac{1}{3}\pi r^2 h$
$V = \frac{1}{3}\pi r^2 h = \frac{1}{3}\pi \times 3^2 \times 30 = 90\pi.$

3. Answer: A
Explanation: Enter the given values into the formula for the volume of a sphere: $\frac{1}{3}\pi r^2 h$
$V = 36{,}000\pi.$

4. Answer: B
Explanation: To find the height, use the modified formula for the volume of a cylinder: $\pi r^2 h$
$h = \frac{V}{r^2 \pi} = \frac{396\pi}{36\pi} = 11.$

5. Answer: 12
Explanation: To find the radius, use the modified formula for the volume of a cylinder: $\pi r^2 h$
$r = \sqrt{\frac{V}{h\pi}} = \sqrt{\frac{1152\pi}{8\pi}} = \sqrt{144} = 12$

6. Answer: D
Explanation: To find the height, use the modified formula for the volume of a cone:
$\frac{1}{3}\pi r^2 h$
$h = \frac{3V}{r^2 \pi} = \frac{3 \times 192\pi}{16\pi} = 36.$

7. Answer: 15
Explanation: To find the radius, use the modified formula for the volume of a cone:
$\frac{1}{3}\pi r^2 h$
$r = \sqrt{\frac{V}{h\pi}} = \sqrt{\frac{3 \times 300\pi}{4\pi}} = \sqrt{225} = 15.$

8. Answer: B
Explanation: To find the radius, use the modified formula for the volume of a sphere:
$\frac{4}{3}\pi r^3$
$r = \sqrt[3]{\frac{3V}{4\pi}} = \sqrt[3]{\frac{3 \times 12348\pi}{4\pi}} = 21.$

9. Answer: 47,916π
Explanation: Enter the given values into the formula for the volume of a sphere: $\frac{4}{3}\pi r^2$

10. Answer: A
Explanation: Enter the given values into the formula for the volume of a sphere: $\frac{4}{3}\pi r^2$

11. Answer: B
Explanation: Enter the given values into the formula for the volume of a cone: $\frac{1}{3}\pi r^2 h$

12. Answer: C
Explanation: Enter the given values into the formula for the volume of a cone: $\pi r^2 h$

13. Answer: A
Explanation: The formula for the volume of a cone is $\frac{1}{3}\pi r^2 h.$

14. Answer: B
Explanation: The formula for the volume of a sphere is $\frac{4}{3}\pi r^3$. The approximate volume is 707.5 m³.

15. Answer: A
Explanation: The formula for the volume of a cylinder is: $\pi r^2 h$

16. Answer: B
Explanation: Sample response: r = 2, h = 3
$V = \pi r^2 h = 12\pi$
If r = 2, h = 9 i.e., if triple the height
$V = \pi r^2 h = 36\pi$
The volume increased by three times.

17. Answer: B
Explanation: Sample response: r = 2, h = 3
$V = \frac{1}{3}\pi r^2 h = 4\pi$
If h=3, r=2×3=8 i.e., if triple the radius
$V = \frac{1}{3}\pi r^2 h = 16\pi$
The volume of a cone is tripled.

18. Answer: C
Explanation: Sample response: r=3.
$V = \frac{4}{3}\pi r^3 = 36\pi$
If r = 3×3 = 9 i.e., if triples its radius
$V = \frac{4}{3}\pi r^3 = 972\pi$
The volume decreased by 27 times.

19. Answer: 1350.3
Explanation: $\frac{1}{3} \times 3.14 \times (10.2)^2 \times 12.4$.

20. Answer: 17.2
Explanation: $\frac{1}{3} \times 3.14 \times (2.22)^2 \times 3.33$.

7. BIVARIATE DATA

7.1 CONSTRUCT AND INTERPRET SCATTERPLOTS

1. Answer: B
Explanation: A scatter plot shows a negative correlation if y tends to decrease as x increases.

2. Answer: B
Explanation: A scatter plot shows a negative correlation if y tends to decrease as x increases.

3. Answer: A
Explanation: A scatter plot shows a positive correlation if y tends to increase as x increases.

4. Answer: A
Explanation: A scatter plot shows a positive correlation if y tends to increase as x increases.

5. Answer: B
Explanation: A scatter plot shows a negative correlation if y tends to decrease as x increases.

6. Answer: C
Explanation: A scatter plot shows no correlation; there is no obvious pattern to the behavior of the variables.

7. Answer: C
Explanation: A scatter plot shows no trend if there is no obvious pattern.

8. Answer: A
Explanation: Look for a point that is separated from all other points in the data set. That point could be an outlier.

9. Answer: C
Explanation: Look for a point that is separated from all other points in the data set. That point could be an outlier.

10. Answer: B
Explanation: Look for a point that is separated from all other points in the data set. That point could be an outlier.

11. Answer: D
Explanation: Find the slope using the two given points,4,0 and $(2,6)$. The slope is -3. Then, find the y-intercept, which is 12.

12. Answer: A
Explanation: Find the slope using the two given points,0,10 and $(8,2)$. The slope is -1. Then, find the y-intercept, which is 10.

13. Answer: B
Explanation: Find the slope using the two given points,2,0 and $(9,10)$. The slope is $\frac{10}{7}$. Then, find the y-intercept, which is $-\frac{20}{7}$.

14. Answer: A
Explanation: Find the slope using the two given points,2,2 and $(8,10)$. The slope is $\frac{4}{3}$. Then, find the y-intercept, which is $-\frac{2}{3}$.

15. Answer: B
Explanation: The data shows a strong positive linear correlation because the pattern of the points is distinct and relatively close to the trend line. The line of best fit is centered inside the pattern of the data points.

16. Answer: D
Explanation: The data shows a weak positive linear correlation because the pattern of the points is distinct but not all close to the trend line. The line of best fit is centered inside the pattern of the data points.

17. Answer: C
Explanation: As the amount of candy increases, the cost of the candy increases as well. A line with a positive slope would be used to model this situation.

18. Answer: C
Explanation: A scatter plot shows no correlation; there is no obvious pattern to the behavior of the variables.

19. Answer: Line b
Explanation: The numbers of data points above and below Line b are approximately the same.

20. Answer: Line b
Explanation: Neither line is very good, but line b passes through more data points on the scatter plot.

7.2 INTERPRET SLOPE AND Y-INTERCEPT OF LINE OF BEST FIT

1. Answer: C
Explanation: The rate of change is equal to the slope. Slope equals change in y divided by the change in x: approximately $\frac{90}{30} = 3$.

2. Answer: A
Explanation: The rate of change is equal to the slope. Slope equals change in y divided by the change in x: approximately $\frac{80}{100} = 1$.

3. Answer: B
Explanation: The rate of change is equal to the slope. Slope equals change in y divided by the change in x: approximately $\frac{90}{60} = 2$.

4. Answer: B
Explanation: The rate of change is equal to the slope. Slope equals the change in y divided by the change in x: $\frac{40}{20} = 2$.

5. Answer: B
Explanation: The rate of change is equal to the slope. Slope equals change in y divided by the change in x: approximately $\frac{90}{50} = 2$.

6. Answer: B
Explanation: The rate of change is equal to the slope. Slope equals change in y divided by the change in x: $\frac{80}{40} = 2$.

7. Answer: A
Explanation: The rate of change is equal to the slope. The slope shows that the that the value of the motor cycle decreases $1,500 per year.

8. Answer: D
Explanation: As the temperature increases, the sales of hot coffee decrease. The slope shows the rate at which the sales change.

9. Answer: A
Explanation: The slope equals the change in the cost y based on the number of minutes used x.

10. Answer: 46.75
Explanation: Substitute 15 for x into the equation $y = 130 - 5.55x$

11. Answer: The hours of a fully charged battery
Explanation: The variable y represents the hours remaining. When x is zero, the phone is fully charged.

12. Answer: The computer had a 40 % charge when it was put on the charging station
Explanation: The variable x is zero when the computer is placed on the charging station. The y-intercept is the amount of charge the computer had at that time.

13. Answer: B
Explanation: The equation should multiply, not divide, 20 and x.

14. Answer: y=12x
Explanation: Every week, she learned 12 new pieces so multiply 12 by x.

15. Answer: y=10x
Explanation: Each phone call takes 10 minutes, so the equation is total minutes equals 10 multiplied by x.

16. Answer: y=3.65x
Explanation: It costs $3.65 for each attendee so multiply 3.65 by x (number of attendees) to get the total cost.

17. Answer: y=14x
Explanation: He reads 14 books each month, so multiply 14 by x (number of months) to get the number of books to read.

18. Answer: y=300x
Explanation: It costs $300 for each guest she invites so multiply 300 by x to get the total cost.

19. Answer: y=15x
Explanation: Each seed packet can grow 15 flowers so multiply x by 15 to get the total number of flowers

20. Answer: y=5x
Explanation: Jose reads 5 books each month so multiply 5 by x.

7.3 CONSTRUCT AND INTERPRET TWO-WAY TABLES

1. Answer: D
Explanation: Mr. Austin surveyed 115 students. If the data were represented by a two-way frequency table, the cell relative frequency of the number of girls who prefer chocolate ice cream would be 9/115 or about 8% of the total population surveyed

2. Answer: B
Explanation: Blake surveyed 37 players. If the data were represented by a two-way frequency table, the cell relative frequency of the number of left-handed Red Sox pitchers would be $\frac{5}{37}$ or 14 % of the total population surveyed.

3. Answer: A
Explanation: Kayla surveyed 66 players, and 28 are right-handed. If the data were represented by a two-way frequency table, the cell relative frequency of the number of right-handed hitters is $\frac{28}{66}$ or 42 % of the total population surveyed.

4. Answer: 0.30
Explanation: The relative frequency is the number of people matching this description out of the total number of the subgroup identified. There are 3,245 students in the "35-55" age group. The proportion representing this frequency is $\frac{1000}{3245}$.

5. Answer: 0.27
Explanation: The relative frequency is the number of people matching this description out of the total number of those identified. The proportion representing this frequency is $\frac{644}{2353}$.

6. Answer: 0.08
Explanation: The relative frequency is the number of people matching this description out of the total number of those identified. The proportion representing this frequency is $\frac{8379}{99421}$.

7. Answer: 0.13
Explanation: The relative frequency is the number of people matching this description out of the total number of those identified. The proportion representing this frequency is $\frac{9986}{77282}$.

8. Answer: The fraction of the number of people surveyed who are men who prefer cats.
Explanation: The relative frequency is the ratio of the number of people surveyed who prefer a given option to the total number of people surveyed.

9. Answer: The ratio of the number of women surveyed to the total number of people surveyed.
Explanation: The relative frequency is the number of people who prefer a given option as a ratio against the total number of people surveyed.

10. Answer: 0.13
Explanation: The relative frequencies add up to 100 %, so the missing relative frequency is 0.13. There are 52 people in this category. $\frac{52}{400} = 0.13$.

11. Answer: 0.28
Explanation: The relative frequencies add up to 100 %, so the missing relative frequency is 0.28. There are 11 teams in this category. $\frac{11}{40} = 0.28$

12. Answer: 0.27
Explanation: The relative frequencies add up to 100 %, so the missing relative frequency is 0.27. There are 12 teams in this category. $\frac{15}{54} = 0.27$.

13. Answer: 0.22
Explanation: The relative frequencies add up to 100 %, so the missing relative frequency is 0.22. There are 12 teams in this category. $\frac{16}{72} = 0.22$.

14. Answer: 0.19
Explanation: The relative frequencies add up to 100 %, so the missing relative frequency is 0.19. There are 12 teams in this category. $\frac{13}{66} = 0.19$.

15. Answer: 0.18
Explanation: The relative frequencies add up to 100 %, so the missing relative frequency is 0.18. There are 12 teams in this category. $\frac{9}{52} = 0.18$.

16. Answer:

		Use social media	Don't use social media
Age	20-25	55	33
	26-32	91	7
	32 and older	90	10

Explanation: The table represents the preferences of the number of people in each of the 3 categories.

17. Answer:

		Kiwis	Cherries	Apples
Age	Under 18	19	20	27
	18-34	30	25	15
	35 and older	12	28	42

Explanation: The table represents the preferences of the number of people in each of the 3 categories.

18. Answer:

		Smartphone	Tablet	Laptop
Age	Under 15	≈0.11	≈0.70	≈0.06
	15-20	≈0.08	≈0.11	≈0.12
	20 and older	≈0.11	≈0.15	≈0.20

Explanation: The table represents the preferences of the number of people recorded as a relative frequency in each of the 3 categories.

19. Answer:

		Girls	Boys
Power	Invisibility	≈0.17	≈0.11
	Superhuman strength	≈0.04	≈0.15
	Telepathy	≈0.17	≈0.08
	flying	≈0.13	≈0.15

Explanation: The table represents the preferences of the number of people recorded as a relative frequency in each of the 4 categories.

20. Answer: Answers will vary. 0.15 and 0.28. The totals for each value are different because they are based on different sample groups.
Explanation: The relative frequency of students who are boys who like pizza is based out of the total of 55 students surveyed. $\frac{8}{55} \approx 0.15$
The relative frequency of girls who like pizza is based out of the total of 29 boys surveyed $\frac{8}{29} \approx 0.28$.

7.4 CHAPTER REVIEW

1. Answer: B
Explanation: A scatter plot shows a negative correlation if y tends to decrease as x increases.

2. Answer: B
Explanation: A scatter plot shows a negative correlation if y tends to decrease as x increases.

3. Answer: A
Explanation: A scatter plot shows a positive correlation if y tends to increase as x increases.

4. Answer: A
Explanation: A scatter plot shows a positive correlation if y tends to increase as x increases.

5. Answer: B
Explanation: A scatter plot shows a negative correlation if y tends to decrease as x increases.

6. Answer: C
Explanation: Find the slope using the two given points, 10,0 and (4,20) . The slope is $-\frac{10}{3}$. Then, find the y-intercept, which is $\frac{100}{3}$.

7. Answer: A
Explanation: Find the slope using the two given points,0,15 and (5,5) . The slope is -2. Then, find the y-intercept, which is 15.

8. Answer: B
Explanation: Find the slope using the two given points, 6,0 and (0,10) . The slope is $-\frac{5}{3}$. Then, find the y-intercept, which is 10.

9. Answer: B
Explanation: An outlier can be thought of as an outsider, but there is no specific formula that defines outliers. However, they are still important to understand when performing a statistical analysis because they affect measures of central tendency.

10. Answer: B
Explanation: An outlier is an extreme point in a data set that is separated from all other points.

11. Answer: B
Explanation: A scatter plot with no obvious pattern has no correlation because the correlation cannot be identified as positive or negative.

12. Answer: A
Explanation: A scatter plot shows a negative correlation if y tends to decrease as x increases.

13. Answer: A
Explanation: A scatter plot shows a positive correlation if y tends to increase as x increases.

14. Answer: C
Explanation: The trend line is the line of best fit between the variables and is used to make approximations.

15. Answer: B
Explanation: The rate of change is equal to the slope. Slope equals change in y divided by the change in x. $\frac{60}{40}$ rounded to the nearest whole number is 2.

16. Answer: C
Explanation: The rate of change is equal to the slope. Slope equals change in y divided by the change in x. $\frac{90}{30}$ = 3.

17. Answer: B
Explanation: The rate of change is equal to the slope. Slope equals change in y divided by the change in x. $\frac{70}{45}$ rounded to the nearest whole number is 2.

18. Answer:
Average growth per week (approx. 1.9 cm)
Explanation: The equation of the line of best fit for this situation is y = 1.9x + 7.1

19. Answer: $\frac{65}{119}$ **= 0.5**
Explanation: There were 119 males surveyed. Sixty-five of them had a positive opinion.

20. Answer: 4
Explanation: Look at the last column and then go to the last row: 22-18=4.

1. Answer: C
Explanation: All the choices are negative numbers. The number -0.004 has the greatest value because it is closest to 0.

2. Answer: B
Explanation: To determine the equivalent fraction for a repeating decimal, multiply both sides of the equation (x = 2.062) by a power of 10 (in this case, 1,000) equal to the number of repeating digits. This gives the equation 1,000x = 2,062.062. To determine the value of x, subtract the original equation from the new equation, and solve for the variable.

3. Answer: 0.01
Explanation: The numerator has a value of 1, and the denominator has a value of 100. $\frac{1}{100}$ is equivalent to 0.01.

4. Answer: D
Explanation: The square root of any number that is not a perfect square is an irrational number.

5. Answer: √161 cm
Explanation: The area (161) is not a perfect square number and has no square factors that would allow its square root to be simplified.

6. Answer: (4.14)(4.14) or (4.14)²
Explanation: The fraction $\frac{1}{7}$ is 0.14. Find the area of the square by multiplying the length of one side by itself.

7. Answer: No
Explanation: The fraction $\frac{1}{5}$ can be expressed as a percent and a decimal, but it is a repeating decimal, so the percent also contains a repeating decimal or a fraction. The correct expression is $20\frac{1}{5}$ % .

8. Answer: No
Explanation: Her formula does not include the correct value for π. The number can be approximated as 3.14. Also, the formula for the area of a circle is πx (radius) x (radius). The radius of the circle is 7 inches.

9. Answer: 530 or 507 or 531
Explanation: Use the exact value of π and then round, or approximate, π using 3.14. Multiply the estimate by 169 which results in 530.66 sq. cm. Round to the nearest whole number. Alternatively, approximate π using 3.

10. Answer: C
Explanation: Substituting the value in for x results in a negative inside the radical. Negative numbers are not in the domain of the square root function.

11. Answer: B
Explanation: y = –3x + 9, When x = 5
y = –3(5) + 9
y = –15 + 9 = –6
y = –6

12. Answer: A
Explanation: Car Wash A will cost: $5.5(0.55×10)
Car Wash B will cost: $15(2.50+5×2.50) for 8 minutes of use, which means Carwash A is a better deal.

13. Answer: C
Explanation: The vertical line test is used to determine whether a graph is a function.

14. Answer: A
Explanation: y = (x+2)² is not a linear function because it contains an exponent other than 1 on a variable.

15.Answer: D
Explanation: The initial value of the function is 49.99 plus 20 times the number of coffees purchased.

16. Answer: D
Explanation: The slope-intercept form provides the y-intercept (a place to start) and the slope (a direction to go) when graphing a line. It is considered a graphing-ready equation.

17. Answer: A
Explanation: The slope of the equation is positive, so the graph is increasing.

18. Answer: B
Explanation: $x=2$ represents a vertical line, so it is linear but not a function.

19. Answer: A
Explanation: The rate of change is the slope. This function is expressed in slope-intercept form ($y = mx + b$), and the value of m, or the coefficient of x, is - 8.

20. Answer: C
Explanation: Substitute the dimensions into the volume formula: $V=(x^3)(3x)(7x)$. Multiply the like bases by adding the exponents. The volume is $V = 21x^5$.

21. Answer: B
Explanation: Square the term inside the second parentheses changing the expression to $(3x^4y)(16x^4y^4)$ Next, multiply the constants and add the exponents with like- bases. The result is $48x^8y^5$.

22. Answer: D
Explanation: Substitute the expression y6 into the area formula for r: $A = \pi (y^6)^2$. Raise the exponential expression to the power by multiplying the exponents. The area expression is $A = \pi y^{12}$.

23. Answer: B
Explanation: Since the number multiplied by 2 gives 12, the cube root has to be 6. The cube root of 216 is 6. When you double 6, you get 12 Therefore, 216 is the answer.

24. Answer: D
Explanation: Substitute 196 for A in the formula, giving. $196=s^2$. To solve for, take the square root of both sides: $s = \pm14$. Delete the negative solution since it does not fit with the situation. The length of the square is 14 inches.

25. Answer: B
Explanation: The farm animals are represented by the system of equations: $c+s =357$ and $s = 2c$. Solving for c using substitution gives 119 goats.

26. Answer: A
Explanation: The first factor is 1.67 and 10^7 indicates that the decimal point is moved to the left 7 places.

27. Answer: C
Explanation: When rewriting numbers in scientific notation, a very large number has a positive exponent in the second factor, and a very small number has a negative exponent in the second factor.

28. Answer: 25.75
Explanation: Substitute 26 for s in: $8.85+0.65s = c$. Calculate the value.

29. Answer: B
Explanation: 270° is one third of a full turn. A full turn is 360°.

30. Answer: A
Explanation: Positive angles are measured counterclockwise, and negative angles are measured clockwise.

31. Answer: B
Explanation: A reflection flips a figure over a line or points to create a mirror image.

32. Answer: D
Explanation: Use the Pythagorean theorem equation $a^2+b^2 = c^2$ to find the hypotenuse: $20^2 + 15^2 = (25)^2$.

33. Answer: 10.39 ft
Explanation: The wall and the ladder make a right-angle triangle. The length of the triangle 12 ft is the hypotenuse of the triangle. The ladder is 6 feet away from the wall. Using the Pythagorean theorem, find the other side of the triangle.
$a^2 + b^2 = c^2$
$a^2 + 6^2 = 12^2$
$a^2 = 144 - 36 = 108$
$a = \sqrt{108} = 10.39\text{ft}$.

34. Answer: 18.439 cm²
Explanation: Use the Pythagorean theorem equation $a^2 + b^2 = c^2$ to find the hypotenuse:
$12^2 + 14^2 = \sqrt{340} = 18.439 \text{ cm}^2$.

35. Answer: 14.1
Explanation: The distance formula is an algebraic expression used to determine the distance between two points with the coordinates $(x1, y1)$ and $(x2, y2)$
$d = \sqrt{(x2 - x1)2 + (y2 - y1)2}$
$\sqrt{100 + 100} \sim 14.1$

36. Answer: 10
Explanation: The distance formula is an algebraic expression used to determine the distance between two points with the coordinates $(x1, y1)$ and $(x2, y2)$
$d = \sqrt{(x2 - x1)2 + (y2 - y1)2}$
$\sqrt{100} = 10$

37. Answer: A
Explanation: Enter the given dimensions into the formula for the volume of a cylinder: $\pi r^2 h$.

38. Answer: B
Explanation: Enter the given dimensions into the formula for the volume of a cone: $\frac{1}{3}\pi r^2 h$. The correct volume is in 528 cubic inches.

39. Answer: A
Explanation: To choose the correct scatter plot correlation, find the outlier. Look for a point that is separated from all other points in the data set, but it is not necessary to remove the outlier to see the correlation.

40. Answer: y = 3x
Explanation: It costs $3 for every guest he invites, so multiply 3 by x.

41. Answer: A
Explanation: An outlier has a large distance from the best-fit line. Just one outlier can have a drastic effect on the correlation and the least squares regression line.

42. Answer: False
Explanation: There are 30 new recipes per week so multiply 30 by x, so, we get y = 30x.

43. Answer: True
Explanation: There are 120 postcards each day of vacation, so multiply 120 by x, so, we get y = 120x.

44. Answer: 8
Explanation: According to the table, 3 males and 5 females prefer apples over oranges.

45. Answer: 23
Explanation: According to the table, 11 males and 12 females prefer cucumbers over carrots.

COMPREHENSIVE ASSESSMENT – II

1. Answer: 8
Explanation: Look at the red row under the pencil column.

2. Answer: 48
Explanation: Look at the column in the second row of the table.

3. Answer: 78
Explanation: Add the numbers in the Prefer Milkshakes column.

4. Answer: C
Explanation: The square root of 49 is a rational number because it $\sqrt{49} = 7$ is a perfect square number.

5. Answer: C
Explanation: Substitute the value in for x and determine the value for y.

6. Answer: B
Explanation: The cost of the gym membership starts at a fixed $15 and then adds $9 each month as a variable cost.

7. Answer: B
Explanation: The graph is decreasing because the equation has a negative slope.

8. Answer: A
Explanation: When multiplying like-bases with exponents, add the exponents. This gives 5^5, which is $5 \times 5 \times 5 \times 5 \times 5 = 3125$.

9. Answer: C
Explanation: According to the problem, the cube root of the number is one less than 5. This means the cube root of the number is 4. The cube root of 64 is 4.

10. Answer: D
Explanation: The cube root of -64 is - 4 because $-4 \times -4 \times -4 = -64$. Then, square -4 to get 16

11. Answer: C
Explanation: The number 1000 times larger than 8×10^7 is equivalent to $8\times10^7(10)^3$ which is 8×10^{10}.

12. Answer: y = 9x
Explanation: The relation in the table satisfies the equation y = 9x. The only choice with a higher slope than 3 is A.

13. Answer: C
Explanation: To solve for g, add 2 to both sides and subtract 5g. The result is g=5.

14. Answer: A
Explanation: Using the Pythagorean theorem equation $a^2+b^2 = c^2$ to find the hypotenuse: $30^2 + 15^2 = \sqrt{1125}$.

15. Answer: B
Explanation: Using the Pythagorean theorem equation $a^2+b^2 = c^2$ to find the hypotenuse: $6^2 + 9^2 = \sqrt{117}$.

16. Answer: $\sqrt{315}$
Explanation: Using the modified Pythagorean theorem equation. 22 meters is the hypotenuse and 13 meters is one of the legs, so $22^2 - 13^2 = \sqrt{315}$.

17. Answer: $\sqrt{11}$
Explanation: The 6 inches are the hypotenuse and 5 inches are the leg, using the modified Pythagorean theorem equation: $6^2 - 5^2 = \sqrt{11}$.

18. Answer: 5.4
Explanation: The distance formula is an algebraic expression used to determine the distance between two points with the coordinates (x1, y1) and (x2, y2)
$d = \sqrt{(x2 - x1)2 + (y2 - y1)2}$
$\sqrt{4+25} \sim 5.38$

19. Answer: 6.08
Explanation: The distance formula is an algebraic expression used to determine the distance between two points with the coordinates $(x1, y1)$ and $(x2, y2)$
$d = \sqrt{(x2 - x1)2 + (y2 - y1)2}$
$\sqrt{1+36} \sim 6.08$

20. Answer: B
Explanation: Enter the given dimensions into the formula for the volume of a cylinder: $\pi r^2 h$. We get 1100 mm³.

21. Answer: 10
Explanation: Add the first row.

22. Answer: B
Explanation: The repeating decimal can be determined by dividing 6 by 8. One digit repeats, so the denominator has one 8.

23. Answer: B
Explanation: has a value of approximately 3.14, when multiplied by 4, the value is 12.56, between 12 and 13.

24. Answer: A
Explanation: Substitute the value in for y into the equation to find the x-value.

25. Answer: C
Explanation: The relation is $y = x^3$, when $x = 2$, $y = 8$.

26. Answer: D
Explanation: All of these items are true about vertical lines.

27. Answer: B
Explanation: First, substitute the expression a^{-4} into the equation for r which is $A=\pi(a^{-4})^2$. Raising an exponent to a power, multiplies the exponents. This gives $A = \pi a^{-8}$. Negative exponents become positive by moving them to the other side of the fraction, resulting in $\frac{\pi}{a^8}$

28. Answer: B
Explanation: The cube root of 512 is 8 because 8×8×8=512

29. Answer: B
Explanation: To solve this equation, get x by itself. To do so, multiply both sides by $x^2=144$ Take the square root of both sides, giving solutions of $x = \pm12$.

30. Answer: A
Explanation: Nine hundred million can be expressed as $(9 \ 108)$. Dividing this number by 10 makes the number 10 times smaller.

31. Answer: $(6 \times 10^2)(5 \times 10^1)$
Explanation: Six-hundredths is expressed as (6×10^2) and 50 is expressed as (5×10^1).

32. Answer: A
Explanation: The table illustrates the relation $y=0.85x$. Insert the 8 value for x, and $y=6.8$.

33. Answer: A
Explanation: Rewrite 4.415×10^{-7} as 0.4415×10^{-8}. Subtract the first coefficient from the second, resulting in $x = 4.415\times10^{-7}$.

34. Answer: A
Explanation: First, distribute the values outside of parentheses. The equation becomes: $2x - 6 = 3x + 6$. Subtract 2x from both sides and add 6, $x = -12$.

35. Answer: D
Explanation: This equation has no solution because subtracting 4x from both sides, eliminates the variable and leaves a statement that is not true: $(5 \neq 2)$.

36. Answer: 0.875 cents
Explanation: First, write 2 equations:
$2h + 2s =6$ and $4h + s = 8.5$. Solve one of the equations for s, and substitute it into the first equation to find h: $s = 2.125$, Sandwich is worth $0.875.

37. Answer: (20,0)
Explanation: The scale factor is 5, and since one vertex is at the origin, all coordinates are multiplied by 5 to determine the new vertices.

38. Answer: (3,5)
Explanation: The scale factor is 4, and since one vertex is at the origin, all coordinates are multiplied by 4 to determine the new location.

39. Answer: B
Explanation: Use the Pythagorean theorem equation $a^2 + b^2 = c^2$ to find the hypotenuse: $14^2 + 18^2 = \sqrt{520}$.

40. Answer: B
Explanation: Use the Pythagorean theorem equation $a^2 + b^2 = c^2$ to find the hypotenuse: $12^2 + 16^2 = 20^2$.

41. Answer: $\sqrt{74}$
Explanation: The dimensions 5 meters and 7 meters are the legs of a right triangle. Find the hypotenuse using the Pythagorean theorem equation: $5^2 + 7^2 = \sqrt{74}$.

42. Answer: 20
Explanation: The lengths 20 ft and 6 ft are the legs of a right triangle. The ladder is the hypotenuse. Find the hypotenuse using the Pythagorean equation: $20^2 + 6^2 = \sqrt{436} = 20.89 \sim 20$.

43. Answer: C
Explanation: The distance formula is an algebraic expression used to determine the distance between two points with the coordinates $(x1, y1)$ and $(x2, y2)$
$d = \sqrt{(x2 - x1)2 + (y2 - y1)2}$
$\sqrt{25 + 49} \sim 8.6$

44. Answer: B
Explanation: The formula for the volume of a cone is $\frac{1}{3}\pi r^2 h$, on substituting the values we get 113.04 ft³.

45. Answer: C
Explanation: The distance formula is an algebraic expression used to determine the distance between two points with the coordinates $(x1, y1)$ and $(x2, y2)$
$d = \sqrt{(x2 - x1)2 + (y2 - y1)2}$
$\sqrt{0 + 4} \sim 2$